Travellers' Portugal

Travellers' Portugal

Anthony Hogg

SOLO MIO BOOKS

Front Cover: Amarante, a Vinho Verde wine town on the Tamega, a Douro tributary.
Portuguese Tourist Office, London

Back Cover: Lamego, Largo dos Reis, top landing of the 686 stepped-pilgrimage staircase leading up to the church of Nossa Senhora dos Remédios. Photograph, Jan Read

First published in Great Britain in 1983 by Solo Mio Books, 1a Little London, Chichester, West Sussex. Revised editions 1986 and 1987.

Art Editors: Chichester Design Associates Ltd, 26a East Street, Chichester, Sussex

UK	Distributors: Ken Dickson (Marketing) Ltd, 14 Crossways, Silwood Road, Sunninghill, Ascot, Berks SL5 0PY. Tel 0990 25421
USA	Boerum Hill Books, PO Box 286 Times Plaza Station, Brooklyn, N.Y. 11217. Tel 718-624-4000
Portugal	Livaria Britanica, Rue da Gloria No 10 R/C, 1298 Lisbon. Tel 37. 23. 86

Printed by: Eyre & Spottiswoode Limited at Grosvenor Press Portsmouth

ISBN 0 9508955-2-0

To Quinta de la Rosa and
all who may wave from your windows

ABOUT THE AUTHOR

Among wine drinkers Anthony Hogg became well-known as the creator of *Wine Mine*, that mine of information, wit and wisdom he edited as a Director of Peter Dominic from 1959 to 1974. This was quickly followed by *Guide to Visiting Vineyards*, virtually a wine tour of Europe still introducing travellers to three hundred establishments pleased to show them round.

Formerly a regular naval officer, his working life has been equally divided between two admirable imbibing and travelling institutions—the Royal Navy and the wine trade.

Portugal is a third, fortunately not equipped for mass tourism except on the Algarve. *Travellers' Portugal* therefore can be no best-seller, but for the discerning few—who have no need to be rich—it does guarantee a memorable holiday.

By the same author

Cocktails and Mixed Drinks
The Hamlyn Publishing Group 1979/80/81/82
'Particularly successful from everyone's point of view except the author's. 90,000 copies . . . royalty about 0.7 per cent . . . Hamlyn have refused to reconsider the terms of the publishing contract or to make any additional payment'.

The Author, The Society of Authors' Quarterly.

Guide to Visiting Vineyards
Michael Joseph 1976–81–82
'No other remotely comparable guide exists: and anyone with an interest in wine who proposes to travel in Europe should carry a copy.'

John Arlott in the *Guardian*

Everybody's Wine Guide
Quiller Press in association with Peter Dominic 1985.
'Completely down to earth . . . covers every aspect of wine you can mention.'

Jack House in the *Glasgow Evening Times*

Contents

Maps

Illustrations

FOREWORD BY JOHN ARLOTT

In recent years Portugal has grown steadily out from its former neglect by British tourists. There they can bask in the sun and eat genuine Portuguese – instead of "British" – cooking. Portugal is Britain's oldest ally and now the former troubles and poverty of the Salazar regime fade away, a much happier state of affairs exists.

Why should British holiday-makers go to Portugal? Importantly – and no one will improve on Anthony Hogg's statement of the case – 'Portugal is beautiful, the people friendly, the climate pleasant, the wines excellent, the food good, and living costs about the lowest in Western Europe.' How? is the question that had not been adequately answered. The *Michelin Guide*, of course, gives the prices; but that is not the full answer.

Portugal is no longer neglected, and this edition of Anthony Hogg's book shows, by comparison with the first, just how great the change has been and how ample the improvement in the tourist's enjoyment.

Travellers' Portugal provides genuine help. Too many guide books are what the publishing trade calls 'scissors and paste jobs'. This is essentially a first-hand book, written with the aim of guiding the traveller as clearly and simply, but also as completely, as possible to the rich and varied pleasures of this country. They will be shared pleasures. Anthony Hogg has been visiting Portugal for more than thirty-five years; and he, and his readers, are both fortunate that he did not have to hurry about it. An enquiring mind led him to turn aside from the main roads, interested to find out what lay beyond them; he found time, then or when he came home, to read the history of what he had seen. So he can give his readers that background of relevant history – not merely antiquarian, but up-to-date, too – which will enable them to understand what they see – an essential ingredient of a civilised holiday. The notes on earlier and famous British visitors reinforce the air of familiarity.

He had experience of giving such guidance before; his *Guide to Visiting Vineyards* has proved uniquely helpful to many travellers in search of wines and those who make them. Now, here again, are all the practicalities; how and where; getting there; travelling; visiting, seeing; eating; wine (highly informed); staying, sleeping; swimming – and *not* swimming – drinking and *not* drinking; above all, enjoying. Of course the tourist will take a copy with him. It is also worthwhile for the first-time tourist to Portugal to study it before he goes.

AUTHOR'S PREFACE (Third Edition)

Four years have passed since *Travellers' Portugal* was published in October 1983. In 1986 we celebrated the six hundredth anniversary of the Treaty of Windsor, England's oldest alliance (see pages 5 and 263). In 1985 our ally joined the European Community. *Soyez les bienvenues!* Or – *Discovering Portuguese* from BBC Television – *Seja Bem Vindo.*

Like Britain, Portugal – with a trading deficit of 377,200 million escudos (225 esc now to the £1) – seeks to progress in today's world, financing her future development and giving her 10,030,700 people life in greater abundance. Ten million people live in their homeland, 100,000 of them suffering wages and salaries in arrears. Another three million – poor and jobless at home – work abroad, remitting much of their pay to keep their families at home. Many successive governments without working majorities have failed to cope with this situation, which is partly a legacy from Salazar, fighting costly wars unsuccessfully to hold the African colonies.

After the emigrants' remittances, tourism is the largest source of income. Increasing about 10 per cent annually, the total topped 10 million people in 1984, exceeding the population for the first time. The British figure is now over 850,000; Americans, Canadians and Japanese too are just beginning to learn of 'some place new' in Europe. Britain's consumption of Portugese wines, increasing steadily year by year, is also a valued asset.

This book aims to be a practical, inexpensive introduction, mainly for people hiring a car on arrival or driving their own through France and Spain, with seven to fourteen days to spare for a sunny land of rivers and mountain greenery, flowers and vines, spectacular views, old churches, ancient convents and castles, monasteries, museums and gaily painted small towns, distinguished by their Manoeline and baroque architecture.

I have also tried to cover in one volume where to sleep, where to eat, what to drink and what to see, in a small country where holidays cost far less than in France and your figure is far less likely to grow larger. Prices in this edition have been updated to 1987 when the exchange rate is 225 esc = £1 and in Portugal inflation 10 per cent. It seems likely to continue, and where my text gives prices e.g. Green Fees on the Algarve potential visitors may need to adjust them.

The book could not have been written without the help and hospitality that my wife Joan, our son Adam and later myself, received from Claire Bergquist, owner of Quinta de la Rosa and, after her death in 1972, from her son Tim and his wife Patricia. Our friendship had a wartime beginning in Arrochar, Scotland at the head of Loch

Long. As a Lieutenant RN burnt in a cordite fire in my first encounter with Hitler's dive bombers, I had been given a spell ashore in charge of underwater weapon trials. During the school holidays, Claire, an attractive mama who was nursing in Glasgow for the duration while her husband (of Swedish extraction) toiled in a munition factory at Greenock, would come to stay in the hotel with her eleven year old son, Tim.

She explained that climbing 'The Cobbler' made them feel less homesick for the hills of her beloved Douro valley, where they lived and made port wine at Quinta de la Rosa. Her maiden name was Feuerheerd, one of the many port shippers forced to merge after the war.

I would take Tim down the loch in HMS *Vesuvius*, a mining trial tender and on return his mother would say, 'Good heavens Tim, where did you learn that disgraceful language?' And he would reply 'From Anthony Hogg and his sailors, of course.'

Returning from the British Pacific Fleet in 1945 when the war was over, I was dismayed within three years to find myself back East again in the cruiser *Birmingham*, based at Trincomalee in Ceylon where there was insufficient accommodation for service families. Hearing I was to spend another 15 months drinking for what remained of the Empire, parted from my family, Claire invited my wife, Joan and our son Adam, aged five out to Quinta de la Rosa, where the two ladies consoled themselves with tawny port until they were as large as pipes themselves. Between whiles they toured the North in those pre-Pousada days when Belloc's fleas that tease in the High Pyrenees were as nothing to the bed-bugs that bite in Bragança. Claire was indefatigable and she had in Joan, a receptive companion who had absorbed Florence with delight at the age of twelve.

Together in 1952 we were able to make the first of many visits to Portugal and La Rosa, accompanied that time by her brother Philip, architect partner of Powell & Moya to help me, a simple sailor, recognise a bowline on the bight hewn in stone if we happened upon one in some Manueline shrine.

Quinta de la Rosa is sited above the single railway line on the *right* bank of the Douro a mile below Pinhão. One of the world's seven *Great Little Railways*, since featured on BBC1 (22.3.83), it follows the Douro through the port vineyards to the land beyond the mountains. By car coming out from England via Guarda, or from Lisbon or Oporto, the approach is upstream on the *other* side, the road passing abreast La Rosa within waving distance across the river. In a car it then takes ten minues to cross the bridge at Pinhão, drive through the town and reach the Quinta on the far side.

Thus arose the custom of blowing a long passing blast on the horn to herald one's arrival and of everybody at the Quinta waving sheets, towels and handkerchiefs to the departing guests as they passed on the far side, always a little sadly, on the way home. Partings are poignant and this one is like that last view of the inland sea going home from Positano, or the finale of Figaro on the last night of another Glyndebourne summer. But so long as people still wave from those windows the Goodbye becomes a perpetual *Au Revoir*; hence the dedication of this book.

Forty years after I had taken Tim down the Loch at Arrochar he was able to return my 10 knot hospitality by taking me up the Douro as far as the new Valeira dam in his 30 knot speed boat.

'None of that disgraceful language', he said. 'My mother-in-law lives in the Close at Norwich, not on the Broads, and she's coming too.'

ACKNOWLEDGEMENTS

My thanks are also due to Mr David Delaforce, an invaluable link in Oporto, to Lord Thomson of Monifieth, Dr Peter Hargrove and Mr Chris Davies for checking my copy in different parts of the Algarve, to Mrs Elizabeth Ray for notes on hotels and restaurants in and around Oporto and to Mrs Elizabeth Kendall and Mr Philip Kendall for their advice.

Helpful travel information was received from Mr Arthur Treagust and Miss Margaret Evans of Chichester Travel and from Mr John Edwards now retired from the Automobile Association.

Nearly all the photographs have been lent by The Portuguese National Tourist office in London, where Senhor Joaquim Santos kindly gave much of his time to their selection. Mr Jan Reid has also been helpful, although colour reproduction unfortunately is far too expensive to make full use of his superb photography. Likewise unacceptable costs have prohibited 'bespoke' maps. I am therefore grateful to J M Dent & Sons for permission to use those originally drawn for their Portuguese Food and Wine books by Carol Wright and Raymond Postgate respectively. My thanks also go to those members of the Wine Trade in Portugal named in my text for their generous hospitality. My wife Joan, making no claim to be a professional at any keyboard, typed the entire book, the second she did for me during her last years of cancer.

Finally, I am most grateful for editorial help from Chichester Design Associates with whom I have worked on wine publications for many years and to both The Society of Authors and Mr Richard Binns for advice on self publishing.

Anthony Hogg
July 1987

Part 1
INTRODUCING PORTUGAL

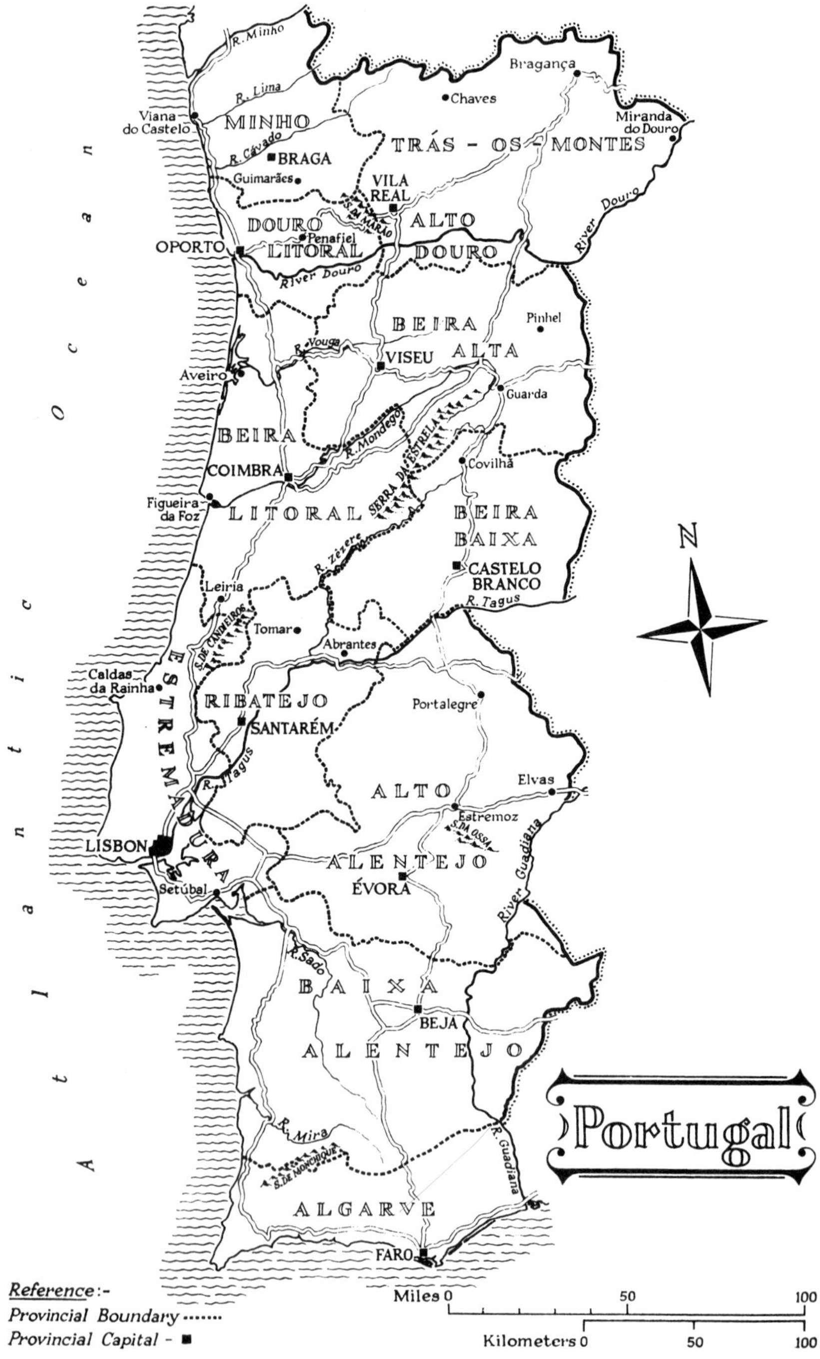
Portugal
A t l a n t i c O c e a n
R. Minho
R. Lima
Viana do Castelo
MINHO
R. Cávado
BRAGA
Guimarães
Chaves
Bragança
Miranda do Douro
TRÁS - OS - MONTES
VILA REAL
S. DA MARÃO
DOURO LITORAL
Penafiel
ALTO DOURO
OPORTO
River Douro
River Douro
BEIRA ALTA
Pinhel
R. Vouga
VISEU
Guarda
Aveiro
BEIRA LITORAL
R. Mondego
SERRA DA ESTRELA
COIMBRA
Covilhã
Figueira da Foz
BEIRA BAIXA
R. Zêzere
CASTELO BRANCO
R. Tagus
N
Leiria
S. DE CANDIEIROS
Tomar
Abrantes
ESTREMADURA
Caldas da Rainha
RIBATEJO
SANTARÉM
Portalegre
R. Tagus
ALTO ALENTEJO
Elvas
Estremoz
S. DA OSSA
River Guadiana
LISBON
ÉVORA
Setúbal
R. Sado
BAIXA ALENTEJO
BEJA
R. Mira
S. DE MONCHIQUE
R. Guadiana
ALGARVE
FARO
Reference:-
Provincial Boundary ......
Provincial Capital - ■
Miles 0 50 100
Kilometers 0 50 100

A LITTLE HISTORY

In the long months preparing plans for the invasion of Normandy in 1944, there was an unwritten rule to ensure harmony in the Joint Allied Staff, 'By all means call a colleague a bastard, but if you call him an American bastard or a British bastard you're fired.'

Happily no such precaution has ever been necessary to maintain the Anglo-Portuguese alliance. Our respective modern histories both spring from bastards and their battles.

In 1066 William of Normandy, the Conqueror at Hastings, became our first Norman king, building Battle Abbey to commemorate his victory.

In 1385 John, Master of the Knights of Avis, won the battle of Aljubarrota, building near this village an abbey which he called Batalha, meaning battle. He then became the first House of Avis king of Portugal. Both men were illegitimate or 'natural' sons as the history books term them. The only difference was that John's *Batalha* preserved the independence of Portugal from Spain, while William's lost it for the Anglo-Saxons.

Expelling the Moors

Some 30 years before William crossed the Channel, Henry I of France had given the Duchy of Burgundy to his brother, Robert, starting a ducal dynasty that was to last until 1381. Styling himself 'Henry of Burgundy', a grandson of Robert went to Spain to fight the Moors, who had been there since the 7th century. Henry married Theresa, a natural daughter of Alfonso VI, king of Leon, whose kingdom ran from Galicia as far south as the river Mondego in the middle of Portugal.

Portucale – as it was then called – being given as a dowry, Henry ruled it as a vassal and dying in 1112, left his wife to govern it during the minority of their son, Alfonso Henriques. But Theresa estranged both Alfonso and his chief supporter, the influential Bishop of Braga, by lavishing wealth and titles on her lover and in 1128 the pair of them were exiled by her subjects.

Meanwhile Alfonso had been fighting his Moorish and Spanish neighbours so successfully that at the peace of Zamora in 1143 he was recognised as being independent of any Spanish sovereign. Aided by many English, Germans and Flemings, who were to settle in Portugal later, his victories over the Moors culminated in 1147 with the capture of Santarém followed by that of Lisbon.

Eight years earlier after his victory at Ourique his troops had proclaimed him Alfonso I of Portugal, a choice now confirmed by the first

Cortes, meeting at Lamego across the Douro from his birth-place, Guimarães. He died in 1185 having made Portucale into Portugal, an independent country from the Minho to the Tagus, even though 80 more years had to pass before the Moors left the Algarve for good.

With his Burgundian roots it was natural for Alfonso to make a vow to St. Bernard after the capture of Santarém that he would give the Domain of Alcobaça to the Cistercians. The order had been founded by Burgundy people in 1098 to follow the teachings of St. Bernard. Their first monastery had been built at Citeaux, near Châlons-sur-Saône. Already settled at Alcobaça, some of these dedicated founders in their grey and white habits began to build their monastery in 1178.

Azulejos

The Moors left to Spain and Portugal a valuable legacy in the art of comfortable living in a hot climate. The patio – its meaning rather stretched in today's self-catering villa – is a roofless, inner courtyard usually with blank windowless walls giving on to the street, and, in old palaces such as the Pousadas at Palmela and Evora, the sound of running water from a fountain. The metal grilles to the lower windows of houses, the blinding white-washed towns of the Alentejo with their flattish roofs, the chimney-pots of high narrow oblongs of mortar in an Algarve town such as Tavira, these are all Moorish in origin.

But the contribution that seems to have appealed most to the Portuguese was their use of glazed tiles for enlivening the scene indoors and out. Their Arabic word *azulejo* meaning 'smooth' is quite unconnected with azure blue, which came to be the prevailing colour.

Designs were often multi-coloured, some with black now being as rare as a black penny in stamp-collecting. There are said to be examples in the Palace at Sintra and near the pool in the garden at Quinta de Baçalhoa, near Azeitão, though after reaching the former on its closed day and the latter when the caretaker could not be found, I cannot vouch for them.

In Portugal they are often part of 19c. railway station decoration depicting the local attractions; the terraced vineyards at Pinhão for example and at Alcobaça inevitably the monastery itself.

Castles in Portugal

After the country was rid of the Moors, the threat from the Castilians was ever present and during the next two hundred years Alfonso Henrique's successors in the First, or Burgundian, Dynasty built castles for national defence, few towns in Portugal being left without one. Many still survive, those at Palmela and Estremoz on the Lisbon

Fly/Drive being worth the climb for exceptionally fine views over the Tagus and the Alentejo plain respectively. Dinis (1279–1325) married to the Holy Queen St. Elizabeth of Portugal was the most enlightened monarch of this dynasty, encouraging his subjects – grown to a million – in good husbandry, afforestation and the arts. He founded the first University in Lisbon, which later moved to Coimbra and consolidated a frontier that exists almost unchanged today.

National Love Story

His grandson Pedro I, and Inês de Castro, Pedro's murdered mistress and lady-in-waiting to the Aragon princess he had been required to marry, make Portugal's saddest love story. Their tombs, feet to feet in the N. and S. transepts at Alcobaça, though damaged by French soldiers in the Peninsular War, rank with the most beautiful sculptures of the 14c.

Pedro and Inês had four illegitimate children one of whom, John, was destined to be a national hero. When Pedro's successor Fernando died, his widow planned to hand the country back to the King of Castille, who had married their young daughter. The Portuguese wanted none of this and it was John who led them to the great victory over the Castilians at Aljubarrota in 1385 with which this story began.

THE GREAT DISCOVERIES

The Half English Prince (1394–1460)

A number of English bowmen sent by John of Gaunt had made a major contribution to John I's victory and in 1387 he married John of Gaunt's daughter, Philippa of Lancaster, after signing a treaty with England. A cultured, religious woman she bore him six remarkable sons. The fifth son (the third to survive) Prince Henry the Navigator, looked out across the sea from the Sagres headland at the Western end of the Algarve from the international school of navigators, cartographers and shipbuilders that he had conceived and created, determined that there must be a sea-borne route to the East.

From here he planned and dispatched expeditions to explore the coast southwards, which by the end of the century had culminated in Vasco da Gama rounding the Cape of Good Hope and reaching India, Christopher Columbus, Vasco's protegé, discovering the New World, and Pedro Alvares Cabral, of Belmonte in the Beira Baixa province, adding Brazil to an entirely Portuguese empire, known to history as *The Great Discoveries*.

Voyages . . . colonies . . . wealth. The process went on and on. It still does. Though the wealth may no longer be tangible, it can be measured in knowledge and experience. 'Go back and learn some more; go further!' the Prince commanded. In August 1982 when the Atlantic has been crossed singly in a 9-foot sailing boat and the Transglobe expedition has returned safely from a three year circumnavigation via the Poles, his injunction apparently still inspires the brave.

When he died in 1460, his navigators had reached Madeira, the Azores and Cape Bojador (now Spanish Sahara). Better means of navigation and, above all, the evolution of the Caravel, the broad-beamed vessel with one tower forward (the forecastle) and two aft, which could tack had, by 1500, made *The Great Discoveries* possible and the Portuguese had begun an age of sail that enabled Europe to dominate the world for three hundred years until the steam engine.

Heavily restored, the house where Prince Henry was born is in Oporto close to the 'Factory House' of the British merchants who have played such a part in the Old Alliance. His tomb with that of his parents is in the Capela do Fundador, the Founder's Chapel in the Abbey of Batalha; his fine portrait by Nuno Gonçalves is in the Museum of Ancient Art in Lisbon. There are too, his statue by the side gate of the Church at Belém and the 1840 monument at Sagres.

Summit of an Empire

The enormous achievements of Portugal's seamen are now probably forgotten if, indeed, they were ever taught in Britain, the English having been engaged at the time with France in The Hundred Years War, with the War of the Roses to follow. João da Nova sighted Ascension (1501) and St. Helena (1502). Tristão da Cunha, giving his name to that archipelago in 1506, went on to discover Madagascar, Mauritius and Socotra. In the next decade the Portuguese reached Goa, Malacca, Siam and Canton. From Goa they went westwards up the Red Sea and the Persian Gulf. In 1522 one of Magellan's ships completed the first voyage round the world. By 1550 their settlements extended along the coasts from Brazil across to Africa and on to Ceylon and Malaya.

Not until 1562 did Hawkins and Drake begin *their* voyages taking African slaves to Mexico, where merciless butchery of captured English seamen by the Spanish Inquisition Drake was never to forget. Thenceforward Portugal had a friend and a protector.

The peak of her prosperity was reached during the reign of Manuel I (1495–1521), the wealth of gold, spices, ivory and precious stones pouring in from East and West. The artists, unable to illustrate the wonders of new lands they had not seen gave expression to the discoveries by introducing the means of achieving them into a new style of sculpture known as Manueline.

Manueline – Portugal's Unique Architecture

The groining of vaulted roofs became knotted cables in stone; stone chains, anchors, sails, coral and even navigational instruments decorated Gothic cathedrals. And to these the architects added what they saw themselves in everyday life – acorns and artichokes, roses, poppies and corn cobs, with trunks of oak and olive as pillars, their leaves and branches twined as tracery.

The leading architect was Boytac, thought to be French in origin, his earliest work being the vaulted Gothic church of Jesus at Setúbal begun in 1494. This was soon followed by the Jeronymite church and cloister of Santa Maria de Belém in Lisbon. Other fine examples of Manueline are the great Portal of the Unfinished Chapels and the tracery in the cloister windows at Batalha.

In the Convent of Christ at Tomar some say the famous Sea Window by Diogo de Arruda of Evora is too grotesque to be taken seriously. There was, for example, the lady – otherwise a Manueline enthusiast – who, denouncing it as 'a stone insanity' had to be revived with brandy after seeing octupuses. A 'ropey' masterpiece would be a better assessment.

Decline and Fall

King Manuel known as 'the Fortunate', hoped to weld Spain and Portugal's possessions together as an Empire under the House of Avis. Unfortunately his own son died in infancy, the inheritance passing to the Hapsburgs, dominated by Jesuit confessors.

Sebastian (1557–1578) not only refused to marry when the dynasty was threatened with extinction, but became quite besotted with the idea of a crusade against the Moors. In this he was killed and his valuable army almost annihilated. The King Cardinal (1578–80), his uncle and holy successor, left the throne vacant favouring Philip II of Spain (1580–98).

Of four other claimants to the throne, England gave weak naval support to Antonio, the Prior of Crato but an invading Spanish army soon put paid to his supporters.

The Sixty Years of Captivity (1580–1640) that followed under the three Spanish Philips, began the decline of the Empire. Philip forbade the Dutch the port of Lisbon so instead of continuing to be the East-West ocean-going carriers of Europe, they joined the English in building a colonial Empire at the expense of the Portuguese. Angola, Brazil, Malacca, Ceylon, all had gone by 1650.

THE RESTORATION 1640–1755

With the Jesuits now supporting Cardinal Richelieu in France, a coup restored the monarchy, the throne going to John IV (1640–56) of Bragança, the richest family in the land, with castles at Barcelos and Guimarães and a Palace with hunting park at Vila Viçosa near enough to Lisbon. All can still be seen. But the war of independence went on with Spain till 1668, leaving Portugal bankrupt. The only saving grace was that the Brazilians revolted against their Dutch masters, throwing them out and retaking Angola for their motherland.

Once more the Portuguese had never had it so good; the gold and diamonds rolled in for another century, sufficing after the disastrous earthquake of 1755 to rebuild Lisbon to Pombal's grandiose plans.

The Golden Age of Baroque

Again the architects rose to the occasion. The Baroque style, begun in Rome about 1630, lasted for two centuries, taking many forms in different European countries as time passed. Light and cheerful in Portugal it has left delightful granite houses occupying whole streets and squares in the small towns of the North, and in the South the white towns of marble are as attractive.

The façades of churches and chapels no less are graceful and dignified; inside, the panelled painted ceilings, the glorious gilt and carved retables around the altars, the choir stalls, the polychrome sculptures and sometimes the organs afford much pleasure even to the non-specialist eye. Not least, seeing São Roque in Lisbon or the little church of Santa Clara in Oporto for the first time is a breath-taking testimony that 'the golden age' was no empty phrase.

A Princess for Charles

With Britain usually at war with France or Holland, the old alliance was firmly re-established in 1663 when Catherine of Bragança (1638–1705) was dispatched to marry Charles II, Britain's price being two million Portuguese crowns (about £300,000) and the cession of Bombay and Tangier. Catherine, as a Roman Catholic amid a Protestant Establishment, was promised freedom of worship.

An unattractive lady compared to his mistresses, Charles gave his wife little attention and she became a recluse. Producing no children she was falsely accused of involvement in Popish plots. But conditions did improve for her and after his death in 1685 she stayed on under William and Mary for another seven years, being welcomed home in 1693.

The Methuen Treaty of 1703 (there were, in fact, two, signed by

Methuen father and son respectively) is now chiefly remembered because in Britain it reduced the duty on Portuguese wines at the expense of the old enemy, France and allowed British woollens into Portugal free of duty. Somewhat of a mixed blessing lasting until 1842, it was fine for the port shippers in Oporto but retarded the development of Portugal's own weaving industry.

THE PENINSULAR WAR

For the peasants the Peninsular War from 1807 to 1812 was a horrible experience with the French invader advancing and retreating on their soil and the British, drunken and destructive, practising a scorched earth policy when they retreated into the lines of Torres Vedras.

Not a Drum was heard not a funeral note!

After the Convention of Sintra in 1808 (see Óbidos) by which Junot's army was sent home in British ships after its defeat by Arthur Wellesley (Wellington to be), the Spanish guerrillas in the north of Spain were so successful for a while against the French invaders that Sir John Moore's army of 22,000 penetrated as far inland as Salamanca.

But Napoleon himself, taking complete command, had reorganised some 120,000 men into seven corps and the guerrillas had been defeated. By December Madrid was in French hands, Napoleon and Soult forcing Moore, and Baird to his north, to fall back on Corunna. In this exemplary rear-guard action through the mountains of Galicia, Sir John Moore was killed, Charles Wolfe's poem* that many boys of my generation had to learn by heart probably being all that people now remember about the Peninsular War. This is why I have included brief details in the Lisbon and Oporto Fly/Drives of Wellington's battles as and where they occurred.

The Queen, Maria I (1777–1816), had religious mania and during the war years the whole royal family had gone to Brazil. By the time they returned in 1821 Brazil had been an independent kingdom for six years. The home country, virtually a British Protectorate and a colony of Brazil, was in a sorry economic state. Then came the Miguelite Wars of the 1830s in which Pedro IV and his brother fought for the throne, after Brazil had proclaimed her own independence in 1822 never to return.

TWENTIETH CENTURY

A brief revolution in Lisbon ended the Monarchy in 1910 two years after Carlos (1889–1908) and his son had been assassinated in Black Horse Square. Thereafter, until Salazar became Minister of Finance in 1928, Portugal's political history was a record of short-lived ministries

* *The Burial of Sir John Moore at Corunna* Charles Wolfe (1791–1823).

and revolutionary outbreaks. During World War I she proclaimed her loyalty to the Allies, fighting the Germans from the outset in Mozambique and Angola and sending 40,000 troops to the Western Front after Germany had declared war on her in 1916.

Salazar's New State

In 1928 Antonio de Oliveira Salazar, born in 1889 in a one storey cottage at Vimiero amid the vines of the Dão valley, was appointed Finance Minister with wide powers. A Doctor of Economics at Coimbra University, within four years he had given his country a new stability, balancing the Budget, reducing the national debt and the cost of living. Promoted Prime Minister in 1932 he ruled Portugal as an authoritarian, pro-Catholic Nationalist dictator until 1968, in spite of seven military and republican coups, one general strike and one assassination, all attempting to dislodge him.

His achievement was to keep Portugal out of World War II yet friendly to Britain. A brilliant financier, between 1950 and 1970 the escudo only dropped from 80 to 68 to the pound. These were years of economic growth for a nation that had grown from five to almost ten million people since 1900. Yet Portugal remained – and still remains – a poor country.

Between 1870 and 1970 the proportion of the population working on the land had fallen from about 72% to under 30%, poverty forcing many of the men to work abroad. Higher wages, mainly in Western Europe and in Brazil enabled them to maintain their families at home. This has not changed much. Others have drifted to the cities, where metallurgy and textiles, the chief industries, are inadequate for full employment.

Illiteracy, estimated at 69% in 1910 had dropped to 25% by 1970; nevertheless one in four remains a dreadful figure for a European country.

The construction of dams for hydro-electricity was begun during Salazar's long term of office, called 'New State' to disguise what in fact was a Police State, with P.I.D.E., the secret police rounding up and holding suspects without trial, an evil that has since become appallingly familiar during the 20c.

1974 AND AFTER

Loss of Colonies

Salazar's big mistake was in trying to hold his colonies by force, draining his national resources of money and materials. India took Goa without a fight in 1961. In Angola (1961), Guiné (1963) and

Mozambique (1964) the Portuguese became involved with nationalist guerrillas. All to no avail, this inevitably led to independence: Guiné (1974), Angola, Mozambique, Cape Verde Islands, São Tomé and Principe (1975). Indonesia invaded and annexed East Timor. (Now, spurred by Britain's Falklands operation, Portugal is attempting to regain the country through the United Nations, in order to offer it self-determination on British–Zimbabwe lines).

By 1974 discontent with the wars had crystallized in the Armed Forces movement (the MFA: *Movimento das Forças Armadas*) which on April 25 overthrew the regime in an almost bloodless revolution. For the next two years the country was a political turmoil with no less than six provisional Governments.

A new constitution in 1976 drawn up by the moderates, hoping to achieve Socialism and democracy, centred on the respected General António Ramalho Eanes as President. A system of proportional representation, with universal suffrage, elected a single chamber of deputies. The Socialists won, and Eanes appointed their leader, Dr Mário Soares, as Prime Minister of a minority Government.

In the election of 1979 the Democratic Alliance, a right-centre coalition defeated the Socialists but their leader, Francisco de Sá Carneiro was killed in an air crash soon afterwards. Since 1980 the Prime Minister has been Francisco Pinto Balsemão. General Eanes remains President. These Governments have had to settle 700,000 refugees from the former colonies, redistribute land and property more equitably after the confusion of the revolution and raise the standards of a poor people during world recession and economic crisis.

Towards the EEC

With an adequate parliamentary majority and three more years to run this Right-Centre Government aimed to steer Portugal into the European Economic Community as planned in 1984. Foreign investment in Portugal has been increasing at a rate of over 100 per cent annually since 1979. Renault are assembling cars and making engines; General Motors have established component plants. Ford are there too, all forming part of the Portuguese Foreign Institute's plan to create a sound industrial base for the country.

Somincor, a joint Portuguese-French venture, is about to mine iron and copper pyrites in the south thus replacing imports and perhaps laying the foundation of a national metallurgical industry. The country has reserves of iron ore, tin, uranium and wolfram in which Rio Tinto Zinc, BP, Shell and others are reported to be interested.

Considerable tin and wolfram deposits to the north of Miranda do Douro are to be brought down river through the locks of the Barragem built for the Douro hydro-electricity scheme. From Oporto the very large self-propelled barges will take their cargoes south to Sines, where a modern port is being built to handle exports. The final energy output of the Douro basin is estimated at 8000 million kilowatts.

General Election 1987

Since the revolution restored democracy in 1974, Portugal has had fifteen free elections, none of them resulting in a Government with a working majority. At last, since Sunday 19 July 1987 it has one. The Social Democrats have 149 seats in the 250-seat national Parliament against 88 in its predecessor. With former figures in brackets, the results were:

Party	Seats	% Poll
Social Democrats	149 (88)	50 (30)
Socialists	60 (57)	22 (20)
Communists	30 (38)	12 (15)
Democratic Renewal	7 (42)	4 (17)
Christian Democrats	4 (22)	4 (9)

Professor Anibal Cavaco Silva, already Prime Minister since October 1985, now appears to have 50 per cent of eight million voters in favour of his Centre Right policies. This 48 year old intellectual and economist who has studied at York University, is the son of an Algarve petrol station proprietor. With luck, for the next four years Portugal should gain prosperity, with the Socialists strong enough to see that the poorest people get their rightful share.

SOCIAL PROBLEMS

At the time of the Revolution many rural areas of Portugal had no electricity, running water, roads and medical services. Workers were poorly paid and no trade unions were permitted.

In the intervening years wages have risen by 300 per cent and there are strong trade unions. Living standards have visibly improved, the men have cars, motorcycles and TV; the children – no longer barefoot except when they want to be – look healthier and better nourished. But the rise of the dollar has brought about 25 per cent inflation, widely destroying these benefits. Vegetables cost ten times more, beef five times more than before 1974.

Education

In Britain we have free compulsory education for eleven years, 5 to 16. In Portugal it is only six years, 7 to 13, which explains why sometimes the page boy aged 14, carrying your bag up in the hotel lift, speaks better English than any older member of the staff.

Their secondary education takes place in State lyceums, commercial and industrial schools and private schools. Coimbra (founded 1290),

Oporto and Lisbon have old Universities; three new ones are in Lisbon, Braga and Aveiro.

After the Revolution masses of people craved an education; students rose from 200,000 to 1,200,000. In Amadora a working class suburb of Lisbon, reported *The Times* 24.2.82, a school built for 1200 had 20,000 enrolled. Students attend in shifts from 7 am to midnight. Lack of teachers and text books, not to mention space, allied to the breakdown of discipline inevitable after any long restrictive regime create great difficulties, slowly being solved it is hoped, with financial help from the Council of Europe.

When political parties were formed, the vote was extended to everyone over 18 but after eight years and 14 governments enthusiasm for democratic government has understandably waned, which is dangerous. The secret police were disbanded but the ordinary police have had difficulties in combating increased violent crime in a land where people still had arms after the Revolution and refugees from the African wars brought them in.

Housing

To combat a great housing shortage, with the Government not having enough money to build nor the people to buy, the Government is trying to get private enterprise to build new houses for renting.

Health

Two new hospitals in Lisbon recently became operational. In the country a number of small hospitals have been built but have no doctors. There is some sort of a health service in which doctors' pay is so poor that they all prefer to work as private practitioners in Lisbon or Oporto. According to a London *Times* survey of 1982 Portugal is not as poor as statistics make out. Corruption and taxation give too high a share to a few.

Agrarian Reform

In the Alentejo – the granary of Portugal – the huge gap between the prosperity of the landowners and the poverty of the land workers created a strong communist party.

The new constitution provided for expropriation of large estates and big capitalist enterprises. Cooperatives have been created, the size of private farms has been limited, small farmers can receive state aid.

Implementing the new law has not been so easy in individual cases and there have been clashes when workers illegally occupying farms have had to be evicted.

Women's Status

Slower to change, has been the status of Portuguese women. As late as the 1950s a woman's property on marriage was administered by her husband and she could not get a passport without his permission. Even upper and middle class women received little education and very few entered the professions. Among the peasants in any mixed working party walking along the road to collect the resin from the pines, the women will be carrying the heavy things – on their heads. Good for the deportment; Claire Bergqvist declared she had once seen a woman with a grand piano on her head! Washing clothes too in the village stream is still their lot.

In the country it may be years before the work of the Government's *Commission for Equality in Labour and Employment* takes effect; in politics matters are very different. Dona Manuela, wife of the former President aids her husband in his public work and in Senhora Maria de Lourdes Pintassilgo, Portugal has had, very briefly, a woman Prime Minister. Across the floor of the bull ring, not 'the House', there has also been Conchita Cintron taking the opposition by the horns but said to be a happy wife and mother.

Outside Parliament where there have been over 20 women deputies, numbers dwindle to very few in local government and among the magistrates. But, of course, it is only four years since the law was passed giving women equality 'in rights to work and employment'.

SOME FORMER BRITISH TRAVELLERS

John of Gaunt, Duke of Lancaster (1340–1399)

The fourth son of Edward III, set sail from Plymouth in 1386 with his wife, several daughters – legitimate and illegitimate – his staff and his army. Having a claim to the Kingdom of Castile and Leon, he already styled himself king but his aim to establish himself needed a little help from John I, King of Portugal, a brave fellow of 36.

After some months of joustings, exchanging gifts and tremendous feasts, during which the two daughters, Philippa and her half sister Katherine, were kept on ice as it were in a monastery, the bargain was struck. The two Johns would join forces against Castile and the Portuguese king could have Philippa as his Queen.

The Portuguese were delighted; Philippa herself escaped both the monastery and the plague in England in due course becoming the mother of five princes, the third, Henry the Navigator, being the genius behind The Great Discoveries.

Alas, poor old John of Gaunt missed his crown! The campaign in Castile was a plague-stricken disaster and the English survivors, either went home with John or joined his daughter's court in Portugal.

William Beckford (1760–1844)

At the age of 11, William Beckford inherited an enormous fortune from his father (also William), an Alderman of the City and twice Lord Mayor of London. Having studied architecture and the arts (including music under Mozart), he became a famous collector of books, pictures and *objets d'art* as well as the author of *Vathek,* a story of a megalomaniac Arabian caliph, who gives himself to the devil (Eblis) and ends tormented by a burning heart with the beautiful Nourini. *Vathek* had an enormous success.

In 1797 when his wife had died after only three years of marriage, this eccentric, compulsive traveller settled into a magnificent mansion at Belém with a retinue of attendants fit for a king. But a homosexual scandal had preceded him; led by Mr Walpole, the Ambassador, British Lisbon society cut him dead.

In retaliation Beckford successfully cultivated the Portuguese nobility yet was unable to obtain the introduction to the Queen, which he could then throw in the face of his countrymen. For posterity the ostracism was a pity; his *Sketches of Spain and Portugal* had already stamped him as an imaginative writer, whose trenchant impressions of the British in Lisbon would have been worth reading.

After a summer at Ramalhão, a residence that later was to become first a royal palace and then a nuns' school for little girls, the Beckford mule train of books, piano, food, wines and staff disappeared to Spain for six years, returning in 1793 with Europe in turmoil, as the French proceeded to execute their Royal family.

In Portugal Queen Maria had gone mad when at long last, in May 1795, the great moment came in the gardens at Sintra where he received the Royal bidding to play hide and seek with the Ladies-in-Waiting. Meanwhile his friendship with 'gifted canons and cardinals' had led to a 12-day trip that was not to be described until 50 years later when *Recollections of an Excursion to the Monasteries of Alcobaça and Batalha* was published. This extraordinary, fanciful travel book by an aesthete who lived like a potentate, makes fascinating reading.

By 1800 he had left Portugal settling down in his own house, Fonthill Abbey near Bath to a life described by Rose Macaulay as 'the fabulous, crazy loveliness of that lotus-eating, comic opera, devout, ridiculous moonish world' he had enjoyed amid the rich 18c. *fidalgos* and prelates.

Today, only in 18c. opera do we get an occasional glimpse of those patriarchal armies of retainers, the troupes of musicians, the banquets, the follies and the extravagancies that amazed and scandalized the respectable world of Jane Austen in the Pump Room of Bath.

George Borrow (1803–1881)

With a knowledge of French, German, Danish, Welsh, Irish, Latin, Greek and the gypsies' Romany, one can hardly blame this Norfolk traveller, linguist and author for omitting Spanish and Portuguese.

That, however, did not deter him, as an agent of the British and Foreign Bible Society, from a tour of Spain, Portugal and Morocco from 1835 to 1840. A business trip really, because he was wedded not to his faith but to his job: the bibles he sold to the Spaniards and Portuguese have been likened to bombs charged with hate for their established churches.

After a fortnight in Lisbon in which he learnt enough of the language to carry out a market survey, accosting people in the street, and to have an enjoyable day off to Sintra, he braved the cold across the Alentejo plain during December. Crossing the Tagus on a mule, with luggage and suitcases full of bibles was hazardous; the muleteer was mad and Borrow was attacked by a large savage dog, quelling the assault the Woodhouse way with 'the calm reproving glance of reason'.

In Evora 200 citizens interviewed were described as apathetic; not surprisingly perhaps, this Reverend Mr Paisley on tour told them repeatedly that 'the Pope, whom they revered, was an arch deceiver and head minister of Satan on earth'.

His report *The Bible in Spain* was published in 1842.

Henry Fielding (1707–1754)

While Southey and Byron, the poets, went to Portugal as innocents abroad aged 21, Fielding – the greatest English novelist certainly of his day – went for his health when 47 and died in Lisbon within two months.

The author of *Joseph Andrews, Jonathan Wild* and *Tom Jones,* born near Glastonbury, spent his early life in Wiltshire and Dorset. Educated at Eton, he became manager of the Haymarket Theatre, but a licensing act of 1737, restricting the number of theatres, put paid to his career as a dramatist.

Next he read for the Bar, practising on the Western Circuit in the 1740s. *Joseph Andrews* appeared in 1742 and *Jonathan Wild* a year later. Then Charlotte Cradwell, his wife, died of a fever and he nearly went mad with grief. He remarried Mary Daniel, her maid and, in 1748 when he became a London JP, they had a free house in Bow Street with £300 pa for the job. *Tom Jones* or *The History of a Foundling* came out that same year.

By 1754 with jaundice, dropsy and asthma he was a dying man, for whom the doctors recommended winter in the warm south. His *Journal of a Voyage to Lisbon* (1755) describes how the Fieldings, his daughter, a maid, a manservant and Miss Collier, who had an eye for the Chaplain, fared.

Mr Stubbs, a leading corn merchant, found them a house near Belém and in spite of the August heat and dust Fielding felt much better. He enjoyed the company of Mr Williamson, the Chaplain, who showed him the magnificence and the squalor of a city that the earthquake would destroy a year later. Possibly depressed because Mrs Fielding wanted to go home to her children, he deteriorated and died on October 8.

His friend, the Chaplain, buried him in the new English Cemetery on the hill but nobody knows precisely where. Could a tombstone have been destroyed in the earthquake? There were several plans but not until 1830 did a *locum tenens* chaplain collect funds to raise the existing monument; a shrine for English tourists, who have included George Borrow (1835), Wordsworth's daughter, Mrs Quillinan (1846) and Alfred Lord Tennyson (1859).

Sir John Croft (1778–1862)

The first John Croft, a wine merchant in York had come out in 1736 to join Phayre and Bradley, whose partnership began in 1678. Presumably they were dead for the firm became Tilden, Thompson and Croft, who is remembered for his *Treatise on the Wines of Portugal* (1788), a valuable historical work.

The red wines known as 'Red Portugal' were weak, and nasty too by the time they reached the London taverns, which explains how Samuel Johnson's contemporaries could drink three bottles and remain sober. Port fortified with brandy did not begin to appear until after his death in 1784; the evolution of the bottle into a shape that could be laid down creating 'vintage port'.

Sir John Croft (1778–1862) is thought to have been a nephew, born in Oporto but working mostly in the York side of the business. In the Peninsular War his intelligence work for Britain and Portugal brought him an English baronetcy in 1818 and the title Barão de Estrêla from the Portuguese.

Wellington, Arthur Wellesley 1st Duke (1769–1852)

The battles of the Peninsular War that occurred on Portuguese soil are referred to in the text under the appropriate place names.

Elizabeth Longford's *Wellington, The Years of the Sword,* the first of two volumes of her Wellington biography published in Panther paperback covers the whole campaign in admirable detail.

Robert Southey (1774–1843)

Much against his will, Southey sailed from Falmouth to Corunna in January 1796. Born in Bristol, this son of an unsuccessful linen draper, had been brought up by his mother's half sister, Elizabeth Tyler in Bath and sent to Westminster School when he was 14. Four years later he was expelled. His crime? An essay in the school magazine against flogging.

His uncle, Herbert Hill, Chaplain of the British Factory House in Lisbon, after paying for his education hoped that young Robert would settle down, having got rid of his dangerous radical ideas and take Holy Orders. In deference to Elizabeth Tyler's wishes, Southey agreed to spend six months in Lisbon with the Chaplain, leaving behind his adored Edith Fricker, whom he had only just married secretly.

From Corunna after a sea-sick passage in January weather, the journey to Lisbon was overland via Madrid. Unfortunately King Carlos of Spain and his court happened to be in front, eating all the food and leaving behind their dead mules in the dirty inns. This experience was enough to turn Robert into a rabid republican.

The first night in Lisbon produced an earthquake tremor which alarmed him as much as the Portuguese, for it was only 40 years since the capital had been destroyed. After an upbringing in Bath and four years at Balliol, the dirt, the dogs, the beggars and near misses from slop pails descending from above disgusted him, as it did Byron (Harrow and Trinity, Cambridge) at the same age ten years later.

While the mornings passed pleasantly in his uncle's library, Southey found no kindred spirit in the English colony. Conversation was commerce, their pastimes dancing and cards and they took no interest in the country of their adoption. As to the Church this humanist, poet laureate to be, hated the institution as superstitious, reactionary, cruel and obsessed with the 'diabolical belief in eternal punishment'.

Nevertheless the first sight of the convent on the hill at Arrábida evoked a poem of delight and his uncle's little house at Sintra among laurels and lemons, with a stream in the garden, afforded great pleasure. Longing for his bride, the young man went home in April, soon to develop kinder second thoughts about Portugal when confronted with a smoking, overcast Bristol. As with wine – the one thing he had enjoyed – his vision of Portugal slowly matured from rough and rude to elegant, sweet, delicious. Three years later he returned with Edith, staying from April 1800 to June 1801 in a little house in the Lapa district (formerly Buenos Ayres) westwards of the Estrêla church on a hill overlooking the Tagus. Reading for the law in England had made him ill, a useful excuse for avoiding the English social life. While he worked at one window, Edith, a devoted but simple soul, looked out of another at the people in the streets.

My Edith here
Thinks all things queer,
And some things she likes well;
But then the street
She thinks not neat,
And does not like the smell.
Nor do the fleas
Her fancy please,
Although the fleas like her . . .

In the summer they had the house at Sintra to themselves; a British army having been in Portugal since 1797 to help fight the Spaniards, the chaplain had so many children to baptize and to bury that he was unable to leave Lisbon. Southey was extremely happy, the climate made him feel fit again as he explored the region on an ass. The melons and the grapes were glorious. Only good fresh English bread and butter were missing.

All this time he was hard at work on his history of Portugal and went to Coimbra, Batalha and Alcobaça, where the tomb of Inez could have inspired the poet. He like Monchique and intended to go north, having become so absorbed in the country that to his friend, Coleridge, he could write 'I would gladly live and die here'. But by May 1801 the international situation was grave, with a Franco–Spanish army approaching Badajoz and the Lisbon British in danger of expulsion to appease the enemy.

So the Southeys went home and in time became used to Keswick's 'horrid latitude and incessant rains'. Failing to get a suitable job in Portugal, he persevered with the history which was never finished. The manuscript has never been found and posterity is left with *Letters from Spain and Portugal* (1797).

George Gordon Byron 6th Baron (1788–1824)

Lord Byron went to Portugal on July 2 1809 arriving in Lisbon on July 7. It was not exactly the best time to be there. Napoleon had declared war on Portugal on October 20 1807, Junot's troops occupying the city soon afterwards killing all the dogs and behaving as invaders usually do. A year later, after the Convention of Sintra, they had been evacuated by sea, only to be replaced by Arthur Wellesley's troops who were little better. It was a time of mistrust; the British thought the Portuguese should have resisted the French and the Portuguese had had enough of foreign armies.

Byron was only 21; lame from birth with a nasty temper, strenuous holidays in the Highlands had enabled him to play cricket for Harrow at Lords and his swimming was good enough to tackle the Tagus and the Hellespont. Moreover his Latin and Greek were good enough to converse with the monks of Mafra.

The title had come from a great uncle the previous year at the age of 20 and after taking his seat in the Lords in January, he set off from Falmouth that summer with a Cambridge friend, John Hobhouse, a butler, a valet and a German of some kind. They were only in Lisbon for a fortnight, long enough for this rather priggish Lothario to take a jaundiced view of the Portuguese and a city that was probably no filthier than London. It was certainly dangerous; armies lived off the land by plunder and violence and Lisbon citizens were as capable of cutting a military throat as the English and the Irish of robbing them.

Sintra was another matter. Gil Vicente, the Portuguese Shakespeare had called it an earthly garden of Paradise in 1529, Southey (q.v.), in Lisbon a dozen years before Byron, had fallen likewise; Byron was to put it on the map in *Childe Harold's Pilgrimage,* trying to knock the Portuguese off it at the same time:

> Poor, paltry slaves! yet born 'midst noblest scenes—
> Why, Nature, waste thy wonders on such men?
> Lo! Cintra's glorious Eden intervenes
> In variegated maze of mount and glen.
> Ah, me! what hand can pencil guide, or pen,
> To follow half on which the eye dilates
> Through views more dazzling unto mortal ken
> Than those whereof such things the bard relates,
> Who to the awe-struck world unlock'd Elysium's gates?
>
> The horrid crags, by toppling convent crown'd,
> The cork-trees hoar that clothe the shaggy steep,
> The mountain-moss by scorching skies imbrown'd,
> The sunken glen, whose sunless shrubs must weep,
> The tender azure of the unruffled deep,
> The orange tints that gild the greenest bough,
> The torrents that from cliff to valley leap,
> The vine on high, the willow branch below,
> Mix'd in one mighty scene, with varied beauty glow.

Joseph James Forrester (1809–1862)

This baron to be was only 22 when he went out in 1831 to join his uncle's wine firm, Offley Forrester. A young man after Robert Southey's heart, he quickly learnt to speak the language, and went about the country making friends with everybody irrespective of nationality or station. A brilliant cartographer, he mapped the Douro from the Spanish frontier to the Atlantic, studied the vine and its diseases and painted portraits in his spare time.

If the honour of being first in the port trade belongs to the West Country represented by the Hunts, Roopes and Newmans of Dartmouth, who first traded in 1654, any awards for distinguished service go to Yorkshire; John Croft being from York and Forrester from Hull.

He arrived just in time for the Miguelite civil war, in which Oporto was besieged for 18 months, its population reduced to eating their dogs, cats and donkeys. Many of the poor died from cholera and starvation.

In Brazil, D. Pedro, having declared that country's independence in 1822, had surrendered the Portuguese crown to his daughter, Maria Gloria (aged 7). His young brother Miguel, however, supported by the rich and the priests, had then, in 1825, set himself up as an absolute monarch.

With the help of a £2,000,000 loan and some ships from Britain, Pedro's 7500 'Liberators', determined to depose his young brother, landed north of Oporto in March 1832. When they marched into the city unopposed, the people rang the bells with delight and shot the Public Executioner. But the 13,000 strong Miguelite garrison, having prudently retired across the river to set up their gun batteries at Vila Nova de Gaia, was strong enough to cut off Oporto completely, except from the sea.

Naturally the shippers' concern was 'business as usual'. For Forrester this meant liaison between his uncle in Oporto and the Lodges in Gaia held by the Miguelites, whose shells were apt to fall on the Rua Nova dos Inglezes, in the lower part of Oporto where the British did business. Many of those killed were children playing in the streets of this crowded quarter. The only British casualty was a Mr Wright of Crofts, who lost an arm and the glass of port it held when a shell came through his dining room.

Fortunately the Miguelites had no navy and no good general, which enabled Captain Charles Napier RN in charge of the Liberators' squadron to make a diversion that led to the fall of Lisbon.

27,000 pipes of port were lost when the Miguelite gunners set fire to some of the Lodges as a parting gesture; but the following year, 1834, with the war over and the vintage good, it was at last 'business as usual', so prettily portrayed by Forrester in that best known of port paintings, *English Merchants in the Rua Nova Dos Inglezes.*

For a decade there was peace, until in 1844 Forrester opened fire with his pamphlet, *A Word or Two on Port Wine, showing how and why it is adulterated and affording some means of checking its adulterations.* In effect, because of a slump in sales he was reiterating the complaint of Pombal's time – too much brandy, too much sugar and too much elderberry juice.

His accusations were, of course, resented by the shippers, leading to a war of recrimination fought with denials, protests and vituperation, which went on for some time.

Today's verdict, I think, is that he was right in saying that the shippers encouraged the farmers to adulterate their wine with elderberry juice and sugar. The demand from Britain was for darker, sweeter wine and this was one way to achieve it. But there were other reasons for the decline in quality, such as blending with inferior wine brought in from areas outside what is now the demarcated region.

In wanting to do away with brandy altogether, Forrester was quite wrong. The result would have been a light dry table wine of little quality replacing a fortified wine that is unique.

That he had the courage to raise the storm and court unpopularity is greatly to his credit. No elderberry has since been permitted; port, its fermentation stopped by blending with local brandy when there is enough natural sugar, has remained unchanged in its constituents for over a century.

Gradually the row subsided. Back at work painting portraits, Forrester was made a Baron by the King of Portugal and many lesser honours were bestowed by royalty from other countries.

On May 12 1862 he was drowned in the river he had mapped for posterity. After lunch at Quinta de Vargellas, the boat capsized in the rapids of Cachão da Valeira. His companions, Baroness Fladgate and Dona Antónia Adelaide Ferreira of Quinta do Vesúvio, floated to safety buoyed up by their crinolines. The Baron, wearing a belt full of golden sovereigns with which to pay farmers or employees, was drowned.

Today the narrow sinister gorge between high rocks lies just above the Valeira dam, the rapids replaced by placid waters between dams. An inscription, which might be a memorial carved in the rock, is dated 1790; it merely records the point where further navigation upstream was impossible until further rocks had been cleared.

Edward VII (1841–1910)

Albert Edward, King of Great Britain and Ireland, and of the British Dominions beyond the seas, Emperor of India, the eldest son and second child of Queen Victoria and Albert was a tremendous traveller.

Educated in succession by four private tutors, two of whom were clergymen, followed by Christ Church, Oxford, and Trinity, Cambridge he had been to Italy, Spain, Canada and the United States by the time he was 21.

With Queen Victoria in retirement, there was a lull after his marriage in 1863 to Princess Alexandra, the King of Denmark's daughter, followed by a nearly fatal attack of typhoid before Christmas 1871. Still Prince of Wales, of course, he made his first visit to Portugal in 1876 on the way home from a 10,500 mile tour of India the previous year.

From February onwards English technicians descended in droves upon Lisbon to prepare all the panoply of a Royal visit – pavilions, illuminations, fireworks, bands – until one Portuguese journalist wondered whether they would produce an English fog.

The Royal entourage, travelling from Madrid in a Spanish Royal train having changed to a Portuguese Royal train at the frontier, duly arrived in Lisbon at 3 pm on April 30. King Luis met the train, the people were out in full to watch the processions, the British merchants lined the windows and battleships of many nations in the Tagus fired royal salutes.

But there was one hitch, giving great pleasure to Senhor Ortigão, the one vociferous Anglophobe journalist, which he developed a little later into a not undeserved diatribe against British arrogance in his *Epistola a John Bull,* probably never translated into English. Rose Macaulay describes it beautifully as the Patriotic Horse:

> There was only one hitch, which very likely entertained the gazing street crowds more than if all had gone smoothly. The procession was halted abruptly in the square outside the station by the obstinate decision of one of the horses of the royal carriage not to proceed. He stopped dead. We have of the distressing contretemps the delighted account of Senhor Ortigão, who found it the one incident in the prince's visit that he could applaud. He respected and admired the resolution of this fine horse, who, in the face of all persuasion, threats, blows, prods from bayonet points and parasols, remained inflexibly stationary. The coachmen, the police, the military, officials, ordinary citizens and their families, all had a try to move him. They recited to him, says Senhor Ortigão, the law, the police regulations, extracts from the patriotic speeches of Senhor Thomaz Ribeiro; they praised the monarchical regime, telling him that under it he might become a consul like the horse of

Caligula; they reminded him that he was a public servant, that he must on no account incur the odium of a traitor. It was no good; he resisted everything, neighing, biting, rearing, tearing his harness. The only thing was to unharness him and proceed a horse short.

The newspapers next day, to minimize the scandal, said the horse had gone mad. But, said Senhor Ortigão, that was not true. He had himself observed the horse being led quietly home, wearing an expression reflective and composed. The horse was in full possession of his faculties. He did not draw the prince's carriage because he did not wish to. 'And that', said Senhor Ortigão, 'seems to me important, John' (he was addressing John Bull), 'that among those who triumphantly received His Royal Highness, there was one who protested.'

Otherwise the visit was a great success with naval and military reviews, banquets afloat and ashore, English jockeys at the races, Royal donkey rides at Sintra and nuns invited to take tea with the officers on board the flagship *Serapis,* an invitation the Mother Superior hastily regretted their order did not permit.

Returning to England in the flagship there was an extra passenger, the donkey the Prince of Wales had bought at Sintra for his children to ride at Sandringham. This employment had not occured to Senhor Ortigão.

'How would this poor expatriate working class *burro* feel, idling at the English court after carrying common or garden Sintra tourists all those years? Or could it be that he would be run in the Royal colours at Epsom races?' he asked.

After his coronation in 1902, King Edward's first state visit abroad was again to Lisbon *en route* in the new Royal yacht, *Victoria and Albert,* for Gibraltar and Malta. The weather was glorious during those four days from April 2. King Carlos went out to the yacht in his Royal barge, its figurehead a Bragança dragon, and the two monarchs drove from Black Horse Square to the Ajuda Palace in the old painted coaches now in the Coach Museum.

Amid the usual round of functions and festivities Edward VII opened the park that still bears his name and this time both the Press and the horses were Anglophile.

HM Queen Elizabeth II and HRH Prince Philip, Duke of Edinburgh

The Queen and her Consort went to Portugal on a three day official visit to Lisbon in February 1957, to repay that of the Portuguese President, General Carveiro Lopes to London.

Protocol at that time allowed Heads of State to visit only capital cities, so it was with great enthusiasm that on February 21 Oporto turned out when Her Majesty decided to pay a brief informal call on the way home. The royal couple, driving in a closed car from the airport, received a warm welcome. They were shown round the Bolsa and the Factory House, where there was time to sign the visitors' book and to taste the Factory's finest port.

Though Portuguese monarchs attended great balls in their honour in the 1860s and Manuel II, the last of all, had been entertained in 1908, this was the first visit of a reigning British monarch. And when they agreed to return to the airport in an open Portuguese military 'pick-up' the Portuguese gave them a tremendous send-off.

On Tuesday, March 26 1985 they arrived at Lisbon once again in the Royal yacht *Britannia* on a four day State visit, moving north to Oporto by air for the last day, which included a reception for the business community at the Bolsa, headquarters of the Commercial Association (page 96).

TRH The Prince and Princess of Wales

During a four day tour this Royal couple were in Lisbon on St Valentine's day February 1987 to commemorate the six hundred years of the alliance. After staying in the Palácio Nacional at Sintra, they flew to Oporto to open a British Trade Exhibition.

WHY GO TO PORTUGAL?

Briefly the answer to this very sensible question is because it's beautiful, the people are friendly, the climate pleasant, the wines excellent, the food good and the cost low.

The cost was low in 1980–81 when there were 100 escudos to the pound; it is even better value now that devaluation gives 218 to the pound, though inflation has increased prices to some extent.

And, of course, Portugal is Britain's oldest ally with whom we have never been at war unless England's football team supporters have started one by the time these words appear in print.

Roughly a rectangle 362 miles long and, on average, 117 miles wide, Portugal's 34,000 square miles cover about one seventh of the Iberian peninsula, Spain's 197,000 square miles being the rest. Wales, also surrounded on three sides by salt water, is much the same size in relation to England.

For holidays Wales and Portugal have much in common – hills, valleys, rivers, lakes – but not only is Portugal three times bigger than Wales but the mountains are higher, the valleys deeper and the lakes larger. Her latitude 37°N to 42°N – rather warmer than Wales – drawn from north to south on a Mediterranean map would run from north Corsica to Tunis. In reality the Atlantic breeze cools her down, bringing a good deal of refreshing rain to the northern half.

The rainfall, however, becomes progressively less going eastwards from the coast into and beyond the mountains as the influence of Spain's dry Mediterranean continental climate takes over, an advantage seldom enjoyed on holiday in Wales, the English Lakes or Scotland.

Land of Rivers

The frontiers with Spain are partly defined by the courses of four principal rivers, the Minho and the Douro in the north, the Tagus and the Guadiana in the south. Portugal, no less than France, is a land of very beautiful rivers. Most of them rise in the mountains of Spain – the most mountainous land of Europe save Switzerland – flowing westwards into the Atlantic. Coming south on the coastal route from Spain we first reach the Minho at the frontier town of Valença do Minho; rising in the Cantabrian mountains of Galicia it forms the frontier for about 65 of its 170 miles.

Next comes the Lima, its pastoral setting so lovely that the Romans feared to go across lest – like the lotus eaters – they were made oblivious of their own home country. Flowing slowly across the plain, the Lima adds an arcadian charm to the Vinho Verde countryside and to Viana do Castelo, the ancient, colourful town near its mouth.

The Cávado descending from the Serra do Larouca, north west of Chaves through a series of artificial lakes in the mountains on the edge of the Peneda-Geres National Park, reaches the sea beyond Bucelas, yet another delightful town on the Oporto Fly/Drive. Rather shorter, the Ave flows south west close to Guimarães, the country's first capital.

Some of the Douro tributaries are larger than these, notably the Sabor, Tua and Tamega, joining the Douro at intervals along its right bank in the port wine lands between Oporto and the Spanish frontier. The Douro itself, no longer the 'River of gold' albeit rather muddy, has now been transformed by a series of dams – all part of the hydro-electric scheme built to provide Portugal's industrial energy – into a majestic river of uniform level comparable to the Rhine or the Loire.

From the Minho to the Douro the mountains come almost right down to the sea. South of Oporto the coastal plain widens, the next river, the Vouga, ending in a lagoon at Aveiro.

In mid-Portugal the Mondego, the nation's favourite river because it rises in Portugal not Spain, appears out of the Serra da Estrêla (Mountain of the Star) the country's highest massif – 6532 feet, fast becoming a winter sports resort at the top. The Mondego's course, reminiscent of the Derby at Epsom, ends in a straight finish beyond Coimbra, after a U-turn worthy of Tattenham Corner at the beginning. Dão, its tributary, puts a name to the best table wine region.

Also from the Estrêla, another river the Zezere, loops, Mosel fashion, south west through a whole series of artificial lakes, ideal for boating and sailing in summer, past Tomar to join the Tagus near Abrantes.

Lisbon's Market Garden

The plain maintains its width south of Coimbra to the fishing port of Nazaré through Estremadura (Latin *Extrema Durü*: farthest from Douro) the province that runs down the coast to Lisbon and across the Tagus from Leiria. Even so there is still a range of foothills, the Serra do Aire running south west from Coimbra to Sintra which makes the going slow around Fatima and Tomar and catches the fly/driver unawares in the tedious, traffic-ridden Oporto--Lisbon drive.

East of the Serra do Aire lies the Ribatejo (Banks of the Tagus) where wheat, vines, olives and vegetables continue to be cultivated in the hot, alluvial plain, 15 miles on either side of the Tagus. Estremadura becomes a market garden, particularly south of Lisbon to the Arrábida coast.

The coastal forests of pine and eucalyptus, the chestnuts, oaks and poplars growing out of bracken and heather make the north reminiscent of Wales and Scotland, with the olive and vine a pleasant bonus. These now give way to a southern landscape more Moorish than European.

The Hot Alentejo

The flat, arid Alentejo south of the Tagus, a vast expanse of territory stretching away to the hills that protect the Algarve, will just support the sheep, goats and pigs that subsist between the almond, olive and cork oak trees, while in summer the shepherd boy and his dog squat in the shade of a fig tree if they can find one.

The only big river is the Guadiana, which turns south at Badajoz into Portuguese territory to become the frontier, a function it fulfils again at the Spanish end of the Algarve. The Sado, rising between Evora and Beja and ending at Setúbal is a valuable source of irrigation; the Mira, further south, likewise.

A Wealth of Scenery

Few small countries offer such a variety of scenery. This journey of rivers began in the Elysian fertility of the Minho; in Sacheverell Sitwell's view 'beyond argument the most beautiful province of Portugal'. Others may prefer the majestic mountains of the Douro and the wilder beauty of Trás-os-Montes. There and on the lower slopes of the Serra da Estrêla, the wild flowers in spring rival those of Switzerland, while mimosa, camellias and wisteria follow each other in great profusion.

The lagoon and canals of Aveiro, the estuary of the Sado above Setúbal and the inland lake of the Tagus above Lisbon, recall the waterways of Holland. By the coast, between Leiria and the sand dunes of the Atlantic, the extensive pine woods may remind us of the Landes south of Bordeaux; originally the trees were imported from there by King Dinis (1279–1325) to make the sandy soil firmer.

The Algarve, before the tourist development, looked more North African than European. Its name is derived from the Arabic, *El-Gharb* meaning West. Just as in Spain Jerez de la Frontera was on the frontier of the Moors last salient, so *El-Gharb* was the most westerly region they occupied.

Watermills and Windmills

Used mainly for irrigation, wherever there is water in Portugal you are likely to find a watermill. Built originally for the peasants to grind their corn, there are said to be over 20,000 scattered about the land. Earthenware jars lashed at an angle to the slats of the wheel fill up at the bottom of the turning circle, emptying at the top into a tray, from which the water flows on through open troughs hollowed out of trees.

The windmills – about 2000 – are seen mostly along the coast from the Mondego to the Tagus, particularly on the flat land around Óbidos. The earliest could have been 11c. The conical stone tower has a mast carrying four triangular sails which form the wheel.

Where there is neither wind nor water – the Alentejo in high summer for example – one sees horse, mule or donkey doing the circular tour operating a windlass.

Climate

Portugal should not be compared with Spain, a much larger land mass under Mediterranean influence, except for Galicia and the north coast.

Portugal's climate is equable and temperate. Average daily temperature of Lisbon, Coimbra and Oporto is around 15.5°C/60°F, with a swing from 14°C/57°F in January to 23°C/73°F in August. In the Alentejo where there is little breeze, it can be very much hotter. Lisbon's annual rainfall is about 700 mm (millimetres) falling mostly between November and March inclusive. In Oporto it is over 1000 mm, more than in Manchester. The Azores anti-cyclone determines our weather and theirs; moving north-west in summer it ensures them good weather, but from November to May west winds bring the rain to the coast at those unpredictable times such as we know in Britain.

Who goes to Portugal?

In 1981, 7,277,000 people went to Portugal, about 4 per cent more than in 1980. Finding that their neighbour's country is quite different from their own, 5,200,000 of them were Spaniards, the number having increased five-fold since 1976, when passports ceased.

In 1985, British visitors numbered 850,000, 20 per cent up on 1984, some 700,000 probably going by air to the Algarve. Though the popularity of self-catering villas has greatly increased, 80 per cent of British visitors are estimated to have stayed in hotels, including the Government run Pousadas, functionally similar to the Paradors of Spain.

Even in winter, British Airways and Air Portugal between them now have at least twenty eight flights weekly from London to Portugal's three international airports. Additionally Lisbon is an almost daily flight from Aberdeen, Belfast, Edinburgh, Glasgow, Manchester or Newcastle. Direct flights to Oporto are five weekly, with a frequent domestic service between Oporto and Lisbon. The Tourist department has increased accommodation steadily to about 200,000 beds. This, of course, is nothing to Spain where there are three million. And what a terrible mess they have made along the Mediterranean shore!

Determined to learn from Spain's mistakes, the Portuguese planners should be less likely to make them because they only have three stretches of south-facing coast suitable for sea-bathing. The Lisbon stretch, Cascais–Estoril is already as built up as Torbay and not as long. For the second, the 25 miles of still unspoilt Arrábida, only half an hour's drive from Lisbon across the 1966 Ponte 25 de Abril, they will need a second Pombal if the inevitable development is to emerge as a Brighton not a Peacehaven. In the third, 100 miles of the Algarve, the self-catering villas grow apace and the expanding golf courses are reported to be overcrowded. All along the Portuguese coast the cold current curves south from the mid-Atlantic and away towards the Canaries, making the sea either cold or too cold for the swimmer.

Northwards from Lisbon escape to the bracing breezes and large swimming pools built into the rocks is what the 1¾ million people of Lisbon and Oporto – as well as many Spaniards – long for in August. For us northerners, in search of sun and warm salt water, our oldest ally has a perfect solution elsewhere – Madeira, where the sea temperature remains 18°–20°C/64°–68°F throughout the year.

Thus the pleasures of this sunny land lie inland away from the madding crowd: in the hills and valleys among the olives and vines, in the beauty of old churches, ancient convents, monasteries and museums, and in the Manueline and Baroque architecture gracing so many gaily-painted small towns in a setting of rivers and flowers.

Trees – The Cork Oak and The Olive

Prominent trees in Portugal include the 'Common' or 'English' oak, *Quercus robur* and her own oak Q. *lusitanica,* besides chestnuts, birches and maples growing on the high ground up to 1500 feet.

On the coasts as well as inland the pine forests are said to occupy a third of Portugal's land surface. Planted primarily as wind breaks by the Atlantic, the handsome Umbrella pine *Pinus pinea* has become rare, the quicker growing 'Maritime' or 'Bournemouth' variety, *Pinus pinaster* having been planted in thousands. The hard wood makes good timber for carpentry.

Resin, made into pitch and turpentine for export and home use, is collected after tapping certainly once and sometimes twice a year, but not until the last two years before felling. The process lasts a month, the men first cutting a hole in each trunk with a special long-bladed axe before fixing the little metal cup below it into which drips the resin. In spring and autumn one sees the parties of women in black walking along the roads to collect the sticky contents. The axe men reopen the wound twice making three collections in all for the women.

Eucalyptus globulus, the Tasmanian blue gum, first introduced in 1856 has also been extensively planted. It too grows to a vast height without looking at all pretty. The tree, however, makes excellent paper, notably by Eucalyptus Pulp, an Anglo–Portuguese public company whose shares are quoted on the London Stock Exchange. The State now owns at least a third of these forests, run by a commission similar to our own.

The climate is ideal for many fruit trees. Almonds, figs, grapes, lemons, olives, oranges and tomatoes are grown everywhere. In February one of the sights of the Algarve is the almond blossom and in mid-Portugal by late March the camellias are spectacular.

The Cork Oak (Quercus suber)

Portugal provides over half the world's cork and it was the three British 'Rs' – Robinson, Rankin and Reynolds who did much to establish the industry in the nineteenth century. Still British, Rankin founded in 1884, has its factory near Lisbon. The other two, also going strong, have become Portuguese companies with long names. *Quercus suber,* the cork oak, met all over southern Europe, reaches a height of about 30 feet and is chiefly grown in Spain and Portugal. Thriving best in light sandy soil, summer heat is of great benefit because it induces the sap to run between the layers of bark, enabling the outer layer to be removed without damaging the one below, which will then start of itself to develop into cork wood. The acorns nourish the pigs, a familiar sight among the Alentejo trees in autumn.

From the time the acorn is planted, some 25 years must elapse before any stripping takes place. During these years the tree must be pruned to a shape admitting first the sunlight and later the stripper. The first strip is the virgin cork, only suitable for decorative work – e.g. those imitation trees often seen in shop window displays; or for granulated cork for floors, tiles and life jackets at sea.

After this nine more years must pass before the second strip is removed; and so it goes on at nine year intervals, the quality of the cork improving for 150 to 200 years, the life of this remarkable tree.

Possibly met most frequently by many of my readers when brandishing a cork screw, a wine bottle cork will be from the second or later strippings, protection for the finest claret being needed for as much as 25 years, when shrinkage of the original cork makes a new one advisable.

After stripping, the cork wood has to be boiled to flatten it out, simplifying production and closing its pores. Depending on quality and thickness selection can then be made for different purposes. Slicing into strips, punching out the basic cork, polishing to the required length and rectifying the diameter complete the preparation. To this day no substitute has been found with the elasticity and characteristics to do the job of closing a bottle of wine effectively for up to 25 years. Should you chance to open your Cockburn 1955 (now at its best) perhaps the first glass should be raised to its unknown protector, the man who must have planted one *quercus suber* acorn in 1921 or earlier, maturing its progeny for 25 + 9 years after that.

The Olive (Olea Europaea)

Thy wife shall be as the fruitful vine: upon the walls of thine house.
Thy children like the olive-branches: round about thy table.

Psalms CXXVIII.3.

Geographically, that old psalmist of Canaan is still dead right; vines and olives remain as inseparable as Ruth and Naomi. The Phoenicians first took them across the Mediterranean and today they enhance the view in lands far beyond Portugal. Sociologically, however, times have changed. Whatever the Pope may say, wives are not as keen as they were on bearing a 'vintage' once a year; and dining *à deux,* who wants the 'scourges of our declining years' milling round the bottle of Dão, let alone the decanter of Lafite?

The olive harvest comes between the grape vintage and Christmas. The lovely silver-leaf trees need 25 years to bear fruit and severe late spring frosts can make the time even longer. In 1956 many trees in Western Europe were believed dead until they sprouted again up to ten years later. On the tree the olive has been described as 'more bitter than a thousand sloes'; even goats leave the fruit and foliage alone.

Gathered ideally when turning from green to black, smooth but not quite ripe, olives may then be dried in the shade for three days. The first pressing is a light cold pressing yielding in France *huile vierge,* the warm, sweet dark green oil of the highest quality that throws a little sediment.

The heavier, second pressing yielding much more oil, still of first class quality, follows without delay lest the fruit should deteriorate lying in the open. Blended perhaps for uniformity and rightly named 'Pure Olive Oil', this is what we buy at home for the kitchen. In Provence and in Tuscany, where the quality is highest, these conditions obtain.

Spain and Portugal – with Greece next – each making twenty times more oil than Provence, dominate the market. Much of Portugal's oil is required for the sardine canning industry. Whether for this reason or due to habit or because they like it that way, it can be rather rancid. Their traditional method is to shake the fruit on to rag rugs, transporting it to a press where a pair of large stone wheels, revolving vertically, grind it to a pulp on a granite slab. The pulp is then shovelled into rope baskets, two feet in diameter, which are piled one above the other and compressed. The oil drips and is collected in metal butts full of water. Like racking wine, the oil can then be run into clean butts leaving impurities behind in the water.

A second grade olive oil is obtained by re-grinding the pulp left in the rope baskets. This slow process can leave olives lying in heaps waiting to be pressed for far too long, a recipe for perfection being 'two hours from tree to mill'. Even the modern commercial process involving curings, washings, drainings, fermenting in wooden barrels and finally sortings takes a month.

The third pressing is likely to be refined for industrial and medical purposes. 'If you ever have any skin trouble', advised a leading varicose vein surgeon 'Use olive oil, far better than expensive ointments and creams!' People with dry skins, leading to cracked fingers and heels in winter, should rub it in two or three times a week after a bath. Start in summer, it will be too late otherwise.

Olive Harvest. JAN READ

THE PORTUGUESE AND THEIR LANGUAGE

All opinions seem to agree that the Portuguese are easy going, obliging, polite and exceptionally good tempered. Two incidents may serve to substantiate this view.

Driving out of the hotel grounds at Viseu, my host, suddenly realising that he was going through the 'In' gateway not the 'Out', jammed on his brakes nearly throwing us both through the windscreen. Almost simultaneously there was an enormous bang at the back. Thankful to be in one piece, all three parties got out. My host had entirely failed to notice in his mirror the young woman reversing out of a parking place and the two cars had met boot to boot. The damage looked formidable, a few hundred pounds worth to each vehicle.

Italians would have fought immediately; other Europeans would have exchanged incivilities or at least apportioned blame. But the two Portuguese took one look at the cars, then at each other and just roared with laughter.

Fortunately we could both drive away. 'Were they driving their firm's cars?' I asked later. 'Good heavens no', said my host in the merriest tone.

The other occasion was when our self-drive Mini came to a halt, fortunately outside a garage, entering Elvas emitting steam worthy of *The Flying Scotsman*. Nobody there speaking English, the manager soon found a young man who said he spoke a little.

Helping me with a telephone call, at 5 pm on a Saturday, to a car firm in Lisbon, it took some time to explain, translate and agree how and where a replacement would be sent next morning; but, apart from the telephone call, I was not allowed to pay anything. He insisted on taking us into the town in his own car to find a taxi to take us back to our hotel at Estremoz, 25 miles away. Since he would accept no tip, we succeeded – only with difficulty – in getting him to accept a bottle of very good tawny port friends in Lisbon had given us. This he showed, with evident pride and delight, to the taxi driver, telling him how kind *we* were. The taxi driver's charge for those fifty miles there and back was £9.00.

Outside Lisbon and Oporto, the Portuguese are, of course, a country people; there are no other real cities and the many small towns are market towns in a rural and often mountainous setting making transport and communications difficult.

Writing as long ago as 1949 in *The Selective Traveller in Portugal*, Ann Bridge and Susan Lowndes describe the Portuguese agricultural methods as 'biblical'. 'Reaping, gleaning, threshing the grain, fetching the water – all are done as they are in the Old and New Testaments'.

Salazar did very little or nothing to change that. In the flat wheat lands of the south it was thought more economical to plough among the cork oaks with oxen rather than tractors. In the mountainous north, the land is divided into smallholdings; for the port vineyards terraced with dry walls, even ploughs were deemed impracticable and the slopes were dug by hand.

Digging in Portugal is not done with a spade throwing the soil forward, but with a large, glorified hoe, moving it backwards towards the feet. In the port vineyards the working hours were dawn to dusk except on Sundays.

The myth that the human foot alone was essential for treading grapes making port wine was quickly disproved in the Sixties when the owners of the feet left the north of Portugal in search of a living wage abroad. Necessity was the mother of auto-vinificators installed in new Douro wineries making up to 3500 pipes in six weeks with only twenty men to work the machinery. To tread such a quantity it is said that 7000 pairs of feet would be needed. Nevertheless treading is by no means obsolete, some experts still feeling convinced that the best port can only be made that way.

In the Douro valley nowadays bulldozers can be seen clearing slopes for new vineyards. New terracing, too expensive to contemplate, is quite outmoded. Mechanical cultivators dig transverse furrows in which to retain the soil and moisture on the steep hillsides.

Romaria

In summer every town has its *romaria*, a jollification that leaves the English village fete standing at the post, though Helston with the 'fiddle, cello, big bass drum, bassoon, flute and euphonium' of the Cornish Flurry† dance might hold a candle to it. As in all Catholic countries, the festival centres on the church; there is singing and folk dancing, local costumes, processions, pilgrimages with the patron saint paraded from the church, a battle of flowers, a bull fight perhaps and as like as not a firework display to round it all off. Details and dates can be obtained from the Tourist Office in any town.

Markets are another feature of Portuguese country life. In Tomar one Sunday evening two main streets were full up with stalls and people. In Ponte de Lima we could barely see the trees and the river for the weekly market on a Monday. In Barcelos, no distance away, Thursday's market is the biggest of all.

The Language

A poor linguist myself I have quite a good French vocabulary but fail to put the sentences together. Moreover, since the Frenchman's accent

†'Flurry' not 'Floral' I was taught.

is entirely different from those of my English teachers, I seldom understand what is said to me. With Portuguese I quickly gave up on being told that every time I bade the natives a civil 'Good Morning' I was actually saying 'Good God!'

My wife fortunately spoke adequate French and Italian, mixing the two as the whim took her when in Spain and Portugal. It seemed to work; and, of course, when apprehended by a policeman (they are relatively civil in Portugal) for some heinous traffic offence it is best to speak nothing at all.

People no longer hesitate to take holidays abroad because they cannot speak the language. Greece, where even the alphabet is totally different, is full of tourists; those who manage in Greece will at least be able to read in Portugal.

A romance language, i.e. Latin based, with some Arabic and other idioms, Portuguese is also the language of Brazil and the *lingua franca* of Angola, Mozambique and Guinea-Bissau. In England, perhaps the most familiar word is the wine, Dão. To us this is *Day-o* but to the Portuguese, *ã* is a nasal vowel pronounced something like *ung* in lung, making their pronunciation *Daung*, which is extremely difficult for us.

I recommend the well-equipped traveller to take one of two pocket books: Berlitz *Dictionary* £2.25 or, if too expensive, *The Portuguese Travel Mate*, Richard Drew Publishing Ltd., 6 Claremont Gardens, Glasgow G1 4PQ, an A to Z English word/Portuguese/Pronounciation booklet £1.50. Both these are to be found in bookshops, Berlitz also have a cassette No. 214 and LP record No. 239 for learners of Portuguese. But after BBC Television's 1987 series *Discovering Portuguese*, perhaps you are accomplished already.

Asking the Way

This is the car driver's greatest irritation; in other circumstances – filling up with petrol or in a restaurant – one can gesticulate.

The phrase books are too involved. The Portuguese bystander is unlikely to understand your pronounciation, and even if you say *Pode mostrar-me no mapa onde estou*? (Can you show me on the map where I am?) as beautifully as President Eanes, the fellow may turn out to be an illiterate non-map reader. No, keep it simple! 'Strada Setúbal Por favor?' and the reply will be: 'direito' – 'straight ahead.' 'à esquerda' – 'left': 'à diretta' – 'right'. or 'Enganou-se na estrada' – 'You're on the wrong road!

After that should you go straight ahead instead of right, well what is time on holiday?

FOOD

The paragraphs entitled *Accommodation, Food, Wine* appearing at intervals give useful regional information. The following is a summary of what to expect based on five weeks of fly/driving when researching and checking this book from 1979 to 1982 inclusive, and frequently since.

With money no object any Good Food table placing Europe's principal holiday countries in order of merit would find France at the top, followed by Italy and Spain, with Portugal, Greece and Turkey after that. If, however, we also consider Value for Money, Portugal would undoubtedly move up a place or two and whether France remains at the top depends on how rich we are and how gluttonous!

The Coastal Tradition

Portugal's geographical position on the Atlantic brings her fish far better than anything in the Mediterranean. *The Blue Guide*, in whch gastronomic guidance is mainly confined to lists with Portuguese/English names of Fish, Meats, Vegetables etc., gives no less than forty *Peixe & Mariscos*/Fish and Shellfish. *Camarões*/Shrimps, *Gambas*/Prawns, *Linguado*/Sole, *Sardinhas*/Sardines are among the more tempting; and, of course, *Bacalhau* 'the piece of cod that passeth all understanding' is included.

This dry salt cod has been the staple diet of the Portuguese living on the coastal side of the mountains ever since their fishermen first brought it from Newfoundland. They are poor people, having to dry and salt to preserve it through the winter. There are said to be 365 recipes, one for each day in the year, ranging from a heavy dish with boiled potatoes and onions fried in olive oil to the light, delicious *Bolinhos de Bacalhau*. These little balls bought in pastry shops, are made from flaked dried cod, beaten egg white, mashed potatoes and parsley fried in deep fat.

In an article *Cuisine of the Douro** Pat Sinclair – whose husband, Ian, managed Sandeman's in Oporto for many years – recommends them as excellent aperitifs with chilled white port at prolonged cocktail parties.

In the small coastal places the sea fish are simply served, fresh sardines grilled on a charcoal fire or sole grilled or fried with butter being very acceptable without mayonnaise or an aïoli sauce.

In the city restaurants such as Tagide and Tavares in Lisbon, and Garrafão, on the coast outside Oporto, eating is on a higher plane, some of the crab dishes being extremely good.

**International Wine & Food Society Journal Volume 8,* August 1981.

Private Hospitality

Having had the good fortune to stay up the Douro at Quinta de la Rosa many times since 1952, I can certainly testify that the British families of Oporto keep extremely good tables, often training their Portuguese cooks to a standard exemplified by *Soufflé au Grande Marnier façon Conceicão* – usually for ten people when at La Rosa.

The shippers' hospitality in the port quintas (farms) up the Douro is proverbial. Eight guests sat down to lunch with seven members of the Reid family one Easter Sunday at Croft's Quinta da Roeda to a turkey beautifully cooked and carved, with all sorts of salads, a strawberry pudding and a Serra cheese, the lunch cooked by our hostess, Elsa Reid, the staff all being on holiday for Easter. Excepting the cheese, every mouthful came from the estate.

Down the road at Bom Fim, Quinta of the large Dow/Warre/Silva and Cousens combination, after sampling a delicious home made tomato juice as an aperitif, we were only ten at lunch. 'Just a quiet day', Margaret Symington explained. 'Now tomorrow we have to feed 22 Dutch wine merchants.' Bom Fim is not a big house, I wondered whether they'd even have room for their clogs.

Alistair and Gillian Robertson at Taylor's Vargellas, hearing we had never been there, invited the entire La Rosa party to 'pot luck' the next day. A crisp chicken grilled with lemons and rosemary remains as memorable as the spectacular 20-mile drive that takes an hour and a quarter from Pinhão.

These standards do not, of course, obtain in hotels and restaurants. I mention them to show that the ingredients are all there for *Haute Cuisine* should tourism grow sufficiently to create the demand.

Meats of the Mountains

In Portugal beef is rare and expensive, because only the Minho and the lower Tagus valley have the pasture. There is seldom lamb, a sheep's wool for the textile industry being more valuable.

Porco (pork) is the national meat supported by *Cabra* (goat) and *Cabrita* (kid). A *refogado* (roux) made from chopped onion and garlic is the basis of a peasant kitchen that has given the name Portugaise to the world's culinary vocabulary whenever a tomato purée is added to make the sauce.

Coelho (rabbit), *Frango* (chicken) *Pato* (duck) and *Perú* (turkey) are met on menus and in the winter there should be *Lebre* (hare) and *Perdiz* (partridge) in the country. *Frango na pucara* is a chicken stew with vegetables etc. (as in Cozida à Portuguesa) cooked in the *pucara*, a deep earthenware pot with lid used widely in Portugal.

Soups and Sweets

Most meals begin with *Caldo verde*, a potato and cabbage soup with other vegetables in season and sometimes garlic sausage added. Given *broa*, the maize bread of the north to dip in it, *Caldo verde* is often part of the midday meal for workers on the land. Delicious and far more expensive than the soup is *presunto*, the renowned smoked ham of Lamego and Chaves; by June there should be fresh melons to go with it. *Presunto* is sometimes added to the meat, chicken and spiced sausages that, with assorted vegetables, make up *Cozida à Portuguesa*, a popular meat stew.

Whether we get our *pudding* from their *pudim* or vice versa hardly matters but *pudim* usually means an egg custard in the offing. *Pudim flan* has its 365-day joke like *bacalhau*. Not varieties this time, just the number of days it is served in the average restaurant.

Said to have been originated by nuns wishing to please visiting bishops, there are still many sweets made from eggs, sugar and almonds. Names include *Angels' Breasts* and *Nuns' Tummies* doubtless likely to be changed to *Nuns' Bums* if any bright young British marketing director had to promote them over here. These sweets are often served in *casas de chá* (tea shops) tea being by no means the least of Portugal's *Great Discoveries*.

Serra, a sheep cheese from the top of the Serra d'Estrêla is rare and expensive because the sheep can only graze when the snows have melted. Becoming runny inside like a German Brie it is only in season from December to May. There are a few cheddar-style local cheeses.

Dessert is home grown fruit of many varieties. A plain peeled orange is a great Portuguese speciality, which the waiter will peel in front of the guest with all the care and skill of a 'hair stylist' attending to a princess.

Where to Eat

It is always difficult to generalise about catering establishments because a change in management can transform a hotel or a restaurant for better or worse in a matter of days.

The primary purpose of the Government Pousadas, which they achieve very well, is to provide quiet and comfortable overnight accommodation. A good dinner helps and some try harder than others. In general the food is adequate and the menus offer some choice at very moderate prices. In an Estalagem – the privately owned inn too small to be classed as an hotel – standards are better with prices proportionally higher.

As in most countries restaurants are the best value, eating out among the locals when abroad usually being more fun than sitting in a hotel or pousada dining room with one's fellow tourists. A la carte menus also enable one to choose a couple of dishes perhaps, instead of wading through a four course fixed menu and there is never any objection to two people sharing one course.

In Spain sherry, the great wine, comes first and everybody eats late. In Portugal meal times are similar to those of Britain; leaving plenty of time for a glass or two of tawny port with excellent coffee from Brazil at the table or in the bar.

If neither *Accommodation, Food, Wine* paragraphs in this book nor the *Michelin Red Guide* give sufficient information, large lists of hotels and restaurants will be found in Regional Guides free from the tourist offices.

Tipping

Service is included in the bill almost everywhere; additionally a small tip may be left for good service but is not expected.

DRINK

As a wine country Portugal would claim sixth place in any 'World League' of producers. Nearly a quarter of a million people – 20 per cent of actual agricultural workers – are employed in an industry that claims 180,000 small growers. Some 35–40 per cent are members of their local wine cooperative or *Adega Cooperativa*, of which there are about 120 all told. These admirable establishments, active in all the Western European countries, give each member a fair price for his grapes, which can then be vinified and blended by trained oenologists and up to date machinery. In this way the peasant-smallholder receives expert advice and a higher price for higher quality; vinification is centralised and the wine is as good as it can be.

Annual production exceeds eight million hectolitres, of which 1.6 million are exported in the rough ratio four bottles of table wine to one of port, bringing Portugal £135 million of foreign exchange in 1985.

The Demarcated Table Wines

In EEC parlance table wines are known as light wines to distinguish them from fortified wines, e.g. sherry and port in which brandy forms an integral part.

However you find meals in Portugal, there is a wonderful variety of *vinhos maduros* to make them more enjoyable. This term 'mature wine' distinguishes those aged in cask for a year or more from the immature or green *vinhos verdes* of the Minho. AP, the national air line gets the visitor off to a good start with a quarter bottle of red or white free on the 'plane. It used to be Serradayres (Mountain of Air); more recently – even better – it has been Dão from the one large single estate at Santar.

Dão

The pronunciation of this simple three letter word is *Da-ong, Daw-ng* or even *Dung*, though the wine, rest assured, has no trace of *velha cabra* (old goat) in the bouquet. One of Portugal's demarcated regions since 1912, Dão wines have had some form of protection since the 15c. and could well become popular throughout the world because less than a twentieth part of its 376,000 permitted hectares are as yet under vine.

Spread about the area between Coimbra, Guarda and Viseu, the vineyards are mainly in the wide valley of the Mondego, Dão being this big river's chief tributary. Red wines predominate over white, which are dry. UK imports of both red and white increased by about 30 per cent during 1981 and are rising steadily.

In Portugal Dão Tinto and Branco are on every hotel and restaurant list, the better ones offering a wide choice of brands. Every bottle should bear the *selo de garantia*, the words printed on a thin ribbon of paper. The red wines must have a minimum of one and a half years in cask. In bottle they will improve for up to seven years. If you want to try the best red Dão, look for the word *Reserva* on the list and go for one around four years old.

Wine Visit. See Viseu.

Vinhos Verdes

'Pronunciation Veenyoosh vairdsh', declared Raymond Postgate, the Green Wines – mostly lemon in colour – are called green because the grapes are picked young and the wines are drunk young.

The region is the Minho – north west Portugal between the Atlantic and the mountains – made green itself by rain, with added humidity from no fewer than five of Portugal's main rivers and their principal tributaries (in brackets) as follows:

Minho (Cours), Lima (Vaz), Cavádo (Homen), Ave (Vizela) and Douro (Tamego and Paiva). Its charming small towns Barcelos, Viana do Castelo, Ponte de Lima, Penafiel and Amarante are all part of the Oporto Fly-Drive.

Demarcated in 1929, the vines are allowed to ramble up trees and trellises because the fertile soil below is needed for vegetables. Picking the grapes young in this humid atmosphere after a hot summer creates a secondary 'malo-lactic' fermentation in the bottle, producing the

light sparkle or 'prickle' in the wine that soon vanishes after a bottle is opened. Only the Portuguese like the red wines, which are terribly tart; but the white, dry and crisp, sometimes called 'the poor man's mosel' everybody seems to enjoy as a really refreshing warm weather drink before meals or with any fish course. Their low strength, 8° to 11.5° is eminently suited to a reunion of self-driving Chief Constables. As made in Portugal many are too weak to travel and the brands advertised in Britain have been strengthened and sweetened a little with some loss of the original flavour. In Portugal the best Vinhos Verdes are from Moncão, just south of the Minho river, and from the Basto and Amarante, both in the valley of the Tamega. In Oporto, the wine of the Escondidinho restaurant should not be missed.
Wine Visit. See Penafiel.

Bucelas, Carcavelos and Colares

These are demarcated regions from which very little wine is now made, due chiefly to Lisbon's spreading suburbia obliterating the vineyards. The scarcity of Colares – Portugal's best red wine – is explained in the Lisbon Fly/Drive, Day 3.

Setúbal

The small region west of Setúbal between Palmela and Azeitão is demarcated only for dessert wines called Moscatel de Setúbal and Moscatel Roxo. As with port, fermentation is checked with brandy, but fresh Moscatel grape skins are macerated with the wine creating an intensely fresh fragrance. Best served with fruit, when matured in wood for twenty years these wines far surpass the many dessert wines made from Muscat grapes all over the Mediterranean.
Wine Visit. See Azeitão.

Undemarcated Table Wines

Sound local table wines, *vinho corrente*, are met all over Portugal. In the Douro they may be found labelled with the name of the local town eg. Alijó, Vila Real, Lamego (which also has its own sparkling wine).

A Portuguese book, *The Wines of Portugal* published by the *Junta Nacional do Vinho*, with English translation in 1979, describes Oeste as the most important wine region in the land. Oeste is the coastal strip running north from the mouth of the Tagus as far as Leiria, in which there are *Adegas Cooperative* at Torres Vedras, Bombarral, Cadaval and Alcobaça among others. The book illustrates some of the labels; none of them is likely to be familiar except Serradayres, but that does not matter. These 12° ruby-red and straw-coloured whites are good *vinhos de mesa* (wines of the table).

The same can be said of the Ribatejo, further east on either bank of the Tagus, where the neat flat rows of vines extend for miles. The principal *Adegas Cooperative* will be found at Cartaxo, Gouxa and Almeirim. The Alentejo too has potable wines in Borba and Redendo and the Algarve in Lagoa, Tavira, Portimão and others. The Algarve and the Bairrada (near Aveiro) have recently been demarcated making ten regions when Madeira and Douro (for port only) are added.

Rosé Wines

These are made from red grapes by running off the juice before the skins have time to impart the full colour of red wines. The world's most famous, Mateus Rosé, must now need red grapes from many parts of the country to satisfy demand. Besides Vila Real, the original source of Mateus, there are thriving Cooperatives making rosés at Chaves and Bragança.

Port

Port can still be described as 'The Englishman's Wine' – but only just. In the 18 and 19c. the British (more accurately) evolved it and shipped it for their kinsmen at home, ashore and afloat, to pass round the dining table, toasting the Monarch at formal dinners and 'Absent Friends' – if I remember rightly – *en famille*.

The decanter invariably contained 'Vintage port', wine of a good year declared a vintage by the shipper, which matures slowly, imprisoned in a bottle for ten, twenty or even more years. There was never much of it; perhaps one per cent of all port made is 'Vintage' but, drunk by the elite, it established 'The Englishman's Wine'.

Later in Victorian and Edwardian times, the masses – imitating the classes – took to ruby port drunk with lemon or lemonade, regarded as a teetotal drink in many a Lancashire mill town of those days. Lighter altogether and matured wholly in cask, ruby and tawny ports (tawnies being older and finer) are blended, bottled and shipped when ready to drink.

Since the war the French, who appear to us to spend all day in a café contemplating one solitary small glass, have taken to sweet ruby *porto* as an aperitif, downing those glasses so frequently that they now drink three times more port than the British. With the heavy French duty launched on spirits in 1982, even those who prefer their cloudy Pastis may be forced to take to the *porto* habit instead.

In production, however, the British firms, numbering twelve excluding about a dozen subsidiaries still trading, handle about 60 per cent of the Trade and predominate too in the export field. In Portugal, of course, the brands met in shops and bars are those of Portuguese firms; in place of Cockburn, Croft, Graham, Sandeman, Taylor, Warre etc., we find Borges, Ferreira, Compania Velha Real, Calém, Fonseca and Quinta do Noval, some of which do export to us and are names not wholly unfamiliar.

British or Portuguese, the one thing they must have in common in order to be a Port Shipper is a Lodge at Vila Nova de Gaia across the Douro from Oporto. Opening to the public in working hours, most firms receive thousands of tourists in summer giving them a tasting and a film showing the vineyards up the Douro at vintage time and how the wine is made there before being brought to the Lodges.

The visitor will be pleased to be offered port at low prices to take home, though such is the warren of Lodges on this hilly slope that he is ill advised to try collecting with his car.

In Britain port coming last in succession, perhaps after several Martinis or Bloody Marys and a liberal measure of table wine at table, is apt to be blamed unjustly for a 'hang over', caused quite simply by too much alcohol.

A change being as good as a rest when on holiday, Portugal is the place to reduce the aperitif to a glass of dry white port and to increase the post-prandial intake to a good glass or two of tawny port – 'the cure for all ills save death' say the Portuguese, who, poor dears, cannot afford much of it. Regrettably port is a little expensive. Let us drink more to make it cheaper!

Aguardente

Portuguese brandy, *Aguardente* is good, whether drunk as a liqueur or mixed with water or ginger ale. *Bagaceira*, pronounced 'Bugger Seira' is what the French call Marc – a spirit distilled from grape husks, pips and stalks.

An acquired taste for most people, the Portuguese peasant loves this inexpensive, colourless spirit. Its kick must remind him of his mule.

Beers and Minerals

Portuguese beer (cerveja) is good. One guide book's description of tap water as only 'usually safe' seems a good reason for keeping to the many inexpensive spa waters. A spa leaflet gives no less than nineteen of these 'watery' places in Portugal. Money, of course, is saved by buying large bottles in supermarket or village shop. Their waters are either with gas – *com gas* or without – *sem gas*. Castelo de Vide and Luso are *sem gas*, Pedras Salgadas has a slight sparkle.

SPORT AND LEISURE

Bull Fights

Until the middle of the 18c. bull fighting was fought under the same rules as in Spain. Then, after a Portuguese count had been gored to death before the eyes of the entire court, either the king, or his more powerful minister, Pombal, decreed that thenceforward bulls would not be killed in the ring in Portugal. Bull fighting is not therefore a national pastime as in Spain.

The season is from Easter to October, the greatest fights being in Lisbon's red brick ring at Campo Pequeno on the way north to Vila Franca de Xira, the town where the bridge crosses the Tagus into the lush pastures where the bulls are bred. From Vila Franca north to Santarem is bull-fighting country, where most of the towns have their own ring.

In their form of *tourada* the Portuguese regard the bull as the *raison d'etre* for a colourful display of courage, elegance and skill by the human participants, male and sometimes female. The mounted *cavaleiros* enter with the bull, whose horns are protected with *embolados*, leather thongs. The rider soon taunts the bull to charge 'like a black thunderbolt', the horse neatly sidestepping.

Ribboned darts like the Spanish *banderilla* are daringly planted by the *cavaleiros* in the bull's shoulder. Then it is the turn of the *forcados*, eight of them, amateurs who wrestle with the animal in the *pega* and can get hurt in the process.

'Finally the *espada* (sword), equivalent of the Spanish matador plays the bull in the familiar manner implanting darts, but miming the death-thrust with the sword until the exhausted animal is led out of the ring.

I once saw a bull fight in Madrid. The spectators, most of all, make it an unattractive form of sadism.

Club Cricket

In Europe the Corfu Cricket Club, founded soon after Waterloo, is the oldest and the Oporto Cricket & Tennis Club, dating from 1855, the oldest actually *on* the Continent.

In the first representative match (Port *v* Pink Gin 1868) a total of 17 runs against the Channel Squadron's 200 was not an auspicious start. However, between the world wars the high standard and hospitality attracted good Club sides, notably the Cryptics, which included H. D. G. Leveson-Gower, Sir Pelham Warner and England captain, P. G. H. Fender*. The Wine Trade Sports Club's 1983 tour combined

**Died 1985, score 95.*

two matches with three days up the Douro, staying in their hosts' quintas, and a luncheon at the Factory House (q.v.). Their week ended with an exciting draw 151 runs all, against the Lisbon Casuals.

No doubt proposals from comparable wine-drinking cricket clubs would be cordially received by the Secretary.

WHEN YOU GO TO PORTUGAL

To plan *your* holiday the Portuguese National Tourist Office, 1/5 New Bond Street, London, W1. will send you a booklet *Tour Operators Guide*. Published winter and summer, it includes Madeira, the Azores and Macau and gives the sort of holidays in which the Operators specialise.

There are villas and apartments, Fly/Drive, Motor coach, City, Senior Citizens' and Students' holidays. For the energetic there are Golf, Tennis, Fishing, Horse Riding, Windsurfing, Sailing, Sail/Drive, Water Skiing and Walking holidays. For the more intellectually minded **Swan Hellenic** now have an 11-night tour staying in Oporto, Vila Real, Viseu and Tomar, while **Cox and Kings'** 10 nights include Oporto, Braga, Vidago and Buçaco hotels.

Fatima is of course the goal of three religious tours, two of them by air from Dublin to Faro. **Threshold Travel** of Manchester offer Disabled Holidays', 7 or 14 nights in the Hotel Sintra near Estoril.

Cruising has regained its former popularity. P & O's *Canberra* and *Sea Princess* are among ships that call regularly at Lisbon, the Algarve and Madeira in keen competition with – details from CTC Lines, Lower Regent Street, London, SW1 – the Russian ships, *Mikhail Kalinin* and *Mikhail Lermontov*.

The following are among the principal Portugal specialists: **Caravela Tours.** 38/44 Gillingham Street, London, SW1V 1JW. Tel. 01-630 5366.

Associated with Air Portugal and Avis, Caravela offer a variety of Fly/Drive 'packages', particularly in winter. Fly to Oporto, Lisbon or Faro and build your own itinerary with a choice of forty hotels; book in advance a 3, 6, 7 or 13 night tour staying in Pousadas, take a golfing holiday of 3, 7 or 14 days in the Algarve with reduced green fees and a car to get about.

Blackheath Travel Ltd 13 Blackheath Village, London, SE3 9LD. Tel. 01-852 0025, specialise in seven day wine tours by motorcoach, flying to Oporto and spending nights at Ofir, Viseu and Lamego (for the Douro Valley).

John Hill Travel Ltd 223 Lower Mortlake Road, Richmond, Surrey. Tel. 01-948 4146, Algarve holidays from Heathrow, Gatwick, Manchester, Belfast and Dublin.

Lisbon Promotions 13 Sandyford Place, Glasgow, G3 7NB. Tel. 041-226 4187.

Lane's Travel Service 251 Brompton Road, London, SW3 2EY. Tel. 01-584 8541.

Both do Fly/Drive from all three airports.

Meon Valley Holidays 32 High Street, Petersfield, Hants. GU32 3JL. Tel. 0730 66561. Specialise in self-catering holidays in villas with car provided. Their well illustrated catalogues feature properties on the Algarve around Lagos, with some in the hills in Monchique.

The Travel Club Station Road, Upminster, Essex, RM14 2TT. Tel. 86 25000. Algarve and Madeira.

World of Sport Holidays Castle Street, Hereford, HR1 2NW. Tel. 0432 59555, are the people for the energetic holidays already mentioned. **Abreu, Thomas Cook, Cosmos, Lord Bros, Silvair** of Luton, **Sun Tours** of Witney and **Sovereign Holidays** usually feature holidays in Portugal in their catalogues.

The Best Time

Spring and Autumn are ideal for Portugal holidays. My Lisbon fly/drive was checked during the last half of October under a cloudless sky for ten days. The Oporto, in the last half of the following May, in an English June temperature and again no cloud to be seen.

Such conditions cannot be guaranteed but from February to October inclusive sunny days predominate, particularly in and around Lisbon. Further north if greeted by rain in Oporto, it is encouraging to remember that annual rainfall decreases sharply as you go inland away from the coast towards Spain. August becomes hot inland and the coastal resorts crowded as happens almost everywhere in Europe.

PLANNING THE TRIP

Plan in good time. Passport and Driving Licence are required, with an International Driving Permit (from the AA) for Spain. No visas. No inoculations normally.

The Portuguese mainland has eleven provinces, subdivided into eighteen administrative districts. The *Travellers' Portugal* Fly and Sea drive itineraries cover them all except Beira Baixa in the centre adjoining Spain. Castel Branco, the chief town has, to be sure, a fine old Bishop's Palace and Episcopal Garden but is so remote that the only hotel is one star and has no restaurant.

Maps Guides and Town Plans

Portugal: Michelin Map No. 37   1 cm: 5 kms
Spain Portugal: Michelin Map No. 990   1 cm: 10 kms

These national maps, clear and adequate, show all the roads suitable for motoring. Using, in conjunction with *Travellers' Portugal,* the latest *Red Michelin Guide* to Spain and Portugal (issued annually) giving hotel and restaurant prices, further books should not be essential. Moreover the town plans in the *Red Michelin* show one-way streets; those in other guides do not. An i indicates the positions of the Tourist Offices, where, before walking round, it is wise to collect a free town plan if your hotel does not have one.

Maps in this book have had to be reproduced from facsimiles and are not wholly suitable for terrestial navigation.

Further Information

For more thorough study Guides now include:

Blue Guide Portugal, Ian Robertson A & C Black 1988, £9.95, Paperback only.
Fodor's Portugal 1987, £10.45.
A A Baedeker's Portugal, Second Edition, Translated from the German, £9.95.
Michelin Portugal and Madeira, Green Series 1985, £4.85.
Michelin España Portugal, Red Series 1987, £6.95.

Through Your Travel Agent or Motoring Organisation

There are regular scheduled flights by BA from Gatwick and by AP (Air Portugal, full name Transportes Aéreos Portugueses) from Heathrow, working in conjunction, to Lisbon, Oporto and Faro. AP also flies from Manchester to Lisbon and there are seats on many Charter flights. The reduced APEX fare has to be booked and paid for at least a month in advance, the cost varying according to season. Dan Air began a London (Gatwick) – Lisbon 3-days a week service in May 1987.

Arrange flight, Self Drive reservations and, if desired, advance booking at Pousadas. The maximum stay at any one is three days in summer, five days in winter. A Holiday Travel Insurance Policy, covering cancellation due to illness or accident, travel delay, personal accident, medical expenses and loss of baggage or money is strongly recommended for any holiday *abroad.* The AA have a good one, available to non members.

Taking Own Car

Make ferry booking and inquire as to procedure for avoiding arrest and obtaining bail in the event of accident in Spain. Obtain Green

Card from insurers and International Driving Permit (unless waived) for Spain. Arrange car service and spares kit before leaving; GB plate, warning triangle, headlight beam deflectors, first-aid kit, torch.

Camping

There are at least 70 camping sites. Leaflet with details from Portuguese Tourist Office in London or Travel Agents. Having no law of trespass Portugal is advantageous for campers, though the mountain roads are slow enough without having to tow a caravan.

Money

Arrange Travellers' cheques and Portuguese currency (limit likely to be about £140) with your bank. Cashing Travellers' cheques in banks abroad can be slow. Most hotels will accept them at a lower-than-bank rate of exchange. Access and other credit cards are acceptable. When cashing take care to countersign all cheques with your signature as near as possible to your original.

By Rail

A motor rail service operates between Paris and Lisbon (daily June 11–September 24, weekly otherwise). Cars take 50 hours by freight train, driver and passengers travelling by the Sud Express taking 25 hours.

In Portugal standard rail fares are very cheap and with family, tourist and distance deductions can be exceptionally so. Senior citizens showing passport and a Rail Europe card should obtain substantial reductions giving 50 per cent discount on journeys over 100 kilometres. Card obtainable at main line stations. Children 4–12 half price. Under 4 – free.

The summer motorail service Oporto–Lisbon–Faro avoids one of the most tedious road journeys, Oporto–Lisbon, in Europe.

Portuguese rail timetables may be obtained from BAS Overseas Publications, 48/50 Sheen Lane, London SW14 (Tel. 01-876 2131).

By Coach and Taxi

In Portugal comfortable coach services cover the country, details from Lisbon are on page 162. The national green and black taxis ply for hire in cities, towns and larger villages.

Motoring in Portugal

Since the Revolution many more Portuguese have cars and motorcycles. Some have little idea of relative velocity and where to overtake safely. The worst have been described as failed *Kamikaze* pilots making up for lost time. Seat belts must be worn.

Country hazards are unlit carts, people in black walking to and from work, bicyclists shooting out on the right from side roads.

Speed Limits

Built-up Areas:	
Cars and motorcycles	60 kilometres (37 miles) per hour
Cars with trailers	50 kilometres (31 miles) per hour
Single Track:	
Cars and motorcycles	90 kilometres (56 miles) per hour
Cars with trailers	70 kilometres (43 miles) per hour
Highways:	
Cars and motorcycles	120 kilometres (74 miles) per hour

Drinking and Driving

The penalties are now severe in all Western European countries. To risk it anywhere is most foolish.

Frontier Posts

Most are open from 0700 at least to midnight in summer and from 0800–2100 in winter (Nov. 1 to March 31).

Public Holidays

January 1, Good Friday, April 25, May 1, Corpus Christi, June 10 (National Day), August 15, October 5, November 1, December 1 and 8, Christmas Day.

Time

Portugal keeps GMT from the last Sunday in September to the last Sunday in March. From April to September inclusive her time is GMT + 1, as in Britain. Spain is always one hour ahead.

Further Information

Portuguese Tourist and State Information Office 1–5 New Bond Street, London W1. Tel. 01-930 2455. The entrance is in Burlington Gardens almost opposite the Arcade entrance.

Route Tables

The Fly/Drive tables give distances in kilometres; the Sea/Drives from Santander, since British made cars are involved, in kilometres and miles. Conversions are based on 1 km. = 0.62 miles. (P) = Parador or Pousada.

In the text distances are in miles when they are likely to convey more to English speaking readers.

Areas

One hectare = 2.47 acres.

Traveller's Notes

Traveller's Notes

Part 2
SIX ROUTES FROM SANTANDER
(Brittany Ferry Port)

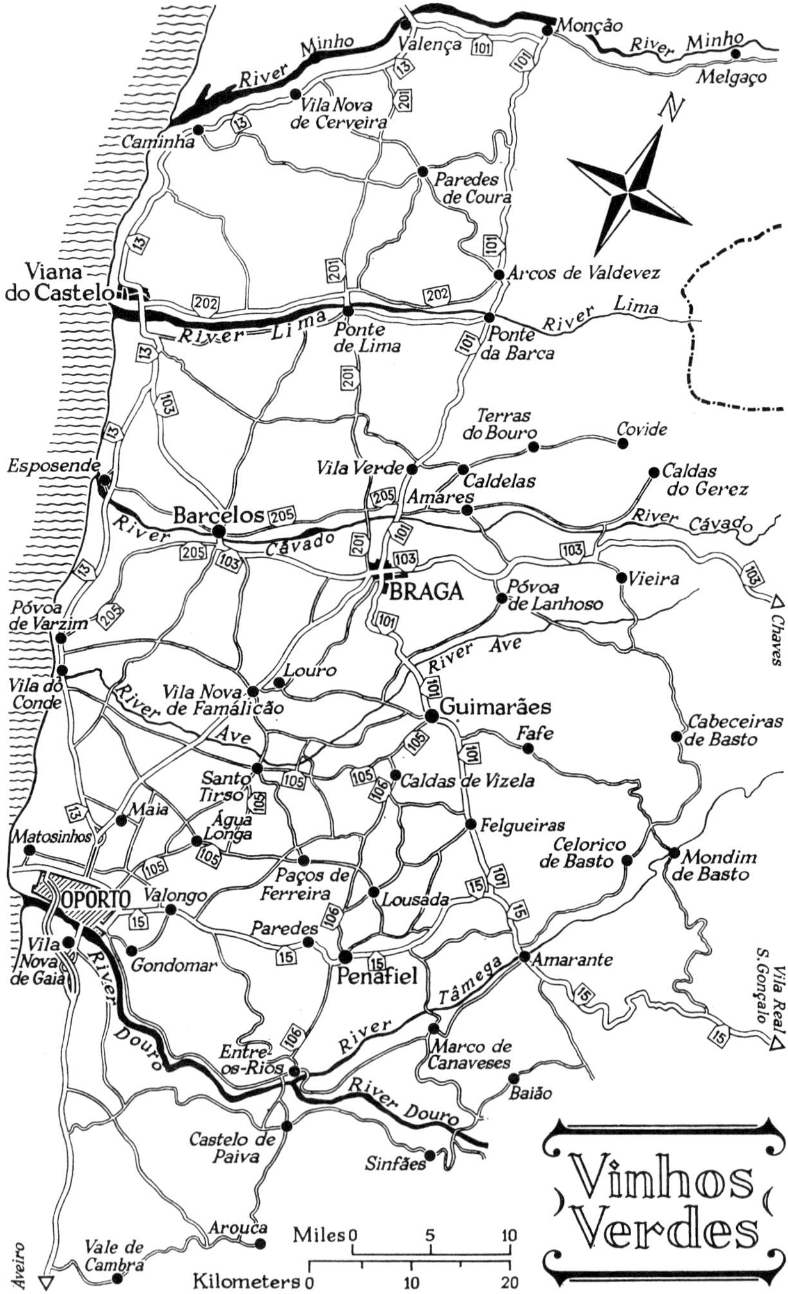

Vinhos Verdes
River Minho
Valença
Monção
Melgaço
N
Vila Nova de Cerveira
Caminha
Paredes de Coura
Viana do Castelo
Arcos de Valdevez
River Lima
Ponte de Lima
Ponte da Barca
Terras do Bouro
Covide
Esposende
Vila Verde
Caldelas
Caldas do Gerez
Amares
Barcelos
River Cávado
BRAGA
Vieira
Póvoa de Lanhoso
Chaves
Póvoa de Varzim
River Ave
Vila do Conde
Louro
Vila Nova de Famalicão
Guimarães
Fafe
Cabeceiras de Basto
Santo Tirso
Caldas de Vizela
Maia
Água Longa
Felgueiras
Matosinhos
Celorico de Basto
Mondim de Basto
Paços de Ferreira
OPORTO
Valongo
Lousada
Paredes
Vila Nova de Gaia
Gondomar
Penafiel
Amarante
Vila Real S. Gonçalo
River Tâmega
River Douro
Marco de Canaveses
Entre-os-Rios
Baião
Castelo de Paiva
Sinfães
Arouca
Vale de Cambra
Aveiro
Miles 0 5 10
Kilometers 0 10 20

		km	m
	From Santander to Oporto		
1	Coastal route via Santiago de Compostela *p57*	761	473
2	Via Verin and Chaves *p63*	687	427
3	Via Zamora and Bragança *p68*	725	451
4	Via Zamora and Miranda do Douro *p74*	780	486
5	Via Salamanca, Guarda and Viseu *p77*	752	467
	From Santander to Coimbra		
6	Via Salamanca and Guarda *p82*	699	434

At present Brittany Ferries sail twice weekly from Plymouth throughout the year except in January and early February. The normal crossing time to Santander is 24 hours, the ship leaving Plymouth at either 0800, 1000 or 1130. Thus travellers should be on the Spanish road during the following morning.

From February to April and from October to December, both inclusive, the return ferry sails from Santander at 1930 but in the High Season (June to mid-September) sailing times change to 1100 or 1400.

Fares for vehicles vary. There are three bands for cars depending on the season while a standard passenger fare applies throughout the year.

There is a wide choice of cabins, mostly two and four berth with wc/shower or wash basin and the restaurant and cafeteria are good.

When it comes to rough weather there is not a great deal to choose between the Bay of Biscay and the English Channel. Even regular sailors feel sea-sick in a gale after long periods ashore or at sea in calm water; any sensible person meets trouble half way by taking travel sickness pills *before* embarking.

If taking the ferry only one way, as the prevailing wind blows from the south west, returning by sea, with the wind on the quarter, should be the more comfortable. A north westerly gale is of course, possible but less likely.

Driving Overland

St. Malo being the nearest French channel port to Spain, Brittany Ferries' Portsmouth – St. Malo service is attractive. Leaving there around 8 am an average of 40 mph should reach the Paris – Bordeaux motorway beyond Niort around noon with motorway or dual carriageway nearly all the way to Burgos from there.

From Burgos the fast straight road E3 leads via Salamanca to the Vilar Formoso frontier near Guarda, and this is unquestionably the fastest route to Portugal from Bayonne.

I include details of it and other ways in and out of north Portugal from Santander beginning with the coastal route via Santiago de Compostela, where millions of Europeans have been before our own times footslogging to the shrine of St. James.

Salamanca and Santiago each have one of Europe's greatest squares worth a place in the first dozen with Lisbon, Nancy, Venice and Siena. Deciding another six could help *you* to pass the journey.

There are alternative routes too before Salamanca, via Zamora. One leads across the new *barragem* at Miranda do Douro; the frontier posts are on either side, the Pousada standing dramatically on the hill high above them. Another is to Bragança, that ancient capital across the mountains, which gave Portugal a dynasty and England a queen for Charles II.

Within Portugal there are different ways to take depending on if and where you prefer to join my fly/drive from Oporto.

All these I take in turn working clockwise from Santander limiting my descriptions in Spain to routes, scenery and accommodation because this is a book about Portugal and there are many guides to Spain. (P) indicates Parador or Pousada at place named.

Driving from Santander

The red Michelin's plan of Santander shows the berthing place of the ferry; the long slow trek eastwards up the main street is unavoidable. Torrelavega too is an unavoidable bottle neck in spite of the 15-mile motorway between it and Santander.

All my Sea/Drive routes, except the first along the coast, lead to Palencia. From there those heading for Oporto or further north could turn west for Benavente to join the now excellent Madrid–Corunna road, C620/N525 (pages 63/64). A superb piece of engineering through the mountains, with little traffic, this route via the frontier Verin–Chaves, is forty miles less to Oporto than via Salamanca. Becoming slow of course in Portugal, new modern roads from Oporto to Braga and from Vila Real to Amarante are being built.

SEA/DRIVE 1

Coastal Route to Oporto via Santiago de Compostela

km	m			Total km	Total m
		Spain			
0	0	Santander	N611/A67	0	0
27	17	Torrelavega	N634	27	17
50	31	Unquera	N634	77	48
131	81	Oviedo	N634	208	129
104	65	Luarca	N634	312	194
52	32	Ribadeo (P)	N634	364	226
67	42	Villalba (P)	N634/NVI	431	268
16	10	Baamonde	NVI	447	278
12	7	Guitiriz	NVI/C544	459	285
73	45	Santiago de Compostela (P)	C479	532	330
59	37	Pontevedra (P)	N550	591	367
46	29	Túy (P)	N550/N13	637	396
		Portugal			
2	1	Valenca do Minho (P)	N13	639	397
122	76	Oporto	N13	761	473

Few people will come this way to Portugal except to see **Santiago de Compostela.** The town's French name – no longer in brackets on the Michelin map of Spain and Portugal – is St. Jacques-de-Compostela, but in Spanish James is Iago, Spain's patron saint.

About 40 miles inland from Cape Finisterre, the town is close to Arosa Bay, one of the many big bays or *rias* along this coast, sometimes visited I remember between the wars, by British battleships on passage to Gibraltar. Legend has it that St. James or St. Iago was shipwrecked in Arosa Bay and his relic, allegedly discovered in the 9c., led to long pilgrimages to Santiago from all parts of Europe in the Middle Ages. The monks cared for the pilgrims in their monasteries; the emblem, three or four cockle shells, still survives as *Coquilles St. Jacques*. Whether passing along the coast or inland through Burgos and Leon, today's travellers – more precisely their tyres – tread 'The Way of St. James' following in the footsteps of a half to two million pilgrims a year in the 12c.

Santiago has one of Europe's greatest squares, the Plaza de España, bounded on the East by the 12c. Cathedral, where John of Gaunt was crowned King of Galicia in 1386, and on the North by the Hospital Real, built to house the pilgrims by command of Ferdinand and Isabella and completed in 1511. Since 1954 it has been a luxurious Government-run hotel, Los Reyes Católicos (the Catholic Kings) converted with the visual good taste associated with Spain's Paradors exemplified here by its four different quadrangles lit up at night. Los Reyes Católicos has 157 rooms, prices being similar to those of the best Paradors.

On our first visit in June 1959 I drove from Santander in one day, taking the best part of 12 hours in a Vauxhall Victor and, still in my forties, climbed out of a car for the first time feeling dead beat. The 1980 *Blue Guide to Spain* still says do not attempt this drive in one day.

Ribadeo. Wiser 12 years later, we drove off the ferry (at Bilbao then) about 0900, reaching the Parador at Ribadeo about 1800. Beautifully sited on what could be a Scottish sea loch but for its warmer climate, it has 47 rooms and my wife, whose memory for such matters was remarkable, declared that our bedroom with its views and furnishings was the best in all our European travels. The Parador was also the only hotel we remember where a whole fresh lobster a person was part of the Table d'hote menu. I think the Mayor and Corporation were dining there that night or else the manager was a philanthropist, doubtless long since replaced by an accountant. Even so, this Parador could still be the perfect night stop on the Way of St. James.

It was mid-May and we drove to Santiago next morning for the Whitsun weekend, spending two nights at the Reyes Católicos, where an American tour sat playing bridge. The weather was bitterly cold and, having left our coats at home, we were plagued by a bar juke box playing incessantly that early thirties pop song:

> Button up your overcoat
> When the wind is free.

Normally the prudent traveller to Galicia, Spain's wettest province, brings a mackintosh and is glad of the protection of Santiago's arcaded streets.

ACCOMMODATION, FOOD, WINE

After the Reyes Católicos the other big hotel (148 rooms) is the Peregrino almost a mile from the centre on the Vigo road. Neither the Compostella (99 rooms) nor the Gelmirez (138 rooms) have restaurants, but there are plenty in Santiago, Alameda being one we found quite adequate.

Wines are Rioja, white and red, sold under the names of the companies marketing them: e.g. Bodegas Langunilla, Bilbainas, Paternina.

The last named has a sound brand, Banda Azul, sometimes costing a little less than the others.

SANTANDER–OVIEDO

After Torrelavega N 634, good and fast, undulates among cypresses through pretty olive and orange groves. With time in hand – more likely if returning this way – note the alternative route via Santillana del Mar, where there is a 22-room Parador. As at Lascaux in the Dordogne, the caves of Altamira have been closed. The prehistoric cave wall paintings, circa 12000 BC, of boars, bisons and other wild animals were deteriorating; a means of preserving them will have to be found before the caves can be re-opened.

From Unquera the 30 mile stretch past Llanes, the sea on the one hand, the Sierra de Cuera on the other is delightful. Turning seawards before Ribadesella, N 632 winding its way to Gijon will lead to *Los Hórreos*, a restaurant on the coast with a fish tank and a Michelin star.

OVIEDO–RIBADEO

After Oviedo, the main N 634 – still good – regains the coast shortly before Luarca (65 miles) after climbing to 2200 feet at La Espina through mountain scenery. From Luarca, a fishing town in a cove, 32 more coastal miles reaches Ribadeo across a new bridge (opened July 1987) at the mouth of its estuary. This Atlantic coast abounds with inlets *(rias)* and this bridge saves the former twenty mile circuit round this one. The small town of Ribadeo is not very exciting but the Parador has superb views of the estuary and the mountains beyond; when the sun shines over Galicia, it might be Itchenor without people and not a suburban villa in sight.

RIBADEO–SANTIAGO DE COMPOSTELA

At Barreiros, less than ten miles beyond Ribadeo, N634 turns south west along the valley of the river Masma, through well wooded country at times. Villalba has a small Parador with only six rooms. In another ten miles we turn west along E50, the Madrid–La Coruña road. La Coruña is now linked to Santiago by a motorway planned to continue south to the frontier at Túy. We need not use it; turn left after Guitiriz at the first signpost to Santiago.

SANTIAGO DE COMPOSTELA–VALENÇA

For the first 37 miles the road runs south through pleasant wooded country not far from the sea to Pontevedra, an attractive town at the mouth of the river Lerez, its quiet old sandstone Parador (47 rooms) close to the bridge. The Casa Solla, a restaurant specialising in fish soup and Minho lampreys (December–March) has a Michelin star.

In another 30 miles we reach the Spanish frontier town of Túy where there is a small Parador (16 rooms). The motorway (1987) is completed only from Pontevedra to Vigo, shortening the journey a little.

INTO PORTUGAL AT VALENÇA DO MINHO

The river Minho is the frontier and we cross it on Eiffel's international 1885, 333 metre bridge to what is a very small town of 2000 people that has looked back across the river at Galicia since 1095. This was the date when the King of Leon gave the land north of the Minho to his legitimate daughter and that south of it to his illegitimate, a move welcomed by the Portuguese as giving them independence from a larger neighbour.

The Pousada S. Teotónio (Portugal's first saint) is in the small 17c. fortified town of which Valença largely consists and in a car the Pousada signs lead in by a tortuous road through the well preserved ramparts. There are some charming squares, a Romanesque church and lovely views over Túy and the Minho. In the Pousada brochure, 'a region famous for its excellent cuisine' could lead to disappointment; Portugal is not France: nor are its prices. In short a pleasant place for a first night and if its 22 rooms are all let, Viana do Castelo with three hotels is only 33 miles down the main road to Oporto.

MINHO AND LIMA VALLEYS – HALF DAY EXCURSION

km	m			Total km.	Total m
0	0	Valença do Minho	N101	0	0
17	11	Monção	N101	17	11
35	22	Arcos de Valdevez	N101	52	33
4	3	Ponte da Barca	N203	56	36
17	11	Ponte de Lima	N202	73	47
23	13	Viana do Castelo	N202	96	60

This is a pleasant half day excursion, joining the Oporto Fly/Drive along the Lima valley. From Valença N101 running eastwards follows the south bank of the river Minho upstream to Monção, another little fortified town like Valença. A deviation left gives marvellous views from the top of Monte do Faro, 1854 feet.

In **Monção** – an ancient little wine town – visitors can be made as fortified as the walls, its reputation for vinho verde and bagaceira goes back to the 18c. There is a good inn called Albergaria Atlántico with 24 rooms, all with bath, and the lampreys (December to March) at local restaurants are unsurpassed.

The Lima from the town of Ponte de Lima. Women washing clothes in the rivers remains a familiar sight in Portugal. JANREAD

Two miles towards Arcos de Valdevez the great granite mansion on the right at Pinheiros was built to be like the Ajuda Palace in Lisbon. Completed in 1834, 12 years after Brazil became independent, thenceforward this Palace of Brejoeira was the last great country house any Portuguese could afford to build.

At Ponte da Barca we reach the Lima valley; the routes onwards are part of the Oporto Fly/Drive which you can now follow as and how you wish.

Watch out for the hazards of mule carts, bullock carts, dogs, donkeys and the two footed drivers with no traffic sense! Alegria! the car drivers just cannot help it; the others have probably just nodded off to sleep.

Valença do Minho to Viana do Castelo. 52 kms. 42.5 miles. From Valença N13, the direct route to Braga or Oporto, runs south west along the south bank of the broadening Minho estuary through Vila Nova da Cerveira, Lanhelas and Caminha, where it turns sharply down the coast. Cerveira and Caminha each deserve a visit, the former for its beautiful 18c. church and microscopic citadel, the houses unchanged for centuries; the latter for its enchanting square and great fortified church looking back across the Minho to Santa Tecla and La Guardia in Spain.

Return to Santander by Santiago and the Coast. On this long journey out I have suggested 226 miles to Ribadeo on the first day leaving 172 on the second to allow at least a good lunch time break at Santiago de Compostela.

Returning by this route the last overnight stop may need to be in or near Santander if the ferry's sailing time is am next day. Comillas, 30 miles from Santander, has a quiet hotel only open mid-June to mid-September and a flowered restaurant with 11 rooms, open May to September inclusive. Santander itself has a good choice of hotels and the wide choice of fish restaurants that should ensure a last good meal.

Return to Santander via Leon. If the ferry sails at 1930, the last night could be spent in Leon, easily reached from Salamanca, Zamora or Benavente. The stained glass windows of the Gothic cathedral are as fine as at Chartres and its hotels include San Marcos, a superbly appointed Parador reasonably priced; though for meals try Leon's restaurants.

The motorway from Leon to Oviedo through the mountains should not be missed. The climb begins after 20 miles with spectacular views of peaks up to 8000 feet high as we pass in and out of the tunnels, short and long. Oviedo's restaurants and Romanesque churches may be tempting but allow three hours *at least* for the 127 miles to Santander.

SEA/DRIVE 2

From Santander to Oporto via Verin and Chaves

km	m	Spain		Total km	Total m
0	0	Santander	N611/A67	0	0
27	17	Torrelavega	N611	27	17
179	111	Palencia	N620/610	206	128
60	37	Becilla	N610/C620	266	165
45	28	Benavente (P)	C620/NV1	311	193
85	53	Puebla de Sanabria (P)	C620/N525	396	246
84	52	Verin (P)	N525/C532	480	298
		Portugal			
26	16	Chaves (P)	C532/N103	506	314
127	79	Braga	N103/N14	633	393
54	34	Oporto		687	427

From Santander the fastest route now to Oporto, Lisbon or the Algarve is N611 to Palencia and C620 to Salamanca. For Oporto then follow Sea/Drive 5 page 77; for Lisbon or the Algarve continue South via Cáceres to the Badajoz–Lisbon frontier, see Madrid–Lisbon page 235. Additionally, for the Algarve, leave N4, the Lisbon road, either at Borba for Evora, or further on at Montemor-o-Novo to connect with N120 at Alcácer do Sal.

Verin-Chaves is a relatively minor frontier north of Vila Real but useful for the Peneda-Gerés National Park. I first went this way in 1954, when for many years after the war the Bragança frontier was kept closed and the one at Miranda do Douro did not exist. The Austin 8 headed westwards from Benavente on a bright cloudless morning; a continuous stream of donkey carts re-enacted the Flight into Egypt as we bumped along slowly through flat, scrubby country of brownish-red sandstone and blue rivers. There was lunch at the Parador at Puebla de Sanabria (2946 feet), whence we wound slowly upwards into Galicia through several passes, the slopes of the Sierra de la Cabrera on either side threaded with streams fed by the melting snows of spring.

Returning from Vila Real with an Austin Maestro in April 1987, we found a fast, recently finished three-lane road all the way from Verin to Benavente, giving a cool fast spectacular run from Verin (2008 feet) through passes that rise to 3451, 3957 and 4429 feet. The plain lying beyond Pueblo de Sanabria lacks shade; the one promising picnic site turned out to be a refuse dump fouler than Epsom Downs after Derby day. Traffic was very light for these juggernaut days and with Spain now a democracy, those 1954 donkeys must be OADs drawing unemployment benefit.

Verin (2008 ft.) now has a Parador (23 rooms) delightfully sited near Monterrey Castle, a better overnight stop than the two hotels in Chaves if you do not mind waiting till 10 pm for dinner in Spain. But, before reaching it, the road for Portugal turns south, through the Tamega valley for Chaves, 17 miles on.

PORTUGAL

CHAVES (Pop. 12,000). This old Roman town keeps its bridge still and two great Roman stones, monuments to the people who built it. It has long been a spa, retaining vestiges of Roman baths. In one quarter an old hand pump supplies water to the residents, gushing out so hot that care must be taken not to let it break any glass jug or bottle.

Mineral waters too abound in this region, notably at Vidago, a Portuguese Leamington Spa, where Wright and Swift's reconnaissance of the Palace Hotel did not actually detect any bath chairs although 'there was a spiritual aura of gout, old colonels, hat pins, bound volumes of *Punch* and Dundreary whiskers'.

Set in a fertile basin of the Tamega rather than in a commanding position, Chaves, meaning keys, holds the defensive key to intruders from the north, but its old castle and 17c. fortifications have not always sufficed to deter them.

The sights of Chaves are down near the river; two small connecting squares graced by a Manueline style pillory and the Baroque church of the Misericordia, faced inside with biblical *azulejos*. The other church close by is the 16c. Igreja Matriz, showing a little of its original Romanesque below the belfry and an old organ inside.

ACCOMMODATION, FOOD, WINE

The Trajano (39 rooms) and the Estalagem Santiago (31 rooms) are Michelin 2-turret and modernised, the Portuguese Costa Verde booklet rates the latter, as all rooms are with private bath, at four stars.

Chaves smoked ham, *presunto,* is the best in Portugal if not the world, excluding Lamego where they claim their's is better still.

Traditional wedding dress in the Minho.

CHAVES TO BRAGA N103

km	m		Total km	Total m
0	0	Chaves	0	0
34	21	Lake Alto Rabagão	34	21
37	23	Venda Nova	71	44
20	12	Salamonde	91	56
24	15	Pinheiro	115	71
15	9	Braga	130	80

The first stage of this splendid drive like Caledonia 'stern and wild' is through the Terras de Barroso, where the lyre-horned oxen of the Minho known as Barrosã should be seen making the most of green pastures between clumps of chestnuts. Twenty miles brings us to the head of Alto Rabagão, the largest of many artificial lakes in the Cavado Upper Valley.

Seventy-three miles long the Cavado rises nearly 5000 feet up on the frontier just in Portugal, only ten miles from this lake formed by its tributary the Rabagão. The Cavado then flows south west through a deep rocky valley between the Serra do Gerés to the north and the Serras do Barroso and Cabreira to the south. Its rapid fall from the source was suited to the hydro-electric scheme begun in 1946 that now comprises half a dozen *barragem* and the blue water lakes along this drive. Some 70,000 hectares (1 hectare = 2½ acres) between the lakes and the frontier became the Penedes-Gerés National Park in 1970.

Montalegre. This hill village, involving a ten mile deviation there and back from N103, is of historical interest in that pursuing Soult's army after retaking Oporto, Wellington stayed here on May 18 1809. Driven north up the Cavado and Tamega valleys, the French were fortunate in finding some bridges still intact. At this point Wellington withdrew his troops south to Abrantes, no further battle being fought on Portuguese soil until Bussaco (q.v.) on September 27 1810, the following year.

Along the main road there are *barragem* at the western ends of lakes Alto Rabagão and Venda Nova and the Salamonde reservoir, in which the Cavado and Rabagão meet. About four miles further on a right turn leads to the 18 room Pousada de São Bento standing high above a long thin Canicada reservoir with views over the National Park. Very quiet and isolated this Pousada has a swimming pool and a tennis court. A minor road N308 leads north to Gerés, the small spa town giving its name to the park.

The rest of the journey to Braga, the valley widening, is typically Minho, smallholdings with Vinho Verde vines climbing here and there between the woods.

Parque Nacional da Peneda do Gerés. This green horseshoe of grey granite peaks, glens of silver birches, oaks and evergreens, lakes and rivers is a great holiday district for the Portuguese and for many Dutch, French and German tourists. In August the hotels and the two official camp sites are likely to be full.

For the rest of the year it is pretty peaceful for the permanent inhabitants – golden eagles, wild boars and cats, deer, wolves and the Luso-Galician wild horses, which look much the same to me as New Forest ponies. The two footed inhabitants number 15,000 people spread about a hundred villages. There should be good fishing for real river trout and some winter shooting of the grey partridge.

A point not easily noticed on Michelin Map 37, due to the northern half being on an inset, is that the river Lima splits the Park in two, the Serra de Peneda to the north, the Serra do Gerés to the south. Once inside it is impossible to cross from one side to the other. Points of entry are: Melgaço and Arcos de Valdevez for Penedes: Ponte da Barca and N308 (already mentioned) for Gerés. The Tourist Office in Braga is the best source of further information.

SEA/DRIVE 3

From Santander to Oporto, via Zamora and Bragança

km	m			Total km	Total m
		Spain			
0	0	Santander	N611/A67	0	0
27	17	Torrelavega	N611	27	17
228	142	Valladolid	N611/N620	255	159
30	19	Tordesillas (P)	N620/N122	285	178
67	42	Zamora (P)	N122	352	220
61	38	Alcañices	N122	413	258
		Portugal			
23	14	Quintanilha	N218	436	272
30	19	Bragança (P)	N15	466	291
69	42	Mirandela	N15	535	333
39	24	Murca	N15	574	357
32	20	Vila Real	N15	606	377
119	74	Oporto	N15	725	451

Though Bragança gave Charles II a Queen and the Dukes of Bragança became the Royal House of Portugal from 1640 to the end of the monarchy in 1910, this remote north-east corner of Portugal has no royal palaces, which needed to be near Lisbon and Oporto, so it is little known even to the Portuguese.

Therein lies the satisfaction of Tras-os-Montes, a table land beyond the mountains with two border towns, Bragança and Miranda do Douro (see sea/drive 4), each with a good Pousada. There is little traffic, yet the going is slow amid such mountain scenery.

Bragança to Chaves being only 100 kms./62.1 miles, this route is also sensible and spectacular if making for the Penedes-Gerés National Park.

Assuming a morning departure from Santander, either of the Paradors at Tordesillas (73 rooms) and Zamora (27 rooms) should be within comfortable range for the first night. At Tordesillas where we get a first glimpse of the Douro (or Duero in Spain) two main roads intersect; arrival before 1800 at the Parador or at the quiet hotel, El Montico (34 rooms) could be prudent if no advance bookings have been made.

Zamora, a cathedral town on the Duero, with Romanesque churches and several good restaurants is the more attractive place. Its Parador is a converted 15–16c. palace in a quiet corner of the main square.

From Zamora N122 runs westwards crossing the river Esla, a Spanish tributary of the Duero that rises in the Picos de Europa west of Santander. Considerably dammed in these parts the barrages (*embalse*) have created artificial lakes. After a dozen miles N122 divides near one of them, one part breaking left for Miranda do Douro, the other running NW for Bragança.

We went this way to the Douro valley late in March 1967, driving from Cherbourg in a Rover 2000 through France and Spain under leaden skies. Depressed by the persistent rain we could only joke that the Clerk of the Westmorland weather had hidden himself in the boot, following the example of M. Soustelle who had just escaped from Paris to Switzerland that way in the Algerian crisis.

PORTUGAL

In Zamora my wife, using her celebrated mixture of Italian, Volupuke and dumb Crambo bought bread, ham, wine, cheese and a melon for a picnic. After the Portuguese customs at the frontier bridge in a wooded hollow across the Sabor, first of the Douro's port wine tributaries, the road climbs out of the woods to the open uplands of Tras-os-Montes. It was, I remember, Saturday April 1, the sun shone from a cloudless sky as we ate that picnic under a wayside cherry in full flower, to the buzzing of innumerable bees, the walls of Bragança in the distance. No other car passed that way. Apart from the bees the silence was only broken by a lonely old donkey in a neighbouring field:

> 'He munched the thistles, purple and spiked,
> Would sometimes stoop and sigh,
> And turn to his head, as if he said,
> 'Poor Nicholas Nye!'

Back in 1952 driving to North Portugal for the first time, there had not been a farm tractor to be seen beyond the Pyrenees. Now Old Castile had become mechanised; not a horse-drawn plough in sight until nearing Zamora. In Portugal too the sand pillows, straw mattresses and sanitary arrangements (not even thought about, much less used) that my wife, touring with Claire Bergqvist, had encountered in 1948 had all gone with the building of the Pousada de Sąo Bartolomeu at Bragança.

Besides the quiet Pousada with its glorious view northwards to the snow-capped mountains of the Sierra de la Cabrera in Spain, there is now a Michelin 3-turret Hotel Bragança in this town, architecturally so good that Ann Bridge and Susan Lowndes opine that *The Selective Traveller* should see all nine of its churches.

This is easier said than done. The Tourist Office leaflet mentions only one, omitting its name; the 1982 *Blue Guide* only one or two more, explaining that the local clergy are at loggerheads with the civil authorities as to who should keep the keys and when such places should be open.

BRAGANÇA (Pop. 12,000). The walled town (2243 feet), ancient capital of Tras-os-Montes is so remote that even Michelin Map 37 only manages to include it on an inset. The Costa Verde (Green Coast) booklet, otherwise covering Portugal north of Oporto, omits it altogether as if Tras-os-Montes did not belong. Over the centuries, however, isolation did enable certain Jewish refugees to settle and survive, a synagogue being opened as late as 1927.

The Tourist Office lies on the road from Quintanilha N218 and it is to be hoped a better Bragança leaflet with plan will become available there. John of Gaunt, an early visitor in 1387, would have included the present one in his dying speech as a 'rotten parchment bond'.

The Walled Upper Town can be approached on foot or by car from the Cathedral in the main square. **The Cathedral** or **Sé** in the main square is really the Church of St. John the Baptist, promoted when the Bishop moved from Miranda do Douro in 1770. Good painted panels in Sacristy. **Misericordia.** Founded in 1418 one of the earliest in Portugal. Hospital now elsewhere. Gold renaissance four-storey retable with polychrome New Testament group in church at side. **Largo de S. Vincente.** Plain renaissance façade of church where Pedro is said to have married Inez de Castro (see their tombs at Alcobaça). 1886 ceiling with country-carved figures of Evangelists.

WALLED UPPER TOWN

From the Largo follow Rua Serpa Pinto up to the Torre de Menagem, the square tower of the 12c. castle that dominates Bragança seen from a distance. In the public gardens meet the granite boar with the shaft of the medieval pillory through its body and round hole hollowed out of the snout. (The boar was a symbol of kingship and this may have been for the anointing oil.) See also Murça.

Domus Municipalis. This famous five-sided 12c. building built over a large water cistern is the oldest Town Hall in Portugal and one of the few Romanesque *civic* buildings left (key from house opposite). Alongside it the church S. Maria do Castelo has a good baroque façade and a fine painted ceiling of the Assumption.

Leaving the Walled Upper Town through the town gate the **S. Bento** (1590) has a renaissance granite doorway and a 1763 barrel ceiling inside, painted in Italian fashion. Good 17c. panels and gold rococo High Altar retable.

Museu do Abade de Bacal. Installed in the old Bishop's Palace, this museum is named after the Abbot of Baçal (a nearby village), Francisco Manuel Alves (1865–1947) whose life was devoted to this region. Besides archaeological, ethnographical and numistic collections, there are the curious costumes of the *Pauliteiros,* the dancers who perform the ancient *Dança dos Pauliteiros* here and around Miranda do Douro. Dressed as women their hats garlanded with flowers, the men do this dance with crossed sticks in white skirts and petticoats and zig-zag stockings.

BRAGANÇA TO OPORTO N15

Starting at 2243 feet this undulating road falls pretty steadily to Mirandela (984 feet) – about half way to Vila Real, which is 86 miles from Bragança. After Mirandela up we go again to 2132 feet at Murça and down to 1512 feet at Vila Real. Then there comes a 1400 foot climb to the Pousada de São Gonçalo, the journey's summit, followed by the drop to 330 feet at Amarante. After all this one hardly notices the gentle climb to 1640 feet at Peñafiel before ending at sea level after 259 kms./160 miles of spectacular motoring likely to take 6–7 hours excluding stops.

Bragança's local railway line with many village stations has five level crossings in the first dozen miles of this journey, which made dodging the train rather fun that sunny Saturday afternoon of April 1967. Willows, tall poplars and little shrines with bunches of fading wild flowers grace this road that rolls across the high arable land of the Serra da Nogueira. And as the Sierras of Spain slowly sink astern the sinister looking shoulder of the Marão rises ahead, looming larger and larger through a landscape of chestnuts, cherries and cork oaks, thick with barley. From March to May there is a succession of wild flowers; in autumn the stubble turns the fields a dusty gold.

In 1967 the road surface was excellent, bordered with little hedges of French lavender planted around the shrines. During the revolution roads became sadly neglected. Going the other way from Vila Real to Bragança at Easter 1979, the three hour ride in the back of a self-drive Cortina was at times painfully reminiscent of:

> We're on a bumpy road its true
> But heaven is in view.

from that appalling tenor number, *Three Blind Loves,* in one of the gospels according to Groucho, Harpo and Chico. But during the 1980s road surfaces have been much improved.

Mirandela. This small town (Pop. 6000) on a hill in the wide valley of the Tua tributary with lovely houses and wide streets is worth a stop just to look at the Town Hall and the bridge. The former was the **Palace of the Tavoras,** the rich family with another palace at Viana do Castelo (q.v.). Built of granite well whitewashed, its triple façade, window frames and pediments decorated with coats of arms make it the epitome of 18c. architectural elegance.

The bridge with 70 arches is medieval, possibly built on Roman foundations. The Tua, rising in Spain as the Tuella, reaches the Douro by Cockburn's and Graham's quintas six miles above Pinhão, some 15 minutes away by speed boat. A glance at the map shows that by road, climbing up the Pinhão river valley from the Douro to Alijó and down the Tua valley to the Douro again, the distance is nearly 20 miles taking the best part of an hour in a car. An excellent example of Douro communications!

Murça. The pig being associated with chestnuts, there are sculpted boars in many parts of Spain and Portugal, those at Avila and Bragança being the most publicized. Here the *Porca de Murça* in the public gardens belongs to the Iron Age, 300–400 BC, and is thought to be the oldest.

ACCOMMODATION

My narrative can end at this point with 40 kms./25 miles to Vila Real on the route of the Oporto fly/drive.

Five miles beyond Murça N212 bears south to the village of Alijó 24.5 kms./16 miles from Murça. Pousada Baron Forrester (11 rooms), is in the middle of this village at the heart of the port wine growing region. Indeed its director, João Van Zeller, is part of the family who own the famous Quinta do Noval, a few miles further down the road and can arrange visits by telephone. The alternative to the Pousada is the new hotel Residencial Colombano in Régua, opened in 1982. The mod. cons. of 56 double rooms (half twin, half double beds) and 14 singles, nearly all with private bathrooms at about £15 a double a night may appeal strongly after driving for some days over Iberian hill and dale.

This moreover is the most exciting approach to the Douro. Fastening seat belts after Alijó with the great river in sight far below, we touch down at Pinhão. After which the 15 mile taxi-in to Régua is as straightforward as it is beautiful.

Porca de Murça, pre-Roman sculpted boar.

SEA/DRIVE 4

From Santander to Oporto, via Zamora and Miranda do Douro

				Total	
km	m	Spain		km	m
0	0	Santander	N611/A67	0	0
27	17	Torrelavega	N611	27	17
228	142	Valladolid	N611/N620	255	159
30	19	Tordesillas (P)	N620/N122	285	178
67	42	Zamora (P)	N122/N122-1	352	220
		Portugal			
55	34	Miranda do Douro (P)	N221	407	254
45	28	Mogadouro	N221	452	282
33	21	Fornos	N220	485	303
26	16	Torre de Moncorvo	N220	511	319
18	11	Vila Nova de Foz Côa	N220/N102	529	330
59	37	Celorico da Beira	N102/N16	588	367
55	34	Viseu	N16	643	401
79	49	Albergaria-a-Velha	N16/N1	722	450
58	36	Oporto	N1	780	486

This is a sensible route from Miranda to Viseu. From Miranda to Oporto a cross country route via Mogadouro on N221/N216 to Macedos de Cavaleiros joins N15 in 97 kms. A further 213 kms. on N15 makes the total to Oporto from Miranda 305 kms./189 miles as against 373 kms./232 miles in the table above.

From Santander this route is exactly the same as Sea/Drive 3 until a point about 24 kms./15 miles beyond Zamora where, after crossing the Esla river over one of its dams (*Embalse*), we turn left for Miranda do Douro instead of going straight on for Bragança. Another seven miles brings us to the Esla/Douro confluence near the Embalse de Villalcampo. The frontier is the Douro gorge, another 12 miles on; the two posts are on either side of the new *barragem* that spans it.

For motorists this relatively new post, with an improved road to it, has created the *shortest* route to Portuguese territory from the north east. But it is not the *quickest* route to Oporto, the north or the centre, the mountain roads of Portugal being slower than those across the plains of Spain.

MIRANDA DO DOURO (Pop. 2000). Yet Miranda do Douro in the wildest of the wilds, its Pousada so dramatically perched above the new Douro reservoir created in the gorge by the dam below it, is not to be missed. In mid-April 1979 an 8 am breakfast on the bedroom balcony in warm sunshine with Spain (left) and Portugal (right), divided only by the tamed torrents of the placid lake below, remains a spectacular memory.

Far below – perhaps a mile away at the end of this lake – the national flags fluttering on either side – lay the road across the top of the *barragem*. And below it – like a fat man released from a health hydro – the Douro has been reduced to little more than a trickle as it twists and turns through the gorge.

Having a day's rest from motoring we took a 1½ hour walk to it and back, learning later that the power station by the dam is always open to the public. The Portuguese are justly proud of their hydro-electrical engineering that now supplies much of the power they need.

Wellington's Secret Visit. Miranda has its place in British history. We last left Wellington in October 1810 retiring after the victory of Bussaco to the prepared lines of Torres Vedras; the French, declining to attack, retired to Spain. The battles of 1811 and 1812 had all been on Spanish territory, the British returning to a comfortable winter and replenishment by sea in their salient each year, even after the capture of Madrid and the victory of Salamanca in the summer of 1812.

At the end of May 1813 Wellington, after entering Salamanca with 30,000 men, slipped away riding here to inspect his main force under General Graham, which had marched unseen with their guns through the Tras-os-Montes, a feat few besides Wellington believed possible. Transferring people and stores from ship to ship along a jackstay became commonplace in World War II. It may well have been invented by Wellington for crossing rivers in India. At Miranda the jackstay having been rigged across the gorge between Spain and Portugal, they hauled the Commander-in-Chief across above the rapids in a basket through the spume.

After telling Graham how and where to get his men and guns across the Esla river, the Great Man departed by the way he had come, flourishing his hat with a shout of 'Farewell Portugal for ever!' Graham's outflanking tactic three weeks later led to the great victory at Vitoria, over 200 miles away; the infantry maintaining surprise by advancing through the hills, not the plains, as their descendants were to do once again in the Falkland Islands.

Jesus in the Top Hat. The former 16c. Cathedral, like the Pousada, looks over the ravine but from a different angle. Its endearing attraction is the 'Menino Jesus da Cartolinha'. 'The Little Master Jesus' is a statuette of the child Jesus in a top hat. Beloved locally the people have furnished him with a wardrobe that includes a straw hat too, for summer wear, entitling Miranda, I suggest, to twin with Eton *and* Harrow.

Miranda has its own dialect Mirandés, related to its origins in the Kingdom of Leon; but with so many people leaving the region to work abroad for at least some years of their lives, it seems likely to die out slowly.

Close to the Cathedral there is a street of small houses, 16c. and older.

MIRANDA DO DOURO TO VISEU

The Douro, flowing south west, continues to be the frontier for some 50 miles, N221 to Mogadouro running roughly parallel, with signs at intervals to the next three barragem, Picote, Bemposta and Saucelle. A road from Bragança joins at Mogadouro and after Fornos we must branch due west for Torre de Moncorvo, a town on a hill among orchards close to the confluence of the Sabor and Douro, on another road that comes south from Bragança.

At Torre de Moncorvo we have entered the demarcated port wine region, its easterly point being Barca de Alva where the single line railway, having clung to the Douro from Régua, crosses into Spain. Our road, now N102, crosses the Douro six miles south of Torre de Moncorvo just below the Pocinho *barragem*. Six miles on, N222, now the quickest way from Pinhão to Spain (page 79), crosses our N102 and in another 40 miles we reach Celorico da Beira joining N16, the main road from Salamanca to Oporto. (Fly/Drive 5.)

From Santander to Oporto via Salamanca, Guarda & Viseu

km	m			Total km	Total m
		Spain			
0	0	Santander	N611/A67	0	0
27	17	Torrelavega	N611	27	17
228	142	Valladolid	N611/N620	255	159
30	19	Tordesillas (P)	N620	285	178
86	53	Salamanca (P)	N620	371	231
89	55	Ciudad Rodrigo (P)	N620	460	286
27	17	Fuentes da Oñoro	N620	487	303
		Portugal			
2	1	Vilar Formoso	N16	489	304
45	28	Guarda	N16	534	332
29	18	Celorico da Beira	N16	563	350
51	32	Viseu	N16	614	382
22	13	S. Pedro do Sul	N16	636	395
57	35	Albergaria-a-Velha	N16/N1	693	430
59	37	Oporto	N1	752	467

From the north east this is the fastest route to Oporto or to Coimbra, for which N2 would be taken at Viseu instead of N16. For Lisbon too, N2 and N1 via Coimbra would be the best route through Portugal as opposed to through Spain via Badajoz.

Since a new bridge was built over the river Cõa it is also the fastest route to Régua, Pinhão and the port wine vineyards of the Douro; a route that by turning north on N332 at Vilar Formoso, barely a mile across the frontier, avoids Guarda.

Salamanca, roughly half way to Oporto, is the ideal overnight stop, easily reached for dinner after starting before 1300 from Santander. From the frontier to Oporto is not unduly slow. In 1972 we left Oporto about 0900 in a Rover 2000 with a picnic lunch, stopping in Salamanca for a walk round about 1600 before reaching the Parador at Tordesillas around 1900.

SALAMANCA (Pop. 167,130). 'A lovely university city of golden stone, narrow streets, large and small squares, splendid buildings and exuberantly rich façades, it is a city of domes and spires, of wealth and long tradition of learning still youthfully alive'.

This introductory summary from the *Michelin Green Guide to Spain* could hardly be bettered. Founded about 1230 by Alfonso IX of Leon, the university is the oldest in the Peninsula and during the Middle Ages the walled city was larger than Oxford and Cambridge put together.

Of the squares the big (1720–33) Plaza Mayor by Andrea Garcia de Quiñones must surely be the finest in the Peninsula, earlier by 50 years than Lisbon's 'Black Horse Square', another contender for first place. Salamanca people walk beneath its arcades and even though until 1863 they used it as a bull ring when the occasion demanded, it is now a pedestrian precinct, not a car park, the unworthy fate of majestic 'Black Horse' square.

South from this square, towards the city's river Tormes, runs the Rua Mayor leading to the **Casa de las Conchas** and the two cathedrals, *vieja* (old) and *nueva* (new). **The Casa de las Conchas** is a rare and beautiful mansion of the 15*c.*, its outside decorated with sea shells in the same golden stone as the walls that combine so well with the Isobeline windows and their iron grilles.

ACCOMMODATION

In Salamanca the Tourist Office is in the south east corner of the Plaza Mayor. Close by, just outside the square is the excellent 3-turret Gran Hotel y Restaurant Feudal. *The Michelin Red Guide* also includes the new national Parador, besides hotels and restaurants too numerous to name.

Standing on a hill this Parador looks across the Tormes at the two cathedrals and the celebrated buildings close to them. Under a mile away, walking there solves the parking problem. Apart from being understaffed for Easter week when I stayed there in 1987, the Parador's service was good.

In Spain the last possible stop is Ciudad Rodrigo (pop. 14,776) a little hill town, less than twenty miles from Portugal which has a hotel, Conde Rodrigo (35 rooms) and a Parador (28 rooms) in its castle. This Parador and those at Tordesillas and Salamanca are likely to be the quietest places for a good night's sleep, avoiding moreover the parking difficulties of the big cities.

PORTUGAL

A fast road across the plain leads to Spanish and Portuguese customs at Fuentes de Oñoro and Vilar Formoso, the 30 miles onwards to Guarda becoming slow and winding through wooded hills.

In less than a mile N332, the best road to Pinhão, Régua and the spectacular port vineyards branches north as follows.

km	m			Total km	Total m
0	0	Vilar Formoso	N332	0	0
17	11	Almeida (P)	N332	17	11
19	12	Figueira de Castelo Rodrigo	N332	36	23
53	33	Horta	N222	89	56
22	14	S. João da Pesqueira	N222	111	70
20	12	Pinhão	N222	131	82
22	14	Régua	N222	153	96

Opened in 1987 Almeida's Pousada with 23 rooms is the latest. The next one is at Alijo and the next restaurant at Pinhão. Alternatives for the night are Régua or Lamego, unless pressing on to Oporto 2½ to 3 hours beyond the former.

Running north and northwest for the first 40 miles, with the river Coa, a Douro tributary doing likewise a few miles to the west, we enter the demarcated port wine region beyond Figueira de Castelo Rodrigo. The gap between our road and the river narrows until, after a sharp descent, we cross the Coa with an excellent view of its confluence with the Douro.

Climbing westwards out of the valley Vila Nova de Fozcôa remains to our north as we turn south for two miles along N102 (Celorico de Beira to Moncorvo) before N222 resumes a west/north-west direction to Horta and S. João da Pesqueira. At Touca and Horta roads lead down to the south bank of the Douro about eight miles away; from the latter to the celebrated Vesúvio, largest of the port quintas planted 120 years ago by Dona Antónia Adelaide Ferreira described as the Queen Victoria of the Douro. The house and chapel standing together on the waterfront look superb from the river; Ferreira still own the property and their excellent ports are on sale almost everywhere in Portugal.

The only road bridges across the Douro in the port wine region are 1) between Moncorvo and Vila Nova de Fozcôa, 2) Pinhão and 3) Régua.

For the continuation of this journey see S. João da Pesqueira, page 135.

GUARDA (Pop. 15,000). This frontier was my first introduction to Portugal and Manoeline architecture in March 1952. Claire Bergqvist, who did not drive herself, motored from Pinhão, her *Caseiro* at the wheel of her big pre-war Austin, for a mid-day rendezvous at Vilar Formoso. We came from Le Havre in a new post-war Vauxhall Wyvern, maximum speed only 62.5 mph, keeping her waiting an hour since nobody had remembered the difference in time.

Lunch was therefore imperative. At a suitable stop before reaching Guarda there emerged from the boot of the Austin, tables, linen table cloths and a tremendous spread, with white wine, red wine and several bottles of Quinta de la Rosa's tawny port. It was explained that the port was not only needed for post-prandial purposes but to stop and toast the Douro whenever it was sighted in our travels. Though my wife had spent the winter of 1948/49 with Claire when I was drinking for the Empire out east in HMS *Birmingham,* she and I had not met since 1944. In another cruiser, HMS *Black Prince,* I had returned to the Clyde after escorting convoys to and from Murmansk, where I had swapped my chocolate ration for a large pot of caviar. Claire was still nursing and living in Glasgow; together we devoured the lot.

For half an hour after the picnic I could no more keep awake than a dormouse and my recollection of Guarda may be hazy. Thereafter on subsequent visits one was apt to be in too much of a hurry to get to La Rosa on the way out or to the pleasures of France on the way back.

The Three Beiras. Beira means edge or side and Portugal has three Beira provinces: 1) Beira Litoral on the coast south of Oporto with Aveiro and Coimbra its principal towns, 2) Beira Baixa, the low side along the Spanish border above the Tagus and 3) Beira Alta, by far the largest and highest, graced by Guarda, Viseu and the river Mondego.

The Serras da Estrêla and da Lousa make Beira Alta the highest province of Portugal. Guarda, 1056 m/3467 feet on the eastern foothills of the Serra da Estrêla is the highest town in the land; indeed after Avila, the highest in the Peninsula. But its white buildings that temper the dark grey granite of the Cathedral, together with what is only a 1300 ft. climb coming from the plateau of Spain disguise the altitude.

Feio fria farta e forte 'Ugly, cold, abundant, strong', say the Portuguese of this high spot founded in 1197 to guard against the Moors. But Guarda is not ugly. Visitors to the spacious Hotel de Turismo will find great views over the Spanish plain. Outside, its 16c. cathedral is contemporary with Batalha as shown by the flying buttresses; inside, a hundred years later, the French master, Boytac, gave the Manoelino master touch to the nave and the west door.

Neither is Guarda's granite 'ugly'; certainly not in the 11c.–12c. Romanesque chapel of Mileo, the town's oldest monument, conspicuous beyond the railway station in the long climb up from Vilar Formoso.

An Embattled Frontier. In the Peninsular War this little corner saw more than enough action. There was heavy fighting in the summer of 1810 as Massena advanced into Portugal from Salamanca with 350,000 men. Ciudad Rodrigo fell to the French on July 10; at Almeida, its equivalent Portuguese fortress, half the town and its

Portuguese garrison were destroyed on August 28 after a French shell had ignited a store of gunpowder.

Seeking more time to train his Anglo–Portuguese divisions and to complete the Torres Vedras salient, Wellington's tactics were to delay the advance and there was some bloody fighting along the river Coa before eventually the battle of Bussaco (page 114) gave him victory on September 27.

The following summer the French retreated to Spain holding only Almeida in Portugal. Though the battle of Fuentes de Oñoro in May repulsed them once more, British deployment was faulty, Wellington remarking 'If Boney had been there, we should have been beat'. Almeida retaken immediately afterwards, was also a disappointment because mistakes allowed the French garrison to escape.

Ciudad Rodrigo was finally regained in January 1812 Wellington's forces pressing on to their great victory at Salamanca (July 22) and triumphant entry into Madrid (August 12). Within three months Napoleon was to begin the retreat from Moscow.

During two of these winters Wellington lived in a house at Freinada close to Vilar Formoso, getting to know the terrain like the back of his hand, though ostensibly there for the shooting.

GUARDA TO VISEU

From Guarda N16 drops 1600 feet in the 17 miles to Celorico da Beira. The Mondego river is crossed about half way there, and again at Juncais eight miles beyond Celorico.

Though the surfaces of these roads along the Mondego valley are good and its trees, orchards and vines attractive, there are too many undulations and twists for average speeds above 30–40 mph.

For Viseu to Aveiro and Oporto see Fly/Drive, pages 109–116.

To Coimbra via Salamanca and Guarda

				Total	
km	m			km	m
0	0	Guarda	N16	0	0
27	17	Celorico da Beira	N16/N17	27	17
26	16	(Gouveia)	N17	53	33
13	8	(Seia)	N17	66	41
19	12	(Oliveira do Hospital)	N17	85	53
8	5	(Lourosa)	N17	93	58
45	28	Penacova X-rds.	N17	138	86
27	17	Coimbra	N17	165	103

The places in brackets are just off the N17; the distances refer to the nearest turnings leading to them.

GUARDA TO COIMBRA

Serra da Estrêla. At Celorico da Beira N17 branches south-west along the base of the Estrêla massif, 40 miles long and 20 wide, through the lush Mondego valley.

An entirely Portuguese river, the Mondego rises in the Estrêla above Gouveia at 1360 m./4462 feet, topping Ben Nevis by some 50 feet. It then flows north-east making an astonishing 180° U-turn anti-clockwise before heading south-west for Coimbra and its mouth at Figueira do Foz.

Another river, the Zezere, also rises nearby heading north-east with a U-turn to follow; this turn, however, is clockwise so that the Zezere settles down on the other (eastern) side of the Estrêla below Belmonte and Covilha flowing south-west. It ends in a confluence with the Tagus near Abrantes, after passing through a series of artificial lakes and a last *barragem* by the Castelo do Bode Pousada, near Tomar.

On N17 **Seia,** a pretty little town with a good Estalagem, at the foot of the Estrêla displays plans of the routes over the top, with reports on their accessibility from November to May when the snow can be seven feet deep. The rough roads across the top connecting Seia and Gouveia with Manteignas (modern hotel with 26 rooms), Torre (the summit 1991 m./6532 ft.) and Covilha (good hotels) may not be passable before the end of May. Nevertheless the skiers manage to reach Penhas da Saúde, the winter sports resort.

Cheese and blankets. During the short, but usually hot, dry summer, flocks of sheep not only graze safely, but profitably on this rocky plateau, the result being the excellent *Queijo da Serra,* something like a German Brie, made each winter but very scarce and expensive. Their wool is made into blankets at Covilha (pop. 26,000).

Exploring the Serra by car is slow going.

1) Seia to Covilha. Direct via Torre. 49 kms./30 m. Allow 2 hours.
2) Gouveia to Covilha. Direct via Manteigas. 77 kms./48 m. Allow about 2½ hours.
3) Seia to Covilha via Unhais da Serra. Longer way. 84 kms./52 m. Allow 2 hours.

The Dão Wine Country. Dão being a tributary of the Mondego, almost all this route between Celerico and Coimbra is passing through the Dão demarcated table wine region. As elsewhere in Portugal, except in the Tagus and Douro valleys, vineyard smallholdings appear between the umbrella pines, the olives, the maize and the barley. There are seldom big expanses of vines as in France.

This is the setting of the Pousada de Santa Barbara (16 modern double rooms) on the main road N17, in the village of Povoa das Quartas, east of Oliveira do Hospital, with a fine view of the Estrela.

Lourosa. Four to five miles after the Oliveira turning a small road left leads to this very old village with the remarkable 950 AD Church of São Pedro, the only one of its kind left in Portugal.

ACCOMMODATION, FOOD, WINE

There being no good hotels in Coimbra careful note should be taken of those mentioned along this road and at Viseu.

COIMBRA (Pop. 79,800). Lacking attractive quiet hotels and being irritatingly slow to reach along the congested Lisbon–Oporto road, I have never given Coimbra the time it deserves. Those with a taste for ancient monuments will be rewarded by a visit, taking the *Blue Guide to Portugal*, a more comprehensive aid than the following notes.

Majestically seated above the right bank of its river Mondego, Portugal's former capital and a city of learning has never catered for tourists; indeed perhaps it still prefers to be without them. For tourists this is a pity because 'Queenborough', for that is the pronunciation, makes it the one place name in Portugal an Englishman might manage to pronounce.

Its position reminds me of Blois in France where the traffic converging at the one bridge across the Loire creates chaos in August. Though the Mondego is not so wide nor Coimbra so big, its main square the Largo del Portagem (and the Tourist Office) are also by the one bridge. A first glance at the town plan, with the railway station only 300 yards downstream, gives the impression that the main Lisbon–Oporto line might be there too. This happily is not so; this station merely serves the main line station a mile out of the town. Nevertheless Coimbra is a motorist's nightmare, as cars may be for its inhabitants.

A short stretch of completed motorway now keeps the main Lisbon–Oporto road clear to the west of the town but the approaches can become congested and slow.

LOWER TOWN

From the Santa Clara bridge the narrow shopping street, Rua D. Ferreira Borges (becoming Rua do Visconde) leads north to the church of **Santa Cruz.** Steps on the right climb to the Upper Town with the University at the top, just as they do to the Castles of Lisbon and Edinburgh. On the left, 200 yards beyond the bridge, among the alleyways near the Plaça do Comercio and the little San Tiago church, there are small restaurants and bars that display a sprig of laurel, the old sign of a tavern put out originally after the vintage – as it still is in Austria – to show when the new wine was ready. **Santa Cruz** was founded by Alfonso Henriques (1112–1185) first King of Portugal as we know it geographically today, Coimbra being the capital until 1385. Six kings of that first Burgundian dynasty were born in Coimbra – Alfonso II (1211–23), Sancho II (1223–48), Alfonso III (1249–79), Alfonso IV (1325–57), Pedro I (1357–67), Fernando (1367–83). Alfonso Henriques and his successor Sancho I lie in the Manueline tombs in the chancel.

Coimbra's 16c. School of French sculptors and other artists headed by Jean de Rouen and Nicolas Chantarène are represented by the renaissance fountain in the Cloister of Silence, as well as the pulpit and paintings in the Sacristy.

UPPER TOWN

Though less than a quarter of a mile it is a steep climb to the University buildings at the top and much further by the Av. Sa Da Bandeira that sweeps eastwards to the Praça da Republica.

The best approach is via Sé Velha, least spoilt of Portugal's Romanesque cathedrals, half way up the hill from Santa Cruz, in a small square where little can have changed during the eight centuries of its life. Replaced as the Cathedral by the **Sé Nova** in 1772, it contains a 1508 retable in the Capela-Mór and later works by the Jean Rouen school.

A little higher up is the magnificent **Museu Machado de Castro** displaying medieval sculptures, ceramics and religious paintings from the 13 and 14c. **The University** founded by King Dinis (1279–1325), re-established by John III (1521–57), embellished by John V (1706–50) and reformed by Pombal, 'Coimbra University is the living evidence of Portugal's long history of cultural patronage' wrote Henry Myhill.

Today the Rector, his Deans and some 300 Professors and lecturers attend to the education of some 12,000 students.

English writers – Sitwell, Ann Bridge and Susan Lowndes, Myhill – are at one in condemning the redevelopment that has destroyed so much of value in Portugal. At Coimbra this reached a peak of 'indecent exposure' in the university blocks built during Salazar's time and the Dictator, its former Professor of Economics, born as near to it as Grantchester is to Cambridge, cannot escape the blame.

Fortunately its gem, João V's secular baroque library built between 1717 and 1778, in which Dr Salazar studied, remains untouched. To enter ring the front door bell. **Botanical Gardens** The largest in Portugal (20 hectares/50 acres) and the work of an English architect, William Elsden, though dating from 1774 were only fully planted in 1920. They lie below the University some 500 yards due east of the Ponte Santa Clara.

SANTA CLARA – CONVENT AND CHURCH

Crossing the Ponte Santa Clara to the left bank of the Mondego leads on the left in 250 yards to **Portugal dos Pequenitas** (Portugal in Miniature), a children's playground with a permanent exhibition of scaled-down models of national monuments, such as the Castle at Guimaraes and the Sea Window at Tomar as well as miniature houses and a children's museum.

Across the road to the north is Santa Clara-a-Velha, a beautiful old church, silted up by Mondego floods and almost a ruin. The western rose window is all that remains of a 13c. edifice, where Inês de Castro and St. Isabel, Dinis's widow were buried before their removal respectively to Alcobaça and the new convent of Santa Clara on the hill 300 yards to the north west.

Traveller's Notes

Part 3
FLY/DRIVE FROM OPORTO

Traveller's Notes

INTRODUCTION

Summary of Fly/Drive. Package Holidays and Car Hire.
The Age of the (Douro) Train.

		Night at:
Day 1	Arrival; finding the hotel.	Oporto
Day 2	AM. The City on foot. PM. A taste of Port in the Lodges.	Oporto
Day 3	Lower Douro Drive. A Round Tour via Penafiel.	Oporto
Day 4	South to Aveiro, East to Buçaco and Viseu.	Viseu
Day 5	Viseu. In and around the little Baroque wine town.	Lamego or Régua
Day 6	A *Caminho do Vinho* including Quinta do Noval and Vila Mateus.	Lamego or Régua
Day 7	Olives and vines to Amarante, Guimarães and Braga.	Braga
Day 8	Barcelos, Viana do Castelo and the Arcadian Lima valley.	Braga
Day 9	Departure.	—

From England most of the direct scheduled flights to Oporto leave in the early afternoon landing by 2000 when on time. This tour, which readers can vary to suit their own requirements, spends three nights in the city, walking round and visiting a port wine lodge the next day (Day 2), with a short circular drive up the lower reaches of the Douro on Day 3.

A1, the Oporto–Lisbon motorway is now open southwards for the first forty miles to serve Aveiro, the fishing port joined by a canal to its own large lagoon. After a look round there, we aim to reach the famous Buçaco National Park*, about 25 miles away, for lunch at its unusual Palace Hotel. Built around 1890 as a royal Palace in neo-Manueline style, it became a hotel in 1910 after the last King was murdered. If the plumbing does not always oblige with a royal flush, the forest is venerable and the gardens are delightful.

Merging with the gardens the huge exotic trees are protected by a 17c. Papal Bull and we can see the monk's cell where Wellington slept – his horse tethered to the olive tree outside – before that great victory over Massena on this ridge in the misty dawn of 1810. This is only a 117 mile day yet it may seem longer by the time you reach Viseu, the delightful Dão wine town.

*Also spelt Bussaco and Busaco.

To save the tedium of packing and unpacking daily, my plan was two nights in each of three towns. At Viseu with river trout and Dão to drink in the cool Grão Vasco hotel, you might like to spend longer than the one night in the programme as it has worked out. If so cut out Day 3 (Douro Drive) altogether to give more time to Viseu, Lamego and the port vineyards on Day 5, particularly now that Régua has the modern hotel, Columbano with 70 rooms.

By Day 6 we are looking down the remarkable pilgrimage staircase from the Parque Hotel at Lamego, a town certainly as attractive as Viseu, while the whole spectacular port wine region lies in the Douro valley, ten miles and 1200 feet below, awaiting our inspection. Those with more time to spare for the terraced vineyards, the olive, the fig and the almond of Tras-os-Montes could stay at this simple Parque hotel where Pension terms are under £15 a day for one person.

We visit Quinta do Noval, a famous port quinta and the Palace of Mateus of rosé label fame before moving, on Day 7, to Braga via Amarante, another river town, and Guimarães the historic cradle of the nation.

The Archbishopric makes Braga the Canterbury of Portugal, famed for its torchlight procession in Holy Week. The Portuguese say 'Born in Braga'! to anybody leaving a door open. Why? Because, they reply with a twinkle, 'Braga people all have tails'.

On Day 8 – a little over 70 miles – we meet the Cock at Barcelos, the charming market town on the Cavado, before looking and lunching at Viana do Castelo at the mouth of the Lima. The run up the Lima valley is idyllic; after inspecting the long 14c. bridge at Ponte de Lima we return to Braga via the Vinho Verde country amid the vines growing up trees. Outside Braga there is the other great pilgrimage staircase, Bom Jesus and more to be seen perhaps in the old town.

Including the two days of arrival and departure this fly/drive has worked out at nine days. If the direct flights to Oporto from Britain remain as at present only on Tuesdays, Thursdays, Fridays and Sundays this could be inconvenient. On days when there is no flight home from Oporto a 40 minute internal flight to connect with one from Lisbon can be made.

If, however, it is proposed to shorten the tour by a day, I suggest merging Days 2 and 3, Oporto and its environs. If taking an extra day at the end, the river Minho as well as the Lima could be explored based at Viana do Castelo where there is a good choice of hotels.

Package Holidays and Car Hire

Much of the country described in this Fly/Drive could be seen by those taking Caravela holidays. From April to October inclusive,

Caravela Tours, working with Air Portugal, offer holidays of 7 and 14 nights at the modern hotels, Ofir Europort at Fão (220 rooms) and Vermar Don Pedro at Póvoa de Varzim (200 rooms), both on the coast about 20 miles north of Oporto.

They have private bathrooms and balconies, tennis courts, swimming pools (the sea is too cold and often rough for bathing), bridge rooms, bars and discotheques. Those who like these amenities may well prefer to stay there rather than in Oporto, particularly during August heat. Self-drive cars can be hired for all or part of the time.

With them, the Minho Province – eg. Braga, Barcelos, Viana do Castelo – could be covered by daily trips. Going further afield would need a night or two at Viseu or Lamego as practised by Blackheath Travel, or in the new Columbano at Régua.

Blackheath Travel Wine Tour

Wine tours to many regions are this firm's speciality. Their summer tour, spending six nights at Hotel Ofir and one at the Parque Lamego, covers the Minho (Vino Verde), the port lodges of Vila Nova de Gaia, the Mateus Palace and the port region, finally meeting and lunching with the owners at Quinta do Noval.

The Age of the (Douro) Train

In Britain where the combined efforts of management and two unions not infrequently bring the network to a 'go slow', if not to an entire halt, British Rail's claim is more joke than fact.

Not so the lively Douro trains of the Porto–Barea d'Alva line! One of the seven *Great Little Railways* shown on BBC1 (March 22 1983); also in *Great Railway Journeys of the World,* £9.95 from booksellers. From Ofir a taxi at 0700 should make the 0745 from Oporto's San Bento station (0800 from Campanha 2 kms. away) reaching Régua (107 kms.) at 1008 and Pinhão (130 kms.) at 1042. The train goes on to Tua, Cockburn's quinta (143 kms.) at 1057 and Vargellas, Taylor's quinta (154 kms.) at 1130. Formerly a train back left Vargellas at 1430; this train however now runs from Tua so there is no train back from Vargellas until 1939, not reaching Oporto until nearly midnight.

Trolleys selling beer, soft drinks and sandwiches are now part of the service and at Régua or Pinhão, the heart of the region, a bargain could be struck for a local tour with one of the familiar diesel-engined black and green taxis, which are cheap because the fuel is not heavily taxed.

This railway enables the port shippers to show their quintas to parties of salesmen, agents, hoteliers, etc. in one day from Oporto. For 75 miles, starting near the Carrapatelo dam where the demarcated port wine region begins, to Barca de Alva nearing its end, the single track line clings to the river through this remote, majestic, incredible valley, the terraced vineyards rising upwards on one side or the other, sometimes both. There can be no spectacle like it in the world; the better for the Douro now being the sizeable waterway that the dams have created.

With the nearest airport three hours away, the valley should be safe from large scale tourism, but in practice there are no real planning laws and the ugly wine storage tanks erected at Pinhão are but one example of nasty blots on the landscape.

While the quinta and vineyard-owning community naturally abhor change, the large groups now owning the shipping firms encourage all manner of visitors to vineyards and cellars as proven means of promoting wine sales. Flying from Faro to Oporto short tours of Portugal's wine regions in the north are already feasible staying at Ofir. A 200 room hotel up the Douro would make them more so.

When it comes will it be a worthy 20c. descendant of an 18c. Factory House or just another ghastly tower block like the new hotels at Guimarães and Leiria? I can only say that one English architect, whose work in our oldest universities has been acclaimed, would be enchanted to embellish the Douro which he knows well.

Meanwhile for fly/drivers each year there are more places in which to stay and eat. Besides the Hotel do Parque at Lamego, the new Estalagem Columbano in Régua opened in 1982 is fully up to date and the Messias restaurant by the bridge on the south side (N2) is recommended by English locals. The Pousada Baron Forrester at Alijó is also accessible.

Private Houses

A new Government scheme, growing apace, provides accommodation as paying guests in private houses, ranging from ancient manors to farm *quintas* and ordinary *casas*. The full list exceeds 120, over half being in the Minho, Douro and Beira Litoral, the provinces of this Fly/Drive. The Portuguese Tourist Office, 1–5 New Bond Street, London W1 can supply the latest leaflets.

Most of the manors look delightful. The sort of stately homes where at 7 pm a bewhiskered 'Jeeves' taps on your door and says, 'If you care to partake, Sir, His Lordship has instructed me to open a magnum of the '29.'

DAY 1

Arrival; finding your hotel

Driving a left-hand drive car one does not know into a foreign city one does not know, perhaps in the dark after the plane was hours late can be exasperating. The modern city being a mass of one-way streets, finding the right one, let alone the hotel in it, can be maddening, particularly when not speaking the language.

The essential points to grasp about Oporto are that it is on the northern bank of the Douro and that the airport is 17 kms. to the north near the coast. The city has only two road bridges across the river and by keeping to the dual carriageway and following the signs to Coimbra and Lisbon you come to the last one, the 1963 Ponte da Arrábida, carrying the Lisbon road south, high above the Douro, with Oporto to your left.

It also has a one-way system, reminiscent of Chesterton's 'the night we went to Birmingham by way of Beachy Head'. On no account cross the bridge but leave the double track via the circulatory system at the sign 'Oporto Centro'. This leads eastwards with the Douro below on the right. Follow signs 'Turismo', 'Centro' or 'Hospital' until, in about 3 kms., the one-way Rua da Restauração brings you into Jardim João Chagas square with the big Hospital de Santo António on your left. The road through the square veers a little right passing the Clérigos tower on your right before descending sharply to the Praça da Liberdade, the base of Oporto's main avenue, Avenida dos Aliados, running northwards to the Town Hall.

The red Michelin map, Porto Centro, shows it clearly. Most of Oporto's principal hotels are within a few hundred metres on either side of the topiary and tessellated pavements of the Avenida; for example the grand Infante de Sagres and the little Malaposta in the R. Conceiçao to the left; the Dom Henriques and the Grande Hotel do Porto to the right. Knowing one's position it should not be too difficult, aided by any plan of Oporto to find the one required.

In daylight the direct shorter approach from the airport involving three roundabouts may be tried, but be warned, the one way streets make it easy for strangers to lose their way, even with a good map reader.

(The best way out of Oporto to the Arrábida bridge is along the one way Rua de Dom Manuel II from the Hospital.)

Another key point in getting into, out of and around Oporto is the Praça de Republica. Into its south-west corner up from the south runs the long one way R. dos Martires da Liberdade and out of its south-east corner the R. Almada is another long one way running *down* from the north to the centre. From the Praça's north-west corner the R. da Boa Vista leads to the Av. da. Boa Vista going west to the coast and the Airport. Inwards from that direction comes the R. de Alvaries Cabral.

Whereas the Tagus opens out above Lisbon into a huge lagoon, narrowing to at least a mile abreast the capital, the Douro ends a 485 mile journey, flowing through a gorge about 200 metres wide, before reaching the Atlantic 3 kms. beyond the Arrábida Bridge. On the south bank Vila Nova de Gaia, Cale to the Romans, is now almost entirely composed of Port Lodges or warehouses, their familiar names painted in large letters on their sloping roofs. On the north bank is Oporto, Portugal's second city with much the same population (396,000) as Nottingham, spreading itself up the greater slope.*

Porto to the Portuguese, even though they speak of it as *O Porto* meaning *the* port, became linked with Cale to give the country its first name, Portucale, a land which Alfonso I Henriques extended southwards to Lisbon in the 12c.

In 1415 when the half-English royal princes (sons of Queen Philippa of Lancaster) led the successful expedition that captured Ceuta, the people of Oporto sent all their meat to feed the expedition, subsisting themselves on offal. To this day the name *tripeiros,* eaters of tripe, has stuck. Compared to Lisbon, Oporto is a commercial city, where they say 'Coimbra sings; Braga prays; Lisbon plays and Oporto works', much as Lancastrians say 'What Manchester thinks today, London does tomorrow'. Manchester and Oporto, each 200 miles north of their respective capitals, have much the same annual rainfall. In Oporto it is supposed to fall mostly from December to March but history records how in 1809 as late as May 13, the day after Wellington had liberated the city, torrential rain created havoc among Soult's fleeing army and the British troops attempting pursuit. Almost as lethal as any 19c. battlefield are the narrow pavements of Oporto in the rush hour when the Portuguese put up their black umbrellas, as they are forced to do frequently from November to May when troughs of low pressure move in from the Atlantic. After that, the ridge of high pressure over the Azores brings the summer heat, which inland can be oppressive. Those contemplating the fly/drive in July or August must expect the deep valleys of the Douro and its tributaries to be very hot.

*With suburbs included the figure approaches a million.

DAY 2

A walk in the City and a taste of Port

AM. OPORTO ON FOOT

A day in Oporto can conveniently be divided between a morning's walk and an afternoon visiting a port shipper's lodge at Vila Nova de Gaia across the river.

The walk, being easier downhill than up, can start for want of anywhere better at the small Malaposta Hotel, 300 metres west of the Town Hall in the R. Conceição. This quiet little one-star hotel, with 37 rooms but no restaurant, is ideal for a short stay, an underground garage being opposite†. There are about 15 buildings and monuments of note in Oporto and this is the order in which they might be seen with the aid of the Oporto town plan (from the Tourist Office in London or Oporto) which superimposes them each in its right place on the plan by means of a page of tissue paper.

Soares dos Reis Museum (Museo Nacional Soares dos Reis). 1000–1200; 1400–1700. Closed Monday and Holidays. Free Saturday & Sunday. Some 500 metres westward of the Malaposta in the Rua de Dom Manuel II, close to the large Hospital de San António, this museum is in the Palacio das Arrancas, a fine 18c. building of 1759. Marshal Soult made it his headquarters and it was here that Wellington, liberating Oporto on May 12 1809, ate the dinner which his opponent, making a hasty retreat had left behind.

The well arranged museum, named after a sculptor and artist (1847–1889) contains 18c. and other paintings, coins, medals and ceramics.

The architect of the **Hospital de S. António** was a Yorkshireman, John Carr, who came to Portugal after designing Harewood House and the Mausoleum at Wentworth. From it the R. de Carmo and R. Carmelitas take us past their two 18c. churches to Portugal's highest tower. The later one is covered outside with modern azulejos of nuns taking the veil. **Clérigos Church** (Igreja dos Clérigos). Tower 0900–1800. An island in a sea of circulating traffic, this dark granite church was built in 1748 to the designs of Nicholas Nazzoni, a Florentine who, having settled here, became Nicolò Nasoni in Portuguese. His other works include the Misericordia in the R. das Flores, a loggia in the Sé, the Bishop's Palace outside it and, near Vila Real, Mateus Palace of rosé wine fame.

The 75 metre/246 foot tower in six sections not only gives a view from the top worth (as I write) the five escudos demanded but, when

†It is also a long distance bus terminus.

looking across from Vila Nova de Gaia at the towers, spires and roofs of Oporto is one of the city's three outstanding landmarks.

Bolsa. 0900–1200: 1400–1700 Monday to Friday except holidays. Heading south from the Jardim de João Chagas, a triangular green space, takes us down the R. São Bento to this extraordinary Victorian edifice built as the Stock Exchange, which has now become the headquarters of the Commercial Association of Oporto. The business community, with no certainty of future prosperity, spent millions on their marble and granite *Bourse*. The Arabian Hall, a pastiche of the Alhambra at Granada has to be seen to be believed. It took 18 years to achieve and some of the Koran texts that grace the walls and ceiling are said to be upside down.

Birthplace of Henry the Navigator. Round the corner from the Bolsa, the handsome 18c. building facing a small green space with a statue of Henry the Navigator is the Port Wine Institute (*Instituto do Vinho do Porto*) the government body that controls the entire port trade. Just below in the Rua da Alfandega, next to the street that bears his name is the house where the one English Queen of Portugal, Philippa, gave birth in 1394 to the Infante Dom Henrique. The street was formerly called the Rua Nova dos Ingleses; the house is now a museum for the city's archives.

St. Francis (Igreja São Francisco). 1030–1300; 1430–1800 (1 hour earlier in winter). Further eastwards along Henry the Navigator's street will be seen the twin towers of St. Francis, its rose window between them and the Baroque doorway below. A national monument for many years no longer used for worship, this 14c. Gothic church received a 17c. rococo baptism by being entirely overlaid inside with golden woodwork. Chapels with golden gates, Manueline archways, the glorious procenium arch facing the high altar, flowers, fruit, birds and angels in gilded wood are everywhere.

'A fantastic golden vision, a thing only to be seen in Portugal', wrote Sacheverell Sitwell, at the same time indicating that there was another, even more glittering, to be seen after lunch.

The British Factory House. On the left before the Rua do Infante Dom Henrique disappears into a short road tunnel leading to the quay by the two-tier, D. Luis I, bridge is the British Factory House, erected in 1785 by the British Consul in Oporto, John Whitehead. The name derives from the custom of calling English merchants abroad 'factors', the associations they formed being 'factories'.

A credit to any British Georgian city, if a little austere, this grey stone building has certainly not changed its name nor its function as the headquarters of the British Association in Oporto, whose membership is confined to British firms shipping port wine, of which there

Oporto. Church of St. Francis – 'a fantastic golden vision only to be seen in Portugal'.

are only 12 today, excluding about a dozen subsidiaries.

An imposing granite staircase leads up from the spacious hall to a writing room full of mementoes, a grand ballroom with crystal chandeliers and a drawing room with period furniture. At formal dinners the party moves from the dining room to an identical great mahogany table for dessert and vintage port, unsullied by any odours from the meal.

The Treasurer, Chairman of the House Committee, requests that visitors' arrangements are made through one of the member firms, which in practice means via their agents in the visitors' home country. While lack of resident staff speaking English precludes casual callers being shown round, arrangements are frequently made by tour operators and wine societies for visits by small mixed parties; and, if introduced by a member, these can include a buffet lunch at a reasonable charge in this elegant place.

Otherwise, for men only, the social event of the week is the Wednesday luncheon, an informal friendly affair of trade and wine talk when guests are invited and everybody tries to guess the year and shipper of the vintage port. Good customers of the wine trade prepared to be there on a Wednesday should ask their wine merchant if an invitation is possible. With women Masters of Wine now in the British wine trade, some of them accomplished writers, it is hard to see how port will get a full share of publicity if the male monopoly is maintained much longer at this luncheon.†

Cathedral (Sé). A stiff climb from San Bento reaches the Sé and the War Museum close to it. Cars can be parked in the approaches on the right and in the Terreiro de Sé itself.

In a splendid position looking down on the Douro by the Luis I bridge, aesthetically this cathedral, a 12c. fortress church modified in the 17 and 18c. has few admirers except for its Sacristy. Declaring himself a collector of Sacristies as Algarve golfers might collect courses, Sir Sacheverell puts it among his best four. Baroque is represented by the silver altar piece in the chapel of the Holy Sacrament off the north transept, a marble holy water stoop, the loggia added to the north face by Nasoni in 1726 and the west doorway.

In the square the 1772 Bishop's Palace, now used as municipal offices, is a splendid building standing out with the Clérigo tower in any long distance view of the city from the south.

Museum Guerra Junqueiro 1000–1700. Closed Sunday and Monday. More or less above the tunnel 100 metres below the Cathedral,

†Miss Jancis Robinson became the first woman guest in 1984.
She was the first that ever burst into the Factoree.

Oporto. The 1866 Dom Luis I two-tier bridge with a *barco rabelo* upstream.

this 18c. house displays works of art – 15 and 16c. pottery, 16c. Flemish tapestries, and Portuguese furniture collected by the anti-clerical poet, Guerra Junqueiro (1850–1923).

St. Clara Church (Igreja Santa Clara). Closed Noon–1500. Across the Avenue D. Alfonso Henriques from the Sé, not difficult to find tucked away on the right no distance up the R. Saraiva de Carvalho is a recessed garden with a Police Station. Go through the arch where the policemen congregate and you are in the courtyard of this exquisite church hidden from the street.

Santa Clara is an even greater monument to the decorative arts than the facings of the St. Francis church. The *lamina* of beaten gold (not just sculpted and painted with gold paint) applied here with consumate skill in every carved corner is an art that lasted from the late 16c. to the early 19c. Within this period Francis is late; Clara early.

The plain exterior gives no hint of the beauty beyond, adjudged by Sir Sacheverell as 'one of the major beauties of the baroque art'. Among the details to be admired are the grilles, the studded gold ceiling and the all gold chancel. Among some good polychrome statues Santa Clara herself is in the first chapel on the left. A pair of black saints and two small organs are also admired.

The Three Bridges. Narrow alleys opening into small squares, in which the elaborate and intricate ironwork of balconies, gates and windows bear witness to the skills of Oporto's 18c. craftsmen, bring us through the old town to the quays (Cais) near the two-tier bridge.

Besides the two road bridges already mentioned, there is an older one, the Maria Pia railway bridge, seen about half a mile upstream. Designed by Eiffel (who also did a Bodega for Gonzalez Byass in Jerez) and made entirely of iron, it has been carrying the Lisbon-Oporto trains across the Douro since 1877.

Even though a light engine, replacing the heavy one, pulls the train across at a walking pace in a hold-your-breath ninety seconds, they say the cautious get out at Gaia and the boatmen below need tin helmets to ward off the falling nuts and bolts.

The two-tier Luis I bridge, Belgian built in 1886 with a span of 172 metres/188 yards is, as I discovered, not without its hazards. On our first visit to Croft's Lodge at Vila Nova de Gaia, the existence of the lower tier did not occur to us so we walked from the hotel in Oporto along the narrow footpaths of the top tier between the Charybdis of the traffic passing uncomfortably close on one side and the Scylla of the Douro on the other, a sheer 225 feet drop viewed through the open iron work of the bridge. We walked these 188 yards in single line, eyes fixed dead ahead.

The lower tier holds no terrors, though a tablet commemorates the place where in 1808 thousands of inhabitants, fleeing from their French captors, were drowned when a bridge of boats collapsed.

The 1963 Arrábida road bridge, enabling north/south traffic to avoid Oporto was designed and built entirely by the Portuguese and has one span only of 270 metres/295 yards.

S. Bento Station. Portuguese trains are not particularly exciting, except when crossing Eiffel's bridge perhaps, or up the single line that follows the Douro to Spain. Often for the peasant on foot this line is the shortest distance between two points, local advice if caught in a tunnel being to lie down until the train has passed over you.

By comparison S. Bento station is prosaic with nothing but some 1930 azulejos in the waiting room, described nevertheless by David Wright and Patrick Swift in their 1968 book, *Minho* as 'a rumbustuous masterpiece'.

BREAK FOR LUNCH

Portuguese meal hours being much the same as ours, it is as well to start looking for a restaurant around 12.30. At that moment it would be ideal to have reached the Cais de Ribeira, where the **Taverna do Bebobos** (closed Sunday and September 1–15 and March 15 to April 1) is a small one-star restaurant long established and popular. Other restaurants are suggested on page 107/8.

PM. VILA NOVA DE GAIA. VISIT TO A PORT LODGE

All port wine, though made in the demarcated region some 70 miles up the Douro from Oporto, is brought in cask in the spring after each vintage to the shippers' lodges at Vila Nova de Gaia opposite Oporto. Maturing, blending, probably bottling and finally distribution, in cask or in bottle, by ship or by road, to wine merchants throughout the world is undertaken in and from these Lodges.

There are about 50 port shipping firms, of which about half are British and their Lodges rise hugger-mugger from the quayside up the slope of Vila Nova de Gaia. Nowadays most of the British firms welcome any tourist who cares to call and join one of the guided tours with English, French and German speaking guides that in summer have become customary.

The entertainment usually begins and ends in a reception room, with a 15 to 20 minute colour film and a welcome free sample. The film will show how port is made from the planting of vines to the time it reaches the consumer. Several films have been made and all of them reveal the great beauty of the 'River of Gold' and its steeply terraced vineyards.

The tour showing the maturing cellars, blending rooms, cooperage and bottling lines passes a pleasant hour or so with Cockburn, Croft, Sandeman, Graham, Taylor, Warre or Ferreira according to choice.*

In summer an additional week day attraction is the launch that makes a cruise at hourly intervals between the three bridges. It is run by Ferreira, the old and much respected Portuguese house, whose brands are to be found in shops and bars all over Portugal and in Britain too. Visits to their lodges, half a mile below the two tier bridge, are free; a small charge is made for the cruise which leaves from their pier.

Access to the Lodges from Oporto is best made on foot across the lower part of the two tier bridge or by taxi. By road from the Lisbon direction turn right before reaching the Arrábida bridge and follow the Fonseca port signs. The combination of narrow streets and commercial vehicles makes the parking of cars almost impossible among the Lodges.

Nossa Senhora de Serra do Pilar. While on the Gaia side it is interesting to see the only circular cloister in Portugal and then to look across at Oporto from the corner of this Renaissance convent, now a barracks that stands upstream from and close to the upper tier of the Luis I bridge. This was where Wellington stood, telescope in hand, before recapturing the city in May 1809 when there were no bridges.

The date was May 12. Soult had ordered all boats to be destroyed and during the night his troops had blown up the one pontoon bridge. However, a report reached Wellington from a barber (like Figaro *un Barbiere di qualitá* evidently) that upstream on the Oporto side four large wine barges lay concealed from the French by the overhanging cliffs.

Led by the barber an Anglo-Portuguese party brought them across unobserved. Six hundred British troops then crossed to Oporto in the first hour setting up a bridgehead in an empty seminary. By the time the French reacted, Wellington's howitzers were in position on the Gaia side to deal with them.

Convinced that the British would come by sea, Soult said that the red-coats – by that time crossing the Douro in force with the help of the citizens – must be his own Swiss guards returning from a swim. By 4 pm Wellington was eating the lunch of his retreating opponent. The carnage and savagery among men and beasts fleeing for the frontier through rain, mud and mountains with the British in pursuit was terrible. The French took reprisals on the peasants, who murdered their stragglers and the wounded without mercy.

*Calem, Ferreira, Graham, Taylor and Warre retain guided summer tours; others seem to have given them up.

Pinhão. Quinta de la Rosa ANTHONY HOGG

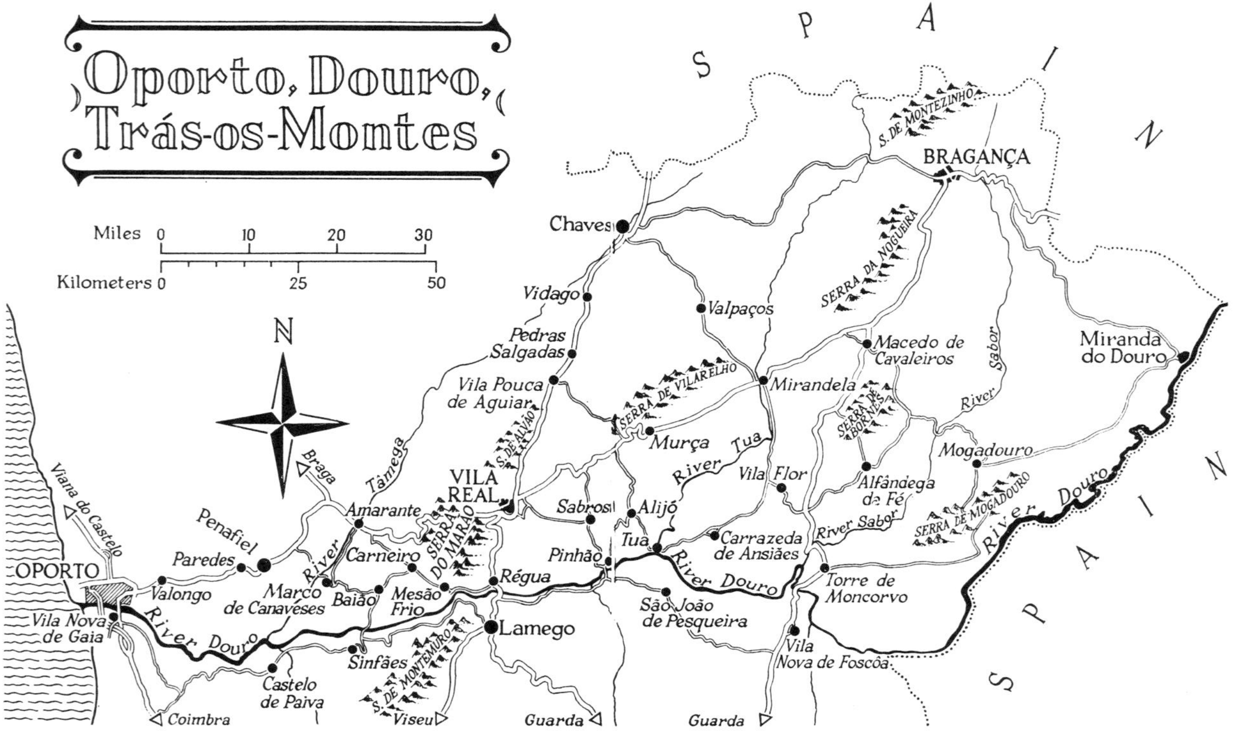
Oporto, Douro, Trás-os-Montes
Miles 0 10 20 30
Kilometers 0 25 50
N
SPAIN
SPAIN
BRAGANÇA
S. DE MONTEZINHO
Chaves
Vidago
Valpaços
SERRA DA NOGUEIRA
Pedras Salgadas
Macedo de Cavaleiros
Sabor
Miranda do Douro
Vila Pouca de Aguiar
SERRA DE VILARELHO
Mirandela
SERRA DE BORNES
River
Murça
River Tua
Mogadouro
S. DE ALVÃO
Vila Flor
Alfândega da Fé
SERRA DE MOGADOURO
River Douro
VILA REAL
Braga
Tâmega
Amarante
SERRA DO MARÃO
Sabrosa
Alijó
Carrazeda de Ansiães
River Sabor
Viana do Castelo
Penafiel
Paredes
River
Carneiro
Pinhão
Tua
River Douro
Torre de Moncorvo
OPORTO
Valongo
Marco de Canavéses
Baião
Mesão Frio
Régua
São João de Pesqueira
Vila Nova de Gaia
River Douro
Lamego
Vila Nova de Foscôa
Sinfães
Castelo de Paiva
S. DE MONTEMURO
Coimbra
Viseu
Guarda
Guarda

DAY 3

Lower Douro drive. A round tour via Penafiel

km			Total
0	Oporto	N108	0
42	Sebolido	N108	42
7	Entre-os-Rios	N108	49
17	Penafiel	N106	66
5	Parades	N15	71
32	Oporto	N15	103 = 64 m

Before making a first trip inland anywhere from Oporto it is important to realise that the mountains stretch across the country from Spain to the sea. The going is therefore as slow as the scenery is superb and the views at times spectacular. To emphasise this by an example, from Oporto at sea level N15, the main road into the interior first climbs to 1640 feet at Penafiel in 38.7 kms. It then drops to 330 feet at Amarante in the next 28 kms. From Amarante a fierce climb over the next 26 kms. rises to 2904 feet at the top of the Marão pass, finally falling to 1512 feet in the 22 kms. to Vila Real. Having met enough hairpins to fill a Woolworth counter, it is not surprising if average speed is no more than 20–25 miles an hour.

Today's route along the lower valley of the Douro, though without great monuments, is historic in that it marks the limit of Moorish northern penetration. Leaving Oporto along the north bank, N108 twists and turns through woods interspersed with vine, olive and cornfields; occasionally there are glimpses of the white villages on the far bank, with a fine view of the valley at Sebolido.

Mateus Rosé. A bottling plant. On the south side a lesser road, N222, runs less close to the river through the village of Avintes, 12 kms. from Oporto, where the firm of SOGRAPE have a huge modern plant that matures and bottles Mateus Rosé at the rate of 160,000 bottles a day. No introduction is required but the drive through Vila Nova de Gaia is slow and the return has to be made the same way.

The historic villa of Mateus Rosé, so familiar from the label, is due to be visited on the sixth day of this fly/drive.

TAMEGA-DOURO CONFLUENCE

Nearing **Entre-os-Rios** (between the rivers) the Douro forms a boundary between the Douro province (Portugal's smallest) and Beira

Litoral, the coastal province of Aveiro and Coimbra. Thereafter to the Spanish frontier it is dividing Tras-os-Montes from Beira Alta, in which lies the Serra da Estrêla, the highest eminence in this mountainous land.

Entre-os-Rios marks the confluence of the Tamega, last and largest of the Douro's many tributaries, which flows from Galicia through the frontier town of Chaves forming a boundary between the Minho and Tras-os-Montes.

For us Entre-os-Rios is important because it has a simple restaurant, the Miradouro, with five rooms, the only likely lunch stop except Penafiel.

On the south side N222 leads to two over-restored Romanesque churches at Souselo and Tarouquela. 7 kms. upstream is the Carrapatelo Dam, penultimate of the eight Portuguese Douro *barragem*, not really worth a detour since that at Régua is on our route later.

A Wine Estate. We now climb north from the valley to **Penafiel**, a town on the main Oporto-Vila Real road with two attractions. The first is its **Misericordia** which has a fine white plaster barrel-vaulted ceiling and a screen of flat painted wood surmounting a rather mediocre carving of the Board pew. It has a lovely Our Lady of Mercy with two children in the centre.

The second is the Quinta da Aveleda, an old and charming estate, open even at weekends and on public holidays where two celebrated Vinho Verde wines, Castel Garcia and Aveleda are made. The estate's winery is not open at weekends, only during weekday working hours. To see over the winery a letter from the agents, Hedges & Butler, Three Mill Lane, Bromley-by-Bow, London EC3, is preferable.

The Quinta is 4 kms. north of Penafiel on the road N106 to Guimarães. This tree-lined cobbled road runs along its wall, in which there is an entrance with a gate keeper. The only direction sign says 'Aveleda 2 km' and it is by the level crossing at the bottom of the hill between Penafiel and Parades. (Closed 1200–1400.)

Paço de Sousa. 6 kms. south of Parades this village has an 11c. Bénédictine monastery with a huge restored romanesque church set by a stream near two 18c. *quintas*. In the church there is a rarity – a romanesque tomb, that of Egas Moniz, the devoted tutor and counsellor to Afonso Henriques, the first king of Portugal and captor of Lisbon in 1147.

ENVIRONS OF OPORTO

Leça de Balio. To the left on the Braga road 8 kms. north of Oporto, this austere monastery church of granite is much as it was in the 14c. Balio meaning 'Bailiff' was the title given to senior Knights of St.

John, the Order remembered for the defence of Malta and Rhodes. There were a number of Portuguese Grand Masters, some being buried here.

The octagonal Manueline style font basins in Ançã stone and their pedestals carved with peculiar animals are admired.

Grijó. About 12 kms. south of Oporto to the west of the Lisbon road this old monastery has an attractive 16c. church and a very fine cloister.

Espinho. On the coast 18 kms. south of Oporto, Espinho is the resort of the region with modern hotels, a casino, tennis and golf. The Oporto Golf Club has a 5000 metre 18-hole course, par 68 and the Miramar a 9-hole course, par 34.

ACCOMMODATION, FOOD, WINE

Oporto's best hotel is the Infante de Sagres, modernised yet retaining its old charm and service. Just off the Avenida dos Aliados in its own little Praça de D. Filipa de Lancastre it could hardly be more central. The other good hotels centrally placed are the four-star Grande Hotel da Batalha on the eastern side of the S. Bento station and the Grande Hotel do Oporto in the Rua de Santa Caterina. Less convenient the Dom Henrique is 600 metres to the north east just off the Rua de Sa. Bandeira, a wide straight street of shops and offices that climbs up from the S. Bento station. There are numerous two-star hotels without restaurants. Albergaria Corcel, R. de Camões being further out than the São José, R. do Bonjardim and the excellent Malaposta already mentioned.

The most famous restaurant in Oporto is the Escondidinho ('The little hidden one') in the Rua Passos Manuel, the best eating-out part of the city. Just one room with a score of tables on the ground floor, its recognition sign, only two trees with no name outside, is easily missed. Its fish soup, trout with Chaves ham and excellent house wines are popular.

For those other than Portuguese, it would be helpful if the staff learnt a little kitchen French or English and refrained from charging a telephone call for a taxi when two people have dined there two nights running, drinking three bottles of wine and six glasses of tawny port.

The Abadia bar-restaurant is also reputed for its fish dishes. Aquario just off the Avenida dos Aliados in the R. Rodriguez Sampãio is quite good and the Rua do Bonjardim has two bar-restaurant-snack bars, A Regaleira and A Brasileira.

Taverna do Bebobos on the quay by the two tier bridge has already been commended.

Further out up the long R. da Alegria, the Portucale, on top of the Albergaria Miradouro with a panoramic view of the city and the Douro, is certainly Oporto's best appointed restaurant making the most of Atlantic fish. Cars may be parked there.

The Degrau restaurant near the Atlantico hotel and that of the Sagres Infante hotel were also commended to me by a leading port shipper.

ALONG THE COAST

Less than 4 kms. from the centre along the Avenida Boa Vista running westwards to the coast is the new Hotel Porto Atlantico, built partly for conventions where delegates can keep awake with the aid of air-conditioning, indoor and outdoor swimming pools, sauna and gymnasium.

The coastal stretch from Foz do Douro to Matosinhos and Leça da Palmeira has become an industrial suburb devoted to sugar refining, textiles, tyres, foundries, fish canning, leather and ceramics. An oil refinery, a wharf for tankers, and docks for smaller vessels have made Lexões into Portugal's second largest port, relieving Oporto which tends to become silted.

Nevertheless sea-faring people like their food and there is no lack of small restaurants offering fish soup, mussels and other crustacea at their best. The port shippers advising on wine tours particularly recommend Garrafão at Leça da Palmeira. Disappointed to find it closed (as most of them are) for a last Sunday lunch before flying home, a passer-by kindly directed us to another where the locals were tucking in with the élan of the French out for a Dimanche déjeuner.

Others are: Varanda da Barra and O Bule at Foz do Douro, and Marujo at Matosinhos.

On the dual carriageway 4 kms. south of the Airport, Via Norte, with a dozen rooms, is a comfortable 3-star estalagem with good food. An overnight stop there after a late arrival could postpone acquaintance with Oporto's traffic system until a better moment.

Further north the coast from Vila do Conde and Póvoa da Varzim to Esposende is being thoroughly spoilt by unplanned industrial and suburban development. North of the Airport, N13 is single track; passing through it is to be avoided and the coastal route until just south of Viana do Castelo forms no part of this Fly/Drive.

DAY 4

South to Aveiro, East to Buçaco and Viseu

km			Total
0	Oporto Motorway A1		0
70	Aveiro	N109/N235	70
	(Anadia 2 kms. N235)		
35	Mealhada	N1/N234	105
8	Luso	N234	113
	(Buçaco 6 kms.)		
29	St. Comba Dão	N234/N2	142
16	Tondela	N2	158
24	Viseu		182 = 113 m.

At last A1, the Oporto–Lisbon motorway, extends south as far as Aveiro, saving at least an hour in a journey of 70 kilometres as well as easing congestion of both the old road, N1 and the coastal road N109. There is a further A1 stretch of 34 kilometres by-passing Coimbra and a final 53 kilometres into Lisbon. This still leaves 156 kilometres of single track out of 330 between the two cities. Where the going is hilly, bumper to bumper processions of cars and heavy vehicles are frequent; across the flat ground elsewhere, fast moving overtakers ignoring double white lines can be a menace.

As far as our day is concerned, if the weather is kind, good use can be made of the time saved by exploring the park at Bussaco.

AVEIRO (Av-ear-o.) (Pop. 30,000.). Primarily a fishing town. Aveiro is the capital of the northern half of the Beira Litoral. After the 11c. when it was a thriving port, the sea slowly receded, a storm in 1575 silting up the lagoon and closing the outlet. Until 1808 when a passage was cleared once more, Aveiro was deprived of its livelihood – cod fishing as far afield as Newfoundland.

Today's fishermen bring in sardines and skate from the sea; eel and perch from the lagoon. Like Nazaré, Aveiro developed its own fishing boats: *esguichos* to ride the waves, *moliceiros* – their swan-neck prows gaily painted – for the salt gatherers and seaweed collectors working in the placid waters of the lagoon. Again as at Nazaré and in some Brittany ports, the natives' dark looks are said to descend from those exploring mariners from Tyre and Sidon, the Phoenicians. And knowing that sailors do get left behind when ships sail, this does not seem improbable.

The Lagoon – Boats and Tours. For some this great expanse of wet and reedy marshland that forms the delta of the Vouga – quite a sizeable stream rising near Viseu – may have a melancholy, monotonous and frequently misty charm; though – as Myhill observes drily – the Norfolk Broads are nearer home. In summer from 15 June to 30 August there is a Boat Tour on weekdays leaving Aveiro at 11.30 and returning at 17.30. It does the 4½ miles to São Jacinto at the mouth of the lagoon before stopping for lunch at the Pousada da Rio along its banks. Motor boats can also be hired to cruise around the islands among the salt pans, the boats and the barges. The town has been hilariously called Portugal's Venice. Portugal's Little Venice (as in London) would be better; its two canals, divided by the bridge and overlooked by 18c. houses, make it attractive. In the second half of July the *moliceiros* muster in the central canal to compete in the La Ria Festival for the best painted prow.

Convent of Jesus 1000–1200: 1400–1700. Closed Monday and holidays. Free Saturday and Sunday. Now a regional museum the former Convent of Jesus is what people come to Aveiro to see. The rococo chapel, while not quite so wonderful as the Santa Clara church in Oporto, is similarly clothed completely – walls, ceilings, altars – with gilded wood.

Having entered this 15 to 17c. edifice through a Manueline doorway, first among a number of Portuguese primitives there is Nuno Gonçalves portrait of Princess, later Saint, Joana. Her father, was Alfonso V (1438–81) and Nuno's other portraits of him, her brother and her uncle are in the Janelas Verde gallery in Lisbon. Sanctity appealed to 15c. royals and Joana, taking the veil in 1475, came to this nunnery where she died in 1489.

Painted on wood, this portrait of the part-Plantagenet princess in a jewelled cap, her hand as delicate as her nose is long, is a sad one anticipating, perhaps, a melancholy future for any princess confined to a convent unaware that at least she would be canonised 200 years after her death.

Elsewhere in the museum there are, to quote Sir Sacheverell Sit-

Canals at Aveiro. 'Swan-neck prow gaily painted'.

well, 'unparalleled treasures in the matter of embroidered vestments and little painted shrines, an incomparable collection of the finest work of women's hands', the majority being 17c. and 18c. nuns.

In the chancel of the chapel a series of little 18c. paintings, possibly by a nun, show the life of the saintly princess from the day when she leaves her father's palace in a golden coach with a black coachman, not for a ball and a princely proposal, but for the hard life of piety.

São Domingo. The 15c. church, promoted to Cathedral and badly modernised is adjacent to the Convent. A finely painted ceiling to the side vestibule and the ten 17c. paintings of the life of S. Dominic are its best features. **Carmelite Church.** Close to the Post Office the 17c. interior is entirely covered with gold woodwork. **Misericordia.** A 16c. church with a façade of blue azulejos. **Senhor das Barrocas.** An interesting baroque chapel (1722–1732) near the railway station.

ENVIRONS OF AVEIRO

Ovar. At the head of the lagoon, 36 kms. from Aveiro, the name of this little fishing town, where the women's native dress is a black pork pie hat, explains why the fish wives of Lisbon have long been known as *Varinhas*, the 'O' having been dropped.

The town has a big parish church on a hill giving good views, some 18c. chapels and sculptures and two handsome old fountains. There is a restaurant 5 kms. out at Torrão do Lameiro on N327, the road that goes south to the Pousada.

Ilhavo. Museum 0900–1200: 1400–1800. Closed Mondays. **Factory Vista Alegra** 0900–1230: 1430–1830. Closed Saturday and Sunday. Another fishing port with 12,000 people (half the population of Aveiro), Ilhavo, on N109 7.5 kms. south of Aveiro, is hardly off our day's route and worth the detour. Its maritime museum showing some brightly painted *moliceiros*, is charming and instructive. While it also contains Vista Alegra porcelain, the Vista Alegra factory, 1½ kms. on towards Vagos, has been making china here since 1824, delivering in the early days by camel to Lisbon and Oporto to avoid breakage. It too has its highly regarded museum.

ACCOMMODATION, FOOD, WINE

From Aveiro the Pousada Ria de Aveiro is about 56 kms. (36 north to Ovar then a U turn with 20 south along the spit that leads nowhere except to the mouth of the lagoon). In brochures, the blue waters lapping below its balconies, it looks pretty, but in spring and autumn it can be cold and grey. We regretted we had not stayed in Aveiro, where the three-star Imperial is central, the Alfonso V peaceful and there are small restaurants in the town. Gala d'Ouro in the Avenida D'Lourenco (main street with easy parking) served us a good sole (*linguada*).

Ovos moles, literally 'flabby eggs' sold in little barrels, are Aveiro's contribution to the world's collection of sweets made in olden days by nuns to please bishops, the only way they had really of pleasing them.

Bairrada Wines. Agueda, Aveiro, Cantanhede, Oliveira do Bairro, Vagos, Mealhada and Anadia comprise an agricultural region called Bairrada that has had extensive vineyards since 950 AD. This region, which exported to the Americas in the 18c., has recently been demarcated, giving enhanced status to 7000 small holders making sound red and white table wines.

Anadia, one of the wine districts of Bairrada, has long made a sparkling wine, so it is not surprising that the huge SOGRAPE company completed a huge new production centre here in 1980. Still very much a family concern under Fernando Guedes, grandson of the founder, SOGRAPE gives practical help to all the smallholders, buying their grapes in the hope perhaps of creating one day, red and white brands as successful as their Mateus Rosé.

AVEIRO TO BUÇACO

N16, the direct route to Viseu, goes inland from Albergaria-a-Velha winding its way through hilly, wooded country up the Vouga valley. With the façade of the Police Station at Vouzela being the best of Baroque, the local cultured constable's lot must surely a happy one. Our own route, aiming to lunch at the hotel in Buçaco National Park, returns to the Oporto–Lisbon road at Anadia before turning inland on N234 to Luso, the spa town of Buçaco where the water from the pump is as good in its way as Anadia's wine.

Buçaco National Park. The Serra de Buçaco† is a wooded ridge about 9 miles long running northwards from Penacova on the Mondego river to the spa town of Luso. The national park, roughly a triangle 2 kms. long by 1 wide at the Luso end, is world famous; among botanists for its huge cypress trees, and in Anglo-Portuguese history for Wellington's victory over the French under Massena in 1810.

Learning that Massena's army was advancing westwards from Spain via Viseu, Wellington deployed his divisions cunningly concealed at intervals along the entire ridge, spending the night of 26 September, 1810 before the battle at the Carmelite monastery, roughly in the centre of the park.

†English books usually spell the name Bussaco or Buscaco pronunciation being Boo-Sar-Co.

Of the monastery the chapel, cloisters and some monks' cells remain; in one of them, lined with cork like those at Sintra to keep out the cold, Wellington slept confidently, his horse tethered to a venerable olive tree near by, his staff occupying the convent as their headquarters.

While his own 55,000 troops had been ordered to take a cold supper and maintain complete darkness, the fires of Massena's 65,000 men could be seen on the ridge to the westward little more than three miles away from Cruz Alta (1800 feet) in the park and the highest of the ridge's many peaks.

At 6 am through a thick mist the first French assaults began, to be repulsed with six pounders and bayonet charges. Whenever a new thrust threatened to gain a foothold, Wellington's dispositions had forces in reserve to remove it. Eventually capturing Sula and approaching Wellington's command post at Sula Mill, disaster threatened until 1800 infantry of the Light Division, charging from the reverse side of the slope, wrought terrible destruction on the French columns almost at the top.

The young British-trained Portuguese troops were as valiant as any and when after two hours the French retired with the loss of 4600 men, British and Portuguese casualties were equal at 626. But Wellington, who regarded Massena as Napoleon's best general, had yet another surprise for him. The allies retreat began next day, not as Massena expected to be embarked by the Fleet but to enter the long prepared lines of Torres Vedras, whence to emerge for final victory when the time was ripe.

At Buçaco the great man planted an olive tree in the Convent garden and left four hundred French wounded in the care of the Prior. Researching her book, Elizabeth Longford* found the inscription on his look-out point still legible and plaques on two sail-less windmills near Moura and Sula commemorating respectively the observation posts of Massena and Crauford, 'Black Bob' C.O. of the Light Division.

Just outside the park by the Sula gate, the obelisk topped with a glass star commemorates the battle and gives a fine view north-east to the Serra do Caramulo and due east to the peak of the Serra da Estrêla 30 miles away. **Military Museum** 0900–1800. Nearby is the small much praised military museum with contemporary maps, weapons and models of the soldiers. The Portuguese were commanded and trained by the English General Beresford and September 27, 1810 was the 21st anniversary of this Anglo-Portuguese army.

The Park. Buçaco has long been a natural forest. 6c. Benedictine monks from the convent at Lorvão built a Hermitage; 11c. priests

**Wellington. The Years of the Sword.*

from Coimbra made good use of oak and pine. But in 1628 the Barefooted Carmelites§ built the convent, now replaced by the hotel except for the chapel, cloisters and the cells already mentioned. The rapid spread of their order in the early years of the 17c. to many parts of the world, particularly to Spanish America, enabled them to obtain exotic seeds from far flung brothers.

The cypresses they added to the oaks and cork oaks are said to be natives of Mexico. To botanists they are *Cupressus Lusitanicus* and presumably word of their size and beauty must have reached the Vatican as early as 1643 when Pope Urban VIII published a bull to excommunicate anyone damaging the trees of Buçaco. The edict is carved in stone by the Porta da Coimbra, the western gateway, where there are cool seats among the trees in summer with views of the hot Mondego plain. Alongside is another Papal Bull threatening penalties to women entering the enclosure lest they should worry the hermits.

In Britain these trees are tender, yet in Hampshire, the Royal Horticultural Journal of October, 1965, recorded a specimen 67 feet high and 4 foot 3 inches wide planted in 1910. In the warmer, watery misty climate of Buçaco they grow to twice that height, towering – as one writer put it – above the rest of the forest like parasols of green lace.

Since 1834, when all religious orders were expelled from Portugal, the State Waters and Forestry Department has been responsible for the forest – some 250 acres/108 hectares altogether – in which there are now some hundred varieties of trees.

Flowers and fountains. In the midst of trees, flowers and fountains stands the five-star Palace Hotel do Buçaco, looking like a late Victorian transplant of Balmoral. A neo-Manueline affair, built between 1888 and 1907 as a palace for the ill-fated monarch, Don Carlos, the designer was a scene painter at the São Carlos Opera House, which may account for its terrible *azulejos*. The approach from Luso is through the Mountain Gate, one of four for traffic through the surrounding wall; the exit being via the Queen's Gate close to the Military Museum.

There are many walks starting from the hotel. Within 500 metres to the north of the hotel are:

The Hermitage of Our Lady of the Assumption. (Ermida de Nossa Senhora de Assunção). This is one of the ten hermitages in the park where monks could retire for contemplation. Beyond is the **Cold Fountain** (Fonte Fria) from which the water cascades down 144 steps

§A split in the order of mendicant White Friars occured in 1593. The reformers, following a stricter contemplative life, took to sandals and were called Discalced or Bare-Footed Carmelites.

to a pool and a path leads on to Fern Valley lake with ferns, rhododendrons, hydrangeas and tall thuya evergreen trees. Beyond the lake runs a 250 metre Fern Alley with fine cupressus trees.

South-west of the hotel a wiggling **Way of the Cross** (Via Sacra) lined with terra cotta figures ends at Cruz Alta 1800 feet up; the all-round view from it is magnificent. A return to the hotel can be made along the other woodland paths past the Silvestre fountain and its waterfall.

Given good weather a short stay at Buçaco cannot fail to be pleasant, peaceful and far removed from our real world in which Wellington's tree – holding out its olive branches to posterity writes Elizabeth Longford – is largely ignored.

ACCOMMODATION

My first acquaintance with the hotel in May 1980 was limited to a dreary table d'hôte lunch when the park might have been an equatorial rain forest. Others have reported log fires and linen sheets were not matched by 'gorgonzola marble' bathrooms with huge baths, furred up pipes and cold water.

Staying there towards the end of March 1985, there were no plumbing problems. The camellias and magnolias still blooming in the warm sunshine around a formal garden below the bedrom windows, its beds silver with *stachys lanata* in a box hedge border, were a lovely sight.

The cellar containing Bucaco wines with their own distinguished labels is also notable; the whites are pleasantly dry, but the reds, full of tannin, take so long to mature that their price is prohibitive. The staff were pleasant. But with no *à la carte*, only a four-course dinner at £7.50, designed to inflate a full dining room of German and Dutch tours was unworthy of a 4-turret Michelin rating.

At Luso the huge three-star **Grande Hotel das Termas** though secluded with swimming pool, tennis courts etc. is only open from May to mid-October. The Eden is a smaller hotel with 56 rooms and the town now has a restaurant called O Casteiro.

The three-star Grão Vasco in Viseu with 86 rooms is a delightful hotel in an agreeable town, 45 not too slow miles further on.

N2 to Viseu, is smooth and fast. With time no object, the vintage motor museum and a grilled trout at the Pousada (order in advance) are well worth the bumpy deviation to Caramulo (page 117).

ENVIRONS OF BUÇACO

Lorvão. The oldest convent here in a deep valley off N235 between Penacova and Buçaco attracts the *cognoscenti*. In 1713 two princesses turned nun, daughters of D. Sancho I (1185–1211) when Coimbra was still the capital, were given new elaborate silver coffins, as incidentally was their sister, Queen Mafalda of Castille interred at Arouca.

Sir Sacheverell contemplating the lovely nuns' grille and their magnificent solid wooden choir stalls pictures them singing 'each upon her stall as upon a raft or platform of past luxury and privilege, and then cut loose and carried out to sea'; all of which sounds like the orchestra still playing in the Marx Brothers' *Night at the Opera*!

LUSO TO VISEU

A straightforward fast run for these parts of 69 kms., the first place, Mortagua, is where Massena halted his army for six days before his attack. Officially he was awaiting supplies; more likely, the road being rough, his mistress 'Madame X', who rode everywhere with them dressed as an *aide-de-camp*, needed the rest. **Santa Comba Dão** was the birthplace of Dr. Oliveira Salazar (1889–1970) and Dictator of Portugal from 1932 to 1968. But the only plaque will be found in the Largo Alves Mateus telling us that an English Queen, Catherine of Bragança stayed here in 1692.

This is also the village where the Mondego's one important tributary, having risen in the hills of Beira Alta, flows gently on to the confluence, its name immortalised in Portugal's best table wine, Dão.

At Santa Comba Dão the N2 turns from east to north east running parallel to the bleak Serra do Caramulo on the left. In Tondela a branch road, N230, climbs 10 kms. to the six room Pousada de São Jerónimo about 2500 feet up just short of the village of Caramulo. Stuart Ross's *Portugal's Pousadas* however gives this one very poor marks – noisy in the night, showers only, food indifferent – which confirms my own 1985 opinion.

The Vintage car museum is much more impressive; fifty cars (and some ancient motorcyles) including Rolls-Royces 1911, 1920 and 1930. A second museum displays by no means the best works of Picasso, Chagall, Dalí and Graham Sutherland among many lesser *objets donnés*, which the curator was too kind to refuse. From the top of the Serra at Carmulinho (1062 metres) there is yet another of Portugal's great panoramas, west across the Bairrada to the coast, south east to the Estrêla massif. **Tondela** has one particularly fine house, the Casa de Corso, with a very beautiful Baroque doorway.

Viseu. The Grão Vasco hotel on the right entering the town, is in its own shady place with its own parking space.

Avis have a car rental office inside, manned – when I was last there – by a helpful and attractive young lady, who spoke good English learnt locally at school.

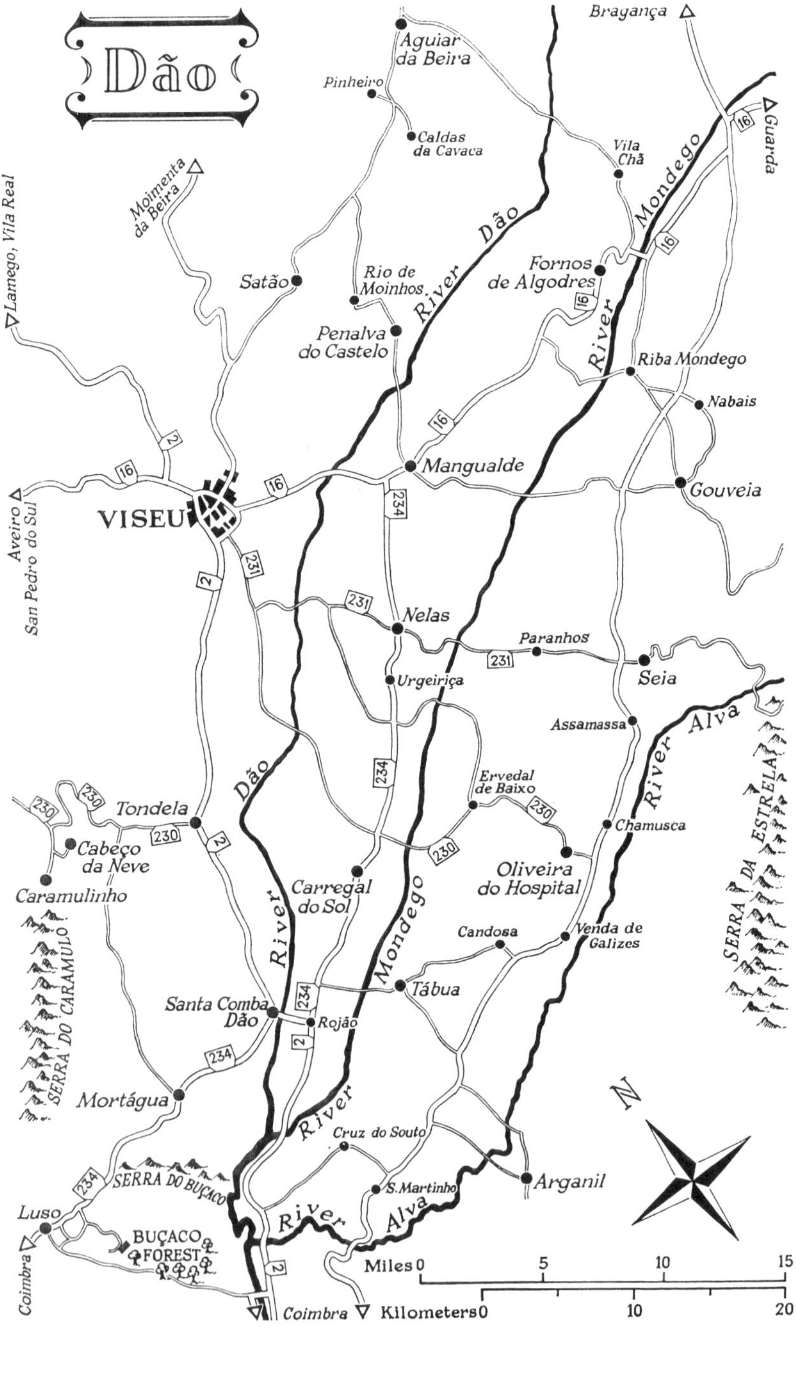
Dão
Bragança
Aguiar da Beira
Pinheiro
Caldas da Cavaca
Vila Chã
Guarda
Moimenta da Beira
Lamego, Vila Real
Satão
Rio de Moinhos
River Dão
Mondego
Fornos de Algodres
River
Penalva do Castelo
Riba Mondego
Nabais
Mangualde
Gouveia
VISEU
Aveiro
San Pedro do Sul
Nelas
Paranhos
Seia
Urgeiriça
Assamassa
River Alva
Ervedal de Baixo
Dão
SERRA DA ESTRELA
Tondela
Chamusca
Cabeço da Neve
Caramulinho
Oliveira do Hospital
Carregal do Sol
River
Mondego
SERRA DO CARAMULO
Candosa
Venda de Galizes
Tábua
Santa Comba Dão
Rojão
Mortágua
River
N
Cruz do Souto
Arganil
S. Martinho
SERRA DO BUÇACO
River Alva
Luso
BUÇACO FOREST
Coimbra
Miles 0 5 10 15
Coimbra
Kilometers 0 10 20
2
16
231
234
230

DAY 5

Viseu. In and around the little Baroque wine town

VISEU (Viz-ay-oo). (Pop. 20,000.) High on the list of charming country towns to be found in North Portugal, Viseu has grown up around and below the compact *old* town, in which the Cathedral, the delightful Baroque Misericordia church and the Grão Vasco Museum are grouped in a simple square at the top of a rocky hill.

It is an agricultural town set in hilly wooded country, farming maize and rye, fruit and cattle, with a lively market on Tuesdays. Local lace, carpets, baskets and black clay pottery will be found in the shops. It is also the centre of the Dão wine region. Even if our own best pronunciation sounds like 'Dung', its excellent table wines are Portugal's best with certainly nothing of the farmyard in the bouquet.* The small river Pavia passing through the north western outskirts is a tributary of the Mondego.

Having sired only one painter of repute, Vasco Fernandes (1480–1543), Portugal has had to make the most of him, and he became known as Grão Vasco – the Great Vasco. To English ears this may sound like an old time music hall star but in fact he was the leader of the 16c. Viseu School of Painting. The Primitives in the Museum are famous, Vasco Fernandes' St. Peter being a great work, even if it does not attain the supreme heights of Van Eyck and the Flemish School.

The town's leading hotel is named Grão Vasco too and, Viseu being the centre of the Dão wine region, Grão Vasco is also an excellent brand made in the local winery, which can be visited.

A good town plan is available from the hotel's Hall Porter or the Tourist Information Office close by.

From the Praça Republica, close to the Grão Vasco hotel ten minutes walk up the cobbled street and through the Porta do Soar, the old gateway in the 15c. town wall, reaches the Cathedral square. **Misericordia Church** (Igreja da Misericordia). Not the most important but the most striking of the three buildings, its 18c. façade of white walls and granite pilasters may already be familiar from Tristram Hillier's painting of the church set against the back cloth of a cloudless blue sky. This picture was reproduced as a frontispiece to Sir Sacheverell's *Portugal and Madeira*. If a Taj Mahal poster draws tourists

*'Farmyardy' is a facetious term once fashionable with wine tasters to describe some wine they disliked.

to India, then this building should do likewise for Portugal, for it could be nowhere else except possibly in Goa or Brazil. **Grão Vasco Museum** 1000–1700. Closed Monday and holidays. Free Saturday and Sunday. On the left from the Cathedral, the Museum occupies a 16c. palace much restored. Among some good Baroque sculpture on the ground floor a 14c. Throne of Grace stands out. The Primitives are on the second floor, Grão Vasco's *Calvary* and *St. Peter on his Throne* being regarded as his two masterpieces.

Gaspar Vaz, his younger partner in running the school, painted *The Last Supper* and *Christ in the House of Martha*. He too did a St. Peter to be seen in the former monastery church at São João de Tarouca, 16 kms. south of Lamego.† Their pupils here are responsible for the less distinguished fourteen paintings of the altar piece.

Cathedral (Sé). The twin-towered cathedral of dark granite embodies styles from 13c. to 18c. and much restoration. Its nave has a remarkable vaulted Manueline roof with prominent stone ropes intertwined. The Renaissance double cloister on the south side can be compared favourably with its counterpart at Tomar. Its *azulejos* are 18c. The sacristy has a beautiful painted ceiling with *azulejos* on its walls in contrasting colours. **Other Churches.** There are said to be five Baroque churches in Viseu, most of them with good *azulejos*. **St. Benedict** (Igreja São Bento) 200 metres east of the Sé is one; another is St. Francis outside the old town between the Grão Vasco hotel and the Praça Republica.

Leave the Cathedral square by the Rua Dom Duarte. A short way down, the tower (Torre de Menagem) has an attractive Manueline window. The mainly 16c. and 18c. houses with their balconies in and around the main Rua Direita make this corner of Viseu very pleasant. **Wine Establishment.** (Vinicola do Val do Dão). This is a business-like winery, by the railway station on the northern outskirts of the town, where red and white Dão wines are made. The vineyards in the demarcated region are scattered between Viseu, Guarda and Coimbra.

Casual visitors, though welcome, would do better to obtain a letter of introduction from UK agents, Hedges & Butler Ltd, 3 Mill Lane, Bromley-by-Bow, London E3. In either case a preliminary ring from the Portuguese hotel Hall Porter is important; they might want to find an English speaking guide for you. The show place of the region is the Quinta owned by the Count de Santar in the village of that name about 15 kms. south of Viseu on the Nelas road. An extensive vineyard in front of a white 18c. house facing a formal garden of rose

†The picture has been removed since 1977 and in 1982 the Church caretaker could not say when it would return.

beds with box edgings, there seems little reason why any passing visitor should not take a peep, the owner usually being away. The vineyard is not enclosed and there are no laws of trespass in Portugal. Condé de Santar is served free on A.P. planes so you may have sampled the wine already.

A morning or afternoon should suffice for sight-seeing in Viseu. Lamego, the next overnight stop, being only 1–1½ hours away; three alternatives are suggested for the rest of the day.

ENVIRONS OF VISEU

km			Total
0	Viseu	N16	0
18	Mangualde	N16/N232	18
	(Casa da Insua 12 kms. N329.1)		
21	T Junction N17	N17	39
	Turn R.		
21	Seia (2 kms. off N17)		60
23	Nelas	N231	83
7	Santar	N231	90
15	Viseu	N231	105 = 66 m.

Mangualde. In this village 18 kms. eastwards along the Guarda road N16, there is an 18c. Misericordia with a small Baroque façade and a finely painted ceiling. The 17c. pink **Palacio Anadia** is a splendid Baroque mansion and the hospital has a pretty little gallery worth a glance.

Yet another Baroque mansion, the **Casa da Insua,** home of the Albuquerque family, requires a 12 km. detour towards Aguiar de Beira to Penalva do Castelo. Illustrated with the Santar estate in at least one Portuguese wine book, both look superb.

From Mangualde N232, crossing the Mondego after 10 kms. meets the main Guarda–Coimbra road N17 just short of Gouveia, where every Thursday there is a market of Serra Estrêla cheeses. Another 13 kms. going west along the foot of the Estrêla hump reaches **Seia,** an attractive little Basque-like town at the foot of the mountain where there is ski-ing in winter. The Estalagem here keeps a good table and is comfortable. Another 45 kms. of easy woodland brings us back to Viseu, via Nelas and Santar.

SHORTER TOUR

At Canas de Senhorim, deep in the country 4 kms. along N234 from Nelas, the quiet three-star Hotel Urgeirica with open fires and Heal mattresses was, at one time, owned and run by an Englishman, a Mr

Harbord. An ideal place from which to explore the Beira Baixa and the Serra da Estrêla, it is now entirely Portuguese with a good report in the 1983 *The Good Hotel Guide* (Which, Consumers Association).

On this occasion, taking the Nelas road N234 from Mangualde, lunching there perhaps and taking a look at the Santar vineyard on the way back cuts the total distance to 62 kms., under 40 miles.

The third alternative, for those tired of motoring is to move on, arriving earlier at Lamego the better to explore this remarkable town on foot and the Douro port vineyards on Day 6.

VISEU TO LAMEGO 71 kms.

Forty-five miles apart both towns are about 1550 feet up and the undulating road N2 between them runs through a fertile countryside of vines, olives, cedars and pines. Traffic is light and the going good.

ACCOMMODATION, FOOD, WINE

We were particularly fortunate in being asked by Senhor José Seradio, when European Sales Manager of SOGRAPE to dine at the Grão Vasco hotel as fellow guests with a party of 30 jolly, all male hoteliers, restaurateurs and sommeliers from the Algarve touring the northern wine places with their one petite, pretty woman courier. After dinner when they had given her various presents and gracious little speeches had been made, the party developed into a sing-song. Maybe there has been no Portuguese Beethoven, but there is no lack of drinking songs with simple tunes which – aided by Dão Tinto and possibly a glass of tawny port – one finds oneself singing as well as Placido Domingo in no time.

Beside the Grão Vasco, the one-star Avenida across the park makes Viseu accommodation normally ample. Only during the festival of São Mateus, in late September when there is a great fair, is it likely to be full. Booking ahead, should the Grão Vasco be full, the Hotel Urgeiriça already mentioned could be best.

The most delightful dish in this region of rivers is fresh river trout, unrelated to the pellet-fed rainbow from the fish farms that now abound from France's Massif Central to the Grampians. The white wine of Dão is a worthy partner; try them both at the Cortico, a good restaurant in the Rua Nova just below the Cathedral.

Any collector of those sweetmeats of nunnish origin should have quite a field day in Viseu. Varieties include: *papos de anjo,* a syrupy baked egg custard, assorted *ovos moles,* the very sweet egg and wine custard with cream, caramel and almonds and *bolos d'amor.* What the Bishop said to the nun about those could not possibly be evidence in any ecclesiastical court.

DAY 6

A Caminho do Vinho including Quinta do Noval and Vila Mateus

LAMEGO (Lam-ay-go) (Pop. 10,000). Lying in a hollow above the Douro to the north, with the 'Lamego heights' growing corn, vines and soft fruit to the south, Lamego is a perfect small Baroque town. Portugal's first national assembly of nobles, clergy and townsmen was held here in 1143, four years after Alfonso I Henriques had declared himself King; he attended in person to proclaim the succession.

Described as a sacred garden, the lower town looks upwards from the Cathedral along a broad two-way avenue, shaded with maple trees to the foot of the double staircase going up to the Pilgrimage Church of Our Lady the Redeemer conspicuous at the top.

N2 (Viseu–Régua) passes the Cathedral and the Museum, where cars may be parked along the avenue before driving through the park from the base of the stairway to the church above and the Parque Hotel alongside it. **The Cathedral** (Sé). Only the belfry remains of the original Romanesque and not much of the Gothic except the handsome 16c. west front. Inside there are some damaged 18c. frescoes by Nasoni, two fine organs and a silver frontal to the Chapel of the Blessed Sacrament. The beautiful Renaissance cloister with a loggia above and still some Gothic detail adjoins the Cathedral on the north side. **The Museum.** 1000–1230; 1400–1700. Closed Monday and holidays. Free Saturday and Sunday. Established in the former Bishop's Palace facing the Avenue and still being reorganised after a fire, the chapel on the ground floor of St. John the Evangelist came from the Chagas monastery demolished in 1925 though the church remains.

Among the furniture, church plate, glass and azulejos, the 16c. Flemish tapestries are outstanding as are the paintings of Grão Vasco – the Annunciation, Visitation and Presentation; and also his Creation of the Animals.

Other fine buildings of granite and whitewash around the Cathedral square are the 17c. Casa das Mores and the 18c. Casa das Brolhas; there are others too south of the Cathedral. **Chapel of the Exile** (Igreja do Desterro). This 1640 chapel in the Rua Cardoso Avelino, further south of the Cathedral towards Tarouca, is decorated inside with 18c. carved and gilded woodwork. The ceiling azulejos, scenes in the Life of Christ, are 17c. **Sanctuary of Our Lady the Redeemer** (Sanctuário Nossa Senhora dos Remedios). Taking the car along the main avenue past the old hospital, now the theatre, gives a fine view of the great double staircase to the church. The vista has been slightly spoilt by the addition in recent years of modern steps at the bottom and some inferior azulejos.

Assuming the pilgrim does not need to say a prayer on each of the 686 steps or to train for the next, and not dissimilar, stairway, Bom Jesus at Braga, we can motor up the road through the park to the square at the top where the Parque Hotel by the Church has a similar view to that of the Largo. **Largo dos Reis.** Known as the 'Court of Kings' this octagonal courtyard surrounded by pillars, arches and huge stone figures of saints forms the top landing, giving the splendid view over the lower town to the hills above the Douro beyond. There are nine landings all told and it is worth going some way down to the sound of falling water from the fountains, to see the balustrades, with their spheres and vases, stairways and terraces.

The Church, finished in 1761, is not of great interest. While the huge granite figures of the saints are considered rather absurd, the architectural concept and execution of the Largo is admired. The Bom Jesus stairway at Braga, having nothing comparable, is less good; although, being much nearer Oporto, it has more visitors.

The pilgrimage over, any thirst after righteousness can be assuaged from a clear spring by the old gnarled chestnut tree in the square. Alternately, or in addition, there is Lamego's dry sparkling wine in the hotel bar.

Balsemão. On the way down to Régua on the N2 (there is also a yellow road alternative see Michelin Map 37) after 4 to 5 kms. a sign right points to Balsemão about 3 kms. at the bottom of a valley. A mule or Shank's Pony is needed for the last kilometre in order to reach a very small 7c. basilica with Visigothic horseshoes, arches and graffiti. A 17c. restoration supplied the painted ceiling and the chancel furniture; nevertheless it is thought to be closer to its original state than another 7c. church, São Frutuoso, at Braga.

Romaria. Every town in Portugal, particularly in the Minho, has its *romaria,* the annual festa during the summer when there is a great gathering out in the open near the shrine of its patron saint, with wine and women, music and dancing. In Lamego the celebration lasts for the first half of September and it takes 40 men to carry and erect all the banners, flowers and streamers associated with the sacred effigy.

ACCOMMODATION, FOOD, WINE

Besides the Parque hotel there is now the Albergaria do Cerrado in the Estrada do Peso da Regua with 30 rooms but no restaurant. The Estalagem de Lamego (7 rooms) is pleasantly sited above the road coming in from Viseu.

Of the Parque's 36 rooms, there are now 12 doubles with bath and it could perhaps merit more than one turret in Michelin. Blackheath Travel's Autumn Port Wine Douro Valley Tour spends a night there.

Standing our friends a bottle of Lamego's *Méthode Champenoise* sparkling wine in the bar (the brand was Caves de Raposeiro Bruto, made by Seagrams, bar about 550 esc., shop price about 300 esc.) we noted that room prices were similar to those of the Malaposta in Oporto – one night 1150 esc. double room with bath. Full pension for two 2150 esc., add 10 per cent May to Mid-October. (1982 prices)

The smoked ham of Lamego is said to rival, perhaps surpass, that of Chaves and there should be no lack of melons by June to go with it.

CAMINHO DO VINHO DO PORTO

Lamego–Pinhão–Vila Real–Lamego

km.			Total
0	Lamego		0
36	Pinhão	N2/N222	36
4	Quinta do Noval	N322	40
32	Mateus	N323/322	72
2	Vila Real	N322/N2	74
40	Lamego	N2	114 = 71 m.

In France whenever one sees the grape there is almost sure to be a tourists' *Route de Vin* not far away. For Portugal I hereby create a *Caminho do Vinho* to beat France hollow for scenery though not, unfortunately, for grub. There being no Routiers signs up the Douro, buy your picnic of smoked ham (*presunto*) and either *pão de centeio,* the rye bread of Tras-os-Montes or *pão de milho,* the crusty, doughy maize bread (*broa*) of the Minho; and butter (*manteiga*). Lamego also has cheeses and with fruits in season and a bottle of wine you will do much better than entrusting the job to the hotel. Portuguese hotels are not good at picnics.

From Lamego our old road, N2, ending eventually at the Chaves frontier, drops dramatically down about 1200 feet to the Douro at Régua in less than ten miles. A bridge below the new *barragem* carries it across the river onwards to Vila Real whence you must return this way unless booked either at the Pousada Baron Forrester above Pinhão or at the Pousada de S. Gonçalo, superbly sited at the top of the Marão pass between Vila Real and Amarante or in either of the two hotels at Vila Real.

Régua having little to commend it other than being the headquarters of the Casa do Douro, which governs the making of port, we turn right (instead of crossing the river) along N222 clinging to the left bank for 23.5 kms as far as the next bridge upstream at Pinhão. This is the heart of the port wine country and if the journey from the coast has been wet, be consoled; in this province of *Tras-os-Montes,* 'Beyond the Mountains', rainfall is 50 per cent less than in Oporto, the climate becoming drier the nearer we get to Spain.†

I recall my own despondency driving over the mountains from Braga to Vila Real in pouring rain one Easter Saturday late in April, with friends who had never seen Portugal before. Previous visits to Pinhão, mostly in March, had been sunny; would we make that plunging descent down the Pinhão valley to lunch at Quinta da Roeda seeing nothing? Fortunately a cloudless Easter Sunday was sheer perfection, in keeping with a lunch prepared by Elsa and Robin Reid, so sumptuous that an Easter parade at jogging pace around the Quinta was needed after it.

This is the Douro – the only region in the world where port can be grown – and nobody describes it better than Sarah Bradford in *The Story of Port**. Of course the eight dams of the hydro-electric scheme now completed have changed a muddy winter torrent that died down in summer exposing great rocks around green pools, into a series of narrow lakes, still waters of uniform level. Yet the olives, oranges and almond trees, the dry walls holding the terraced vineyards covering the steep hill sides, the scent of gum cistus and wild lavender, the scudding clouds and, above all, the silence remain.

For a 100 years until the railway came about 1880, all the wine was taken to Oporto downstream in the old *barcos rabelos,* the flat-bottomed barges with one square sail steered by a man with a gigantic oar. Even with some help from the prevailing strong west wind it is remarkable how they got up beyond Pinhão using oxen on the bank to haul the boats over the rapids. And even more remarkable, each laden with up to 60 pipes,§ were the feats of seamanship that took them safely back over the rapids and through the gorges.

The single line railway from Oporto, joining the right bank at a point about 15 miles below Régua, follows the Douro, on one side or the other, to the frontier at Barca de Alva, 203 kms. from Oporto, Régua being about half way. A life line for the Douro people and often

†Annual rainfall figures in millimetres: Oporto 1200, Régua 900, Pinhão 700 and Barca d'Alva 400. Comparative figures are: England and Wales 912, Scotland 1431.

*First published in 1969 by Macmillan and later in 1978 by Christies Wine Publications.

§A full pipe of port is 115 gallons weighing about 635 kilograms, which is 0.635 tons.

The Douro at Pinhão from the right bank. La Rosa vineyards adjoin, downstream; the main road is visible on the far side. WINE & SPIRIT ASSOCIATION

the shortest route from one village to another, only during the 1970s have the 1880 German 'Puffing Billy' engines been replaced by diesels.

Another 100 years and the road tanker has largely replaced rail and river as the wine transporter. In the next 50, self-propelled barges bringing wolfram from the Spanish frontier through a series of locks already built into each *barragem* will turn the river into a commercial waterway like the Rhine and the peace of the valley could be gone.

RÉGUA TO PINHÃO

Driving from Régua to Pinhão, the Delaforce Quinta da Foz de Temilobos lies a 100 feet above the road near the 7 km. (from Régua) stone, a much better view of it being obtained coming the other way. In general the quintas making the best wines are above the railway on the other (northern) bank, where they get the morning sun. Their modest white houses with adjacent red-roofed *armazen,* in which the port is made and rests before being moved to the lodges at Vila Nova de Gaia, were built – colonial style – mainly by British shippers as places to visit during the vintage, with a few of their trade friends from Britain, and occasionally to shoot partridge in winter. Nowadays when children fly out from school in England and the dams allow fast motor boats to be used for picnics and water skiing, families come up from Oporto more often for holidays.

First of the famous quintas is Boa Vista on your left, just below the point where N323 from Tabuaco comes in on your right 6 kms. short of Pinhão. The vines are said to have been planted by Baron Forrester. His firm, Offley Forrester now absorbed into Sandeman, continue to market vintage ports wholly from this vineyard, as 'Boa Vista'.

N323 climbs up the pretty little Tavora valley, which has a lake and its own *barragem*. Off the beaten track, difficult to find without local knowledge, there are a number of chapels and sanctuaries, notably the 1693 chapel at Santa Leocardia and the Sanctuario de N.S. da Sabrosa, a peaceful picnic place looking north to the distant patterns of earthy brown and conifer green along the hills of the Marão.

Two kms. before Pinhão, as we keep straight on, N222 turns away to the right up the valley of another small tributary, Rio Torto, the twisted river passing some fine quintas and vineyards that include Lages and Bom Retiro.

Next, less than 2 kms. below Pinhão on the right bank, 50 feet vertically above the railway and the river is Quinta de la Rosa, flying a Union Jack alongside the flag of Portugal perhaps because the Bergqvists who own it are as English as Buckinghamshire in which they live. La Rosa was built by Albert Feuerheerd, a descendant of a Hamburg family which had begun in Oporto c. 1750 as general merchants and traders. An early Feuerheerd who became Anglicised without quite mastering the language, declared he would educate his sons at the best English Public Houses.

Albert's daughter, Claire Feuerheerd (1907–1972) who married Eric Bergqvist† of Oporto made La Rosa her home after the war. She was not the first woman to prefer a country quinta to Oporto society; Dona Antónia Adelaide Ferreira (1810–1896) unlike Claire a millionairess, ruled vast estates from the Ferreira Quinta do Vesuvio (q.v.) much further up the valley.

Sold at one time to Croft, the wine of La Rosa has gone to Sandeman for some years now, the property being much improved of late by Claire's son, Tim and his wife, Patricia. Sandeman has become part of the Canadian House of Seagram.

Above la Rosa is Quinta Val de Figueras owned by Alfredo and Jean Hoelzer. The big house lower down by the railway bridge is Quinta da Foz.

We cross over the Douro into Pinhão over the road bridge where the river has made an almost 90° turn eastwards. The quintas on the right bank as you cross are (left) Bom Fim and (right) Roeda. The former belongs to the Symington family, owners of Warre, Graham and Silva & Cosens, better known for Dow's port. Roeda, a much larger vineyard making 220 pipes a year belongs to Croft. Facing them from the left bank is the famous 18c. Quinta das Carvalhas, founded by Pombal to protect the interests of the small Douro farmers; among the largest it makes about 650 pipes a year.

Though Pinhão is an unattractive small commercial town, the railway station's azulejos depicting the valley are amusing and it now has a supermarket and a restaurant. Once through it the Pinhão river valley is superb. The orderly terraces of Noval – the most photographed quinta of all – look down across the confluence of this little tributary with the Douro. Noval's owners, A. J. da Silva, the only Portuguese firm to have long competed successfully in the British market, changed their company's name in 1974 to Quinta do Noval Vinhos.

For some time Quinta do Noval has been the only port quinta to be declared open to all during working hours (Monday to Friday 0930–1300; 1500–1800) so that the public can see the vineyard, the wine making arrangements and the view of, and from, its white walls and terraces, even though the staff may only be Portuguese speaking. The climb by car is certainly worth the 15–20 minutes that it may take for the 4–5 kms.

†British of Swedish extraction, the Bergqvists founded in Oporto the now British public company, Eucalyptus Pulp Mills Ltd.

As Ben Howkins explains in *Rich, Rare and Red,* The International Wine and Food Society's Guide to Port, published late in 1982, Noval intended to concentrate all operations here at the Quinta, moving out entirely from the Lodges at Vila Nova de Gaia. But a change of management reversed the decision. Group visits can be arranged through London agents, H Sichel & Co, York Buildings, London WC2. Casual callers are welcome to admire the view and the vineyard; resident staff speaking only Portuguese precludes explanatory talks.

Who, one wonders, will be the first to provide a port quinta, comparable say to Château Loudenne in the Médoc, as a tourist attraction?

With time in hand having driven through Pinhão, draw off the road and eat your picnic up the Pinhão river; or cross the river, turn left under the railway by Quinta da Foz and follow the right bank road down the Douro towards Boa Vista.

There is no law of trespass in Portugal. You can park the car and climb up any convenient track through the vines. In May among the gum cistus, the white and yellow broom and wild lavender, you should find *anagallis* the vivid blue pimpernel, blue miniature lupins, little gladioli, wild anchusa, lathyrus, wild marigold and other wild flowers I have been unable to identify.

Bullocks, Dogs and Wolves. The bullock cart, still to be seen in the Minho, has become rare in this prosperous valley where brown patches, high up here and there, show that more hectares are coming under vine. Unchanged since they dragged Wellington's guns across Tras-os-Montes, their spokeless wheels are solid wood cut from tree boles, the axle width the same as the Roman chariot. On top of their heads the pair of oxen have *molhelas* (like big boxing gloves) to reduce the pressure of the yoke. Gone too, since the revolution, are the *sol to sol* working hours from dawn to dusk (except Sundays) throughout the year. As a guest one could wake at dawn to the weird squealing, squeaking wheels known as 'the music of the Douro'.

During the night the silence would be broken by the barking of the Serra dogs. Each quinta has at least one of these woolly 'wolf hounds' trained to spend the night patrolling the grounds. I fancy Emelio, the sagacious hound I knew best, made his headquarters on a chair in the porch (much as we used to do on a battleship's quarterdeck when Officer of the Middle Watch in harbour), doing his rounds from time to time. Doors were never locked up the Douro. It is unwise to say 'sit' to these dogs until formally introduced. Their names are usually those of rivers – Douro, Mondego, etc., because dogs with rabies will not go near water and therefore the river's name will protect the dog from infection.

Quinta do Noval. Most port quintas plant a pair of cypress trees, calling them 'Peace and Prosperity'. A. J. DASILVA

Staying at La Rosa I was once rash enough to say I thought that the wolves they talk about were really extinct. Affronted, Claire, our hostess, immediately made a rendezvous for us to see a dead wolf at 6 pm that very day. Somewhere in the hills near Sabrosa we waited, until out of the forest stepped a peasant looking the living image of Clement Atlee – then Prime Minister.

'He's terribly sorry', explained Claire, 'He buried the wolf last week, but if we walk seven miles he'll be only too pleased to exhume it'. A Cordon Bleu cook herself, Claire had trained Conceicão, her own cook, to the same heights.

'But we'll be late for dinner,' said her guests in unison.

It was the only reply that could have saved us. Claire could be very determined and I promised to believe in wolves ever after.

Quinta do Noval. Two roads climb up the Pinhão valley; to our left N323 leads to Celeiros, where Sandeman's have a wine making establishment and, after turning left at Sabrosa, to Mateus and Vila Real. To our right N322 on the other side of the Pinhão river goes to Quinta do Noval and on to Alijó (Pousada Baron Forrester).

The entrance to the Quinta is just beyond the 4 kms. stone from Pinhão. There is a mirror on the left facing the drive, which is a cobbled road on the right under an archway of vines. In front of the house is a magnificent old cedar.

Port being a wine blended by the shippers from many *quintas* large and small, wines from a single quinta are rare and Noval is certainly the finest of them, commanding prices similar to those of Taylor, Fonseca, Croft and Cockburn. Noval belongs to the Portuguese firm of A. J. da Silva owned by the Zeller family whose grandfather planted these terraces. Today the quinta makes 300/400 pipes a year from 350,000 grafted vines and a few more non-grafted, pre-phylloxera vines. (The phylloxera is an insect which devastated the vineyards of Europe between 1860 and 1900. It attacks the roots and the remedy eventually found was to graft the vines on to American root stock which happens to be too tough for the insect to destroy.)

The few pre-phylloxera vines are really retained for historical interest though in practice they have permitted pre- and post-phylloxera wines to be assessed. Tastings have established that the earlier ungrafted vines made an even deeper purple, harsher potion, which took even longer to become drinkable; hence the term 'black-strap' applied to port 100 to 150 years ago.

I include this note on vines and wines in case the staff speak only Portuguese. For visitors the first joy of Noval lies in the landscape – the Douro in the valley below, the conical hill on the far side, the terraces, the vines, the olives, the chestnuts. 'A vista of hills patched with great blue cloud-shadows, like a wilder Tuscany' writes Sarah Bradford.

Mateus. To reach this village a mile or so short of Vila Real, we return to Pinhão, cross the Pinhão river and then take N323 already mentioned. The Vila Mateus is open daily, the small entrance fee being quite insufficient to maintain the fabric properly. To the world the illustration on the flagon label of Mateus Rosé has made Nicolau Nasoni's (1739–43) manor house the best known Baroque building there is and the wine (over a million bottles sold each week) the largest single brand.

The wine was a blend created by Fernando Guedes*, head of the newly formed SOGRAPE firm in 1942. The Portuguese soldier's water bottle inspired the flagon shape and he asked his cousin, the Count, if he could use Mateus as the label. First shipments reached Britain in 1951.

'There is no such thing as a 'great rosé, and anybody who uses the phrase is either drunk or has shares in the company', said Raymond Postgate. Most Portuguese *rosado* wines make pleasant drinking, those from the Vinho Verde country having a slight sparkle.

The villa, on the other hand, its lake and garden surrounded by vineyards and orchards is exceptional. The great coat of arms, the Italianate balconies, balustrades, statuary and the garden façade that looks on to the formal garden combine to make it one of Europe's remarkable private houses. The conducted tour also includes the interior where there are some finely carved wooden ceilings, 18c. four-poster beds from Brazil and 17c. still-life pictures.

The bottling plant at Mateus soon becoming inadequate, the new production centre at Avintes was opened in 1968. In the company of a party from Bass Charrington, now the UK agents, lunching there in 1982 our three hosts were Fernandó, a spritely 80, his son Fernando and his grandson Salvador, all in the business.

I was pleased to hear that in return for the perpetual use of the label SOGRAPE have donated a capital sum to the Mateus Palace Trust, believed to be sufficient to repair and maintain the Count's unique palace. The company's new centre at Anadia is producing the new Mateus white wine already mentioned on page 113.

Vila Real. With 15,000 inhabitants, Vila Real is the largest town of Tras-os-Montes though it may seem little more than a road junction leading north to Chaves and west to Bragança, towns almost as large and infinitely more attractive. This may explain why its most famous

*This charming octogenarian died on July 15 1987, receiving from *The Times* (24.7.87) an obituary as sparkling as his popular pink creation.

son, Diogo Cão, first to reach the mouth of the Congo (1482) went to sea. His great contemporary, Magellan (c. 1480–1521), was born in nearby Sabrosa. Magellan had defected to Spain; of his five ships that sailed west from San Lucar de Barremeda (the sherry town) rounding the horn of South America, only one completed the circumnaviga-tion, Magellan having been killed fighting in the Philippines.

The town now has two Michelin two-turret hotels. Mira Corgo has 46 bedrooms, a swimming pool but no restaurant; Albergaria Cabanelas a restaurant and 24 rooms. Espadeiro, a restaurant, is a relatively new entry.

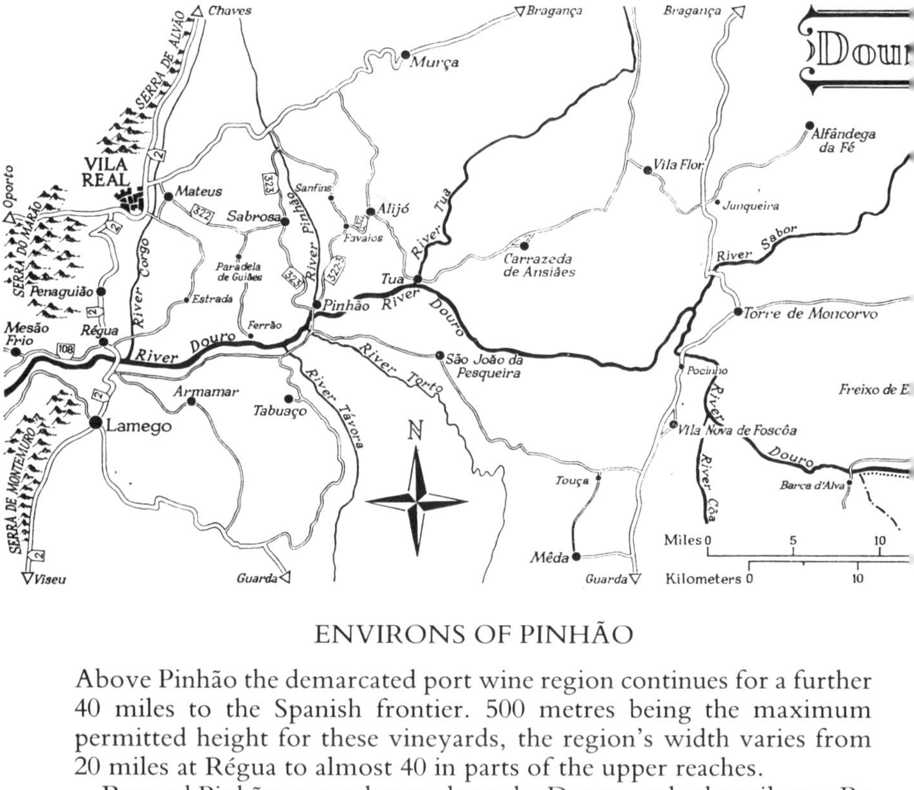

ENVIRONS OF PINHÃO

Above Pinhão the demarcated port wine region continues for a further 40 miles to the Spanish frontier. 500 metres being the maximum permitted height for these vineyards, the region's width varies from 20 miles at Régua to almost 40 in parts of the upper reaches.

Beyond Pinhão no road runs along the Douro, only the railway. By water Tim Bergqvist was kind enough to take me the 16 miles from Pinhão up to the Barragem de Valeira in his 25 knot boat. The weather was poor and the wet hillsides took us back to Loch Long, where almost 40 years earlier I had taken him out in HMS *Vesuvius*, a small mining trials vessel. At the confluence of the Tua on the right bank, Graham's Malvedos and Cockburn's Quinta da Tua (also known as Quinta dos Inglezes) have the railway close at hand and a road that leads up to Alijó. On the left bank Köpke's equally famous Roriz, without a road, has had to roll every pipe down to the *barcos rabelos* and roll out those barrels once more up to the railway trucks on the other side.

Above the *barragem,* built at the Cachão (neck) de Valeira where rapids made further upstream navigation impossible until 1792 when granite obstructions were cleared, Taylor's great Quinta de Vargellas slopes steeply up the south bank above the railway. About 10 kms. above the dam where the Tejo tributary enters, Quinta do Vesúvio looks north across to Quinta da Nossa Senhora da Ribeira.

Vesúvio, owned by the Ferreira firm and the biggest vineyard of them all with a house of château dimensions has been described as 'a vineyard containing between its walls, seven hills and 30 valleys'. Silva & Cosens sold N. S. da Ribeira (though they still buy the wine) which now belongs, as they do, to the Symington's Warre Dow Graham group. Vargellas became Taylor's in 1893 having made only five pipes of port that year due to the phylloxera. Today it makes 200, mostly by treading because Taylors eschew auto-vinification.

To reach by road this historic corner of the Douro where, in 1862, Baron Forrester was drowned in the Cachão takes a good hour from Pinhão and over two from Lamego. There and back would mean virtually a day and either a picnic lunch or a stop at Pinhão's tolerable new restaurant, Ponte Grande, opposite the station.

Such is the hospitality between port people that Alastair and Gillian Robertson of Vargellas invited the entire house party of Quinta de la Rosa at Pinhão – nine people – to lunch, recommending a 'Kwell' for anybody prone to car sickness. From Pinhão N222 climbs the 21 kms. to São João da Pesqueira up the valley of the Torto, the 'twisted' tributary. After 11 kms. and a series of hair-pin bends, the Douro reappears momentarily, a break in the hills giving a glimpse of Croft's Quinta Roeda and the reach above Pinhão, far below on the 'port quarter'. This is the view shown on page 90 of Sarah Bradford's *The Story of Port* (Christie's version).

São João da Pesqueira is a large village with some good 18c. houses, a new small hotel and shops good enough to buy a picnic. Beyond it Michelin map 37 shows a yellow squiggle, N222–3, forking left to the Barragem de Valeira, with a right turn half way down to Vale de Figueira. We take the latter. Far below as if from an aeroplane, we see the Douro above the *barragem,* at a point where a new bridge brings the railway from the north to the south side. The old one (with one span removed) is still there too, liable to be underwater because the hydro-electric scheme has raised the river's level there by 15 feet and much more elsewhere.

Vargellas consists of little more than its railway station, Taylor's small charming house, the Quinta buildings and the vineyard itself, through the earthy patterns of which we descend along their very rough private track for the last 4 kms. Apart from this stretch the surface had been good. From Pinhão time taken 1¼ hours, speedometer recording 40 kms.

After lunch Alastair Robertson took most of his guests in the Taylor speedboat up stream beyond Vesúvio, where the contours in places make the vineyards look like Roman amphitheatres, and down stream through gorges that alternate with longer reaches, to inspect the massive dam.

From the frontier to the sea the Douro scheme comprises eight Barragems on Portuguese territory: Miranda do Douro, Picote, Bemposta, Saucelle, Cachão da Valeira, Régua, Carrapatelo and – last to be finished – Crestuma, just above Oporto. Each has a lock through which 1500 ton self-propelled barges and lesser traffic will be able to pass when deeper channels have been cut below it.

Then 'the old river of gold' will have become another great European waterway like the Rhine and the Loire. The speedboats will make Pinhão from Vargellas in 40 minutes; still time to read what the journey was once like in a *barco rabelo* as described by George Robertson in his excellent book *Port* telling how a Croft/Cockburn party shot the rapids way back in 1953.

For me this warm, cloudless day will remain a memory. Before leaving Pinhão I had looked down on the Douro exactly from the great cedar in front of Quinta do Noval. Later we had seen it again from the heights above Vargellas. In the world of mountains and valleys I doubt whether two such views can be excelled.

WINE TOUR

Satisfactory accommodation at Vila Real (page 134) has improved. Abreu, 109 Westbourne Grove, London W2 4UL, offering Portugal wine tours for the first time in 1986, spends one night there at Mira Corgo, a modern 3-star hotel.

Their 8-day itinerary, flying Sundays Gatwick-Lisbon, includes Bucaco, Dâo, Viseu, and a tasting with lunch at Pinhão in the cellars of Quinta da Foz, next door neighbour of Quinta de la Rosa.

DAY 7

Olives and vines to Amarante, Guimarães and Braga

km.			Total
0	Lamego	N2	0
15	Régua	N108	15
13	Mesão Frio	N101	28
25	Amarante (P)	N101/N15	53
33	Guimarães (P)	N101	86
22	Braga		108 = 67 m.

An early start (0830–0930) is recommended to make Guimarães for a walk round before lunching at the Pousada at the centre of the old town.

Taking once more the steep descent to Régua, we cross the Douro before going downstream along the right bank for about 12 kms., narrow in parts with a level crossing and likely to be slow. The steep climb up and through the narrow streets of Mesão Frio ends at the top of the Quintela Pass (Padrões is marked on the map). The road is wide, the surface good and normally there is little traffic even though this is the quickest route from Oporto to Régua and Pinhão.

Typical Tras-os-Montes country, on our right far below lies a deep valley dotted with the red roofs and white stucco of the farms, the dark gaunt slopes of the Serra do Marão on the far side. At the top a long descent begins through the next valley (Rio Fornelo) to the next river, the Tamega at Amarante. A delightful drive in late April sunshine, the white broom along the roadside and the cuckoo calling like that early morning maiden singing in the valley below.

From Amarante the Vila Real–Oporto road climbs once again, out of the Tamega valley. The Guimarães road, branching right after 9 kms., twists and turns through gentler wooded slopes than in Tras-os-Montes, with Vinho Verde vines growing up trellises seldom far away. Surfaces are good except for patches of cobbles through numerous villages; the going is slow nevertheless.

AMARANTE (Pop. 5000). A brief stop is recommended if only at the café with tables outside it by the Gonçalo Church and the *old* bridge where, with luck, there will be space in the car park. The town lies astride the Tamega, rolling down from Chaves to meet the Douro. From here northwards between the mountains and the sea, all is Vinho Verde demarcated country; Amarante's wine being particularly good with Tamega's true river trout.

Two road bridges cross the river; the modern one upstream carries the main road clear of the town while giving a good view of it. To see Amarante make for the other.

The sex shop has, I feel sure, not so far invaded Portugal and Amarante certainly can have no need of one. For centuries during the *romaria* of S. Gonçalo, the town's patron saint later made that of marriage in the 16c., they baked cakes in the shape of a phallus, which the young men present to the girls; and they, far from being bashful maidens, are only too eager to accept and even solicit them. Nothing, of course, unusual about this today but the custom – an ancient fertility cult – goes back at least to Roman times and could even account for the town's amorous name. The *romaria* occupies the first week in June; at other times there are cakes of conventional shapes called *Lerias, Foguetes Ceria, Galhofas* and *Papos de freira*.

After mentioning this unusual confectionery, the *Blue Guide* goes on to say that S. Gonçalo's erection collapsed in 1763. This, however, refers to the bridge he built, a monumental structure that lasted from 1220 to that date. A fine baroque replacement with three arches, obelisks and niches, built in the reign of Maria I the poor mad queen, leads across the river to his church and convent. At the entrance on the left bank a plaque recalls how in May 1809 after Wellington had recaptured Oporto, Silveira, later the Count of Amarante, whose Portuguese troops were operating with Beresford's, routed the French into a disorderly retreat northwards through the mountains.

San Gonçalo Church and Convent. Built between 1540 and 1620, the pale golden granite buildings rising to the blue and yellow tiled *cupola* and backed by the San Domingo church tower could, when seen across the bridge in sunshine, be somewhere in Italy. The portal of the church too is Italianate renaissance. S. Gonçalo has his statue in a niche and his tomb in a small chapel under the high altar. Architecturally the best features are the arcaded loggia with 17c. figures, the two storey renaissance cloister, its lower storey with rich fan-groining and painted reliefs of saints, a more severe cloister large enough for dancing during the *romaria* and a very fine organ, one of several in this part of Portugal believed to have been built by a Braga firm.

The old convent, now the town hall, has a small museum with paintings by the Cubist, Amadeo de Souza Cardoso, who was born here.

ACCOMMODATION, FOOD, WINE

Cars, lorries and noisy motorcycles using the old bridge and its equally narrow approaches at both ends make this otherwise attractive town horrid for pedestrians including, one supposes, its inhabitants.

On the left bank, 100 metres or so above the old bridge, is **Ze Calcada,** a restaurant with a terrace looking downstream over the bridge to S. Gonçalo. I recall lunching there on Easter Saturday 1979, the rain pouring down but the trout was excellent. Not in the guides, it has been recommended to me by several port shippers for its view, its food and its Pensão. The alternative on the other side of the bridge is the Cacador, an average sort of place with a blaring radio. Amarante's Pousada, São Gonçalo, is 24 kms. up the Pass towards Vila Real.

GUIMARÃES (Pop. 25,000). Regarded as the cradle of Portugal, in 1095 Alfonso VI, King of Leon and Castile gave Portucale to his son-in-law, Henri of Burgundy, who set up a court here, converting a tower into a castle. In 1112 his wife, Tessa Tarega bore a son, Alfonso Henriques, who took over the kingdom from her in 1128, drove out the Moors, captured Lisbon and became Portugal's first King, the succession confirmed, as we have seen, at Lamego in 1143.

Gil Vicente (1470–1540). Poet Laureate, accompanying the court to Lisbon, Tomar, Evora and Coimbra, Gil Vicente, described as Portugal's Shakespeare, wrote 44 plays and was born here.

While Guimarães may be noted for its linen (as advertised by samples of lace embroidery along the road from Amarante) and for its football team, (by its trophies in the Tourist Office window) it is the old town that is worth seeing. The Pousada de Santa Maria, a delightful conversion of old houses in the centre, is very much part of its charm but, even if a town plan can be found (one in the *Blue Guide*), much time can be wasted with a car trying to find the one car park in it. The following instructions should succeed:

From Amarante as we approach the roundabout Praça de Mumadona, the 79 foot tower about 200 metres up the hill on our right is the keep of the 10c. castle built by Henri of Burgundy. Below it, less than 200 metres up the hill from the Praça, the huge bogus-looking building was originally the 12–15c. Paco dos Duques, a palace abandoned by the Dukes of Bragança when John IV (1640–56) became the first Bragança monarch after the rule of the three Spanish Philips (1580–1640). He decided that a palace at Vila Viçosa near Lisbon would suit the court better. From a ruin this palace was badly converted into a residence for Salazar, Now the town's third museum, there are good 16–18c. tapestries, 15 and 17c. Persian carpets, some paintings and a variety of arms.

From the Praça de Mumadona 'straight on' bears slightly right (R. Serpa Pinto). In 150 metres at the next cross roads, with the Convento do Carmo on your right, a road leads up to the castle past a triangular garden. Opposite on your left is the narrowest of streets, the one way

R. de Santa Maria leading directly to the Pousada in 200 metres.

Go slowly down this charming old street through the little square with the imposing former Convento de Santa Clara (now the Town Hall) on your left, until you reach signs on the wall: 1) 'Pousada' straight on, 2) 'Parque de Pousada' turn right. The latter leads to parking spaces, some reserved for the Pousada, outside it in the Largo de São Tiago.

The adjacent smaller square to the south, virtually a pedestrian precinct is bounded by the Pousada's dining room side, facing a building with massive arcades and, on the eastern side, the Collegiate Church of Our Lady of the Olive Tree, which has a Gothic shelter over a Cross in front of its west door.

The Olive Tree Church is so named because Wamba (a Visigoth though he may sound like a Moor) chosen to be King about 670, planted his staff in the ground saying he would not do the job unless it sprouted. Naturally it did and a church had to be built to celebrate the miracle. The interior is now of little interest.

The cloister, chapter house and its conventual buildings, however, form the **Alberto Sampaio Museum.** Guided Tours 1000–1230: 1400–1700. Closed Monday and holidays. Free Saturday and Sunday.

Well restored, the Romanesque cloister was built by João I (1385–1483) victor of Aljubarrota and husband of Philippa of Lancaster (tombs in the Founder's Chapel, Batalha).

The first floor galleries have a remarkable collection of ecclesiastical plate; the silver gilt triptych presented by the King is said to have been captured from the Castilians during the battle of Aljubarrota. It depicts the Nativity, Annunciation, Purification and Temple Presentation surrounded by the Magi and Shepherds. Other exhibits of note are a 16c. silver Manueline cross and Gothic chalice, a Manueline monstrance attributed to Gil Vicente and a tunic said to have been worn by Don João in the battle.

From the roundabout close south-east of the Museum, the circulating Alameda do Liberdade, its dual carriageways separated by chestnut trees and camellias, curves right for some 350 metres, the Tourist Office being on the left hand corner at the end. On a lower level, only three minutes walk across the Avenue from the Museum, is São Francisco, a church so chopped and changed since the 15c. that there is little worth seeing except the 18c. azulejos of S. Anthony feeding the fishes.

Returning to the car, before leaving the old town walk a few hundred metres up the R. de Santa Maria, the narrow street down which you first came. The 14c. and 15c. houses are delightful.

To get out of the town in the car follow the one ways through the

Largo João Franco, the bigger square close west of where you have parked it. This leads into the Largo do Toural, a busy commercial square from which the Braga road runs north-west past the Martins Sarmento Museum.

Martins Sarmento Museum. 1400–1800 Closed Sunday October to June. Closed Monday July to September.

The museum is named after an archaeologist (1833–1899) who in 1875 excavated the Celt settlement of Citania de Briteiros near the Bom Jesus church at Braga. The settlement comprising 150 stone huts resisted the Roman invaders about 2000 years ago. Their *lares* and *penates* assembled here include bronze dolphins, a bull and a hermaphrodite figure holding a bunch of grapes.

ACCOMMODATION, FOOD, WINE

The Pousada de Santa Maria (16 rooms) is a delightful conversion of old houses and one of the best in which I have stayed. The food and service seemed well above average and at night the church's chimes were silent until 6.30 am.

The tall modern block on the Oporto road to the south of Guimarães is the three-star Fundador Dom Pedro. While its 54 rooms and nine 'executive suites' are 'fully equipped for the business man', for the inner man there are only snacks and a bar.

Pride of the Pousadas, recently converted from a monastery, is Santa de Marinha da Costa, 2.5 kms. East towards Pena; 55 rooms, complete with cloisters!

BRAGA (Pop. 64,000). Height 190 m. Braga is Portugal's fifth town, coming after Coimbra and Setúbal. The modern town is a sprawling place subsisting on agriculture and light industry, in contrast to the old town which is compact, ancient and ecclesiastical. Indeed Braga has no less than twelve churches and their twin-towered belfrys look more numerous than Oxford's 'dreaming spires'.

Guimarães and Braga have a special place in Portuguese hearts. Alfonso I Henriques, first King who captured Lisbon from the Moors in 1147 was born and bred in Guimarães. His principal supporter, encouraging the nobles to fight for freedom from the Moors, was the Archbishop of Braga, who had his own vested interest in wishing to become independent of the Archbishop at Santiago de Compostela in Galicia.

Long before the arrival of the Romans in 2c. AD, Galicia and the Minho province were one, first under the Gallarca tribe, then the German Suevi, then the Visigoths and finally the Moors from 711 AD. But by 9c. the Moors had been driven south of the Mondego, Alfonso extending the frontier to the Tagus.

Today the Archbishop of Braga remains the Roman Catholic Pri-

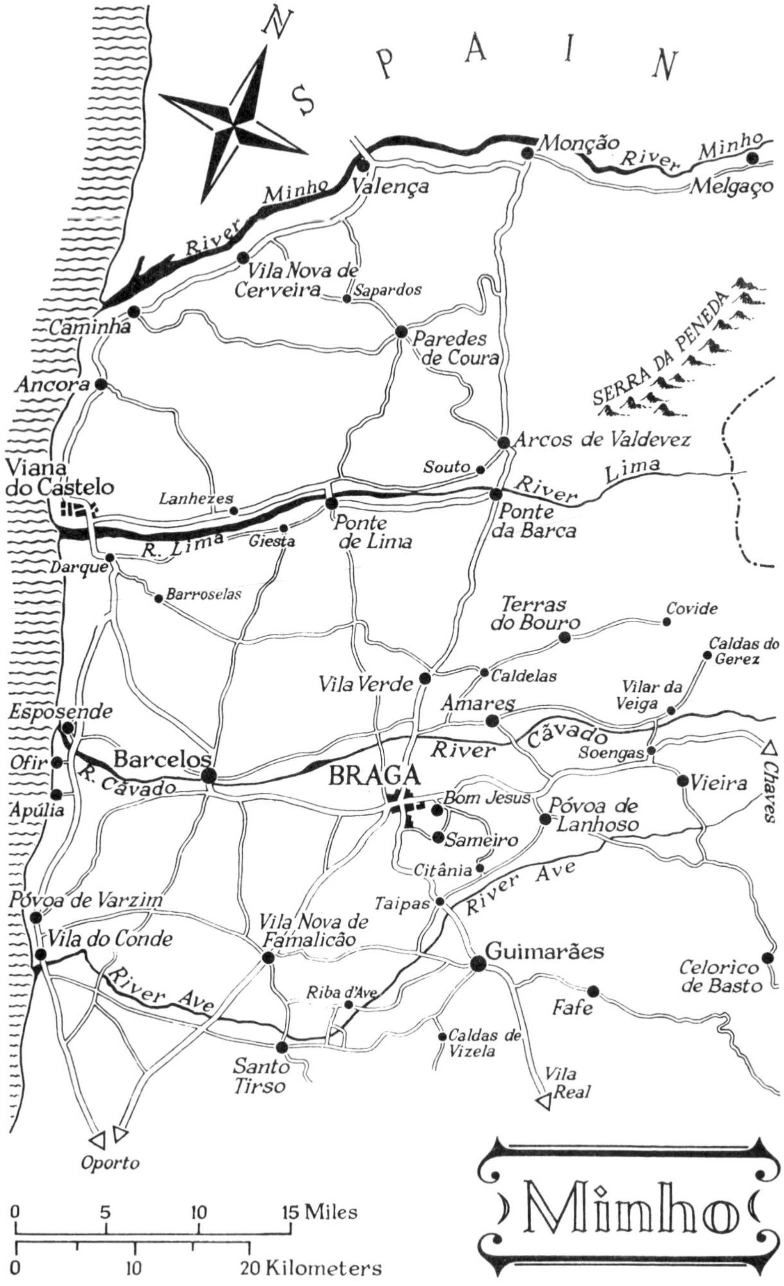
N
SPAIN
Monção
River Minho
Melgaço
Valença
Minho
River
Vila Nova de Cerveira
Sapardos
Caminha
Paredes de Coura
SERRA DA PENEDA
Ancora
Arcos de Valdevez
Souto
Viana do Castelo
Lanhezes
River Lima
Ponte da Barca
Ponte de Lima
R. Lima
Giesta
Darque
Barroselas
Terras do Bouro
Covide
Caldas do Gerez
Vila Verde
Caldelas
Vilar da Veiga
Esposende
Amares
River Cávado
Soengas
Chaves
Ofir
Barcelos
R. Cávado
BRAGA
Vieira
Apúlia
Bom Jesus
Póvoa de Lanhoso
Sameiro
Citânia
River Ave
Póvoa de Varzim
Taipas
Vila do Conde
Vila Nova de Famalicão
Guimarães
Celorico de Basto
River Ave
Riba d'Ave
Fafe
Caldas de Vizela
Santo Tirso
Vila Real
Oporto
0
5
10
15 Miles
0
10
20 Kilometers
Minho

mate of Portugal. The city is capital of the Minho and the best centre from which to explore the province. The credit for much of its ecclesiastical splendour goes to Archbishop Diogo de Sousa, who set the renaissance and early baroque architects to work during his episcopate from 1508 to 1532.

Unfortunately his 18c. successors, having more money than taste 'modernised' most of the churches and, says the *Blue Guide* 1982, 'The interiors of comparatively few – apart from the Cathedral – merit the attention of the visitor'.

On the other hand Braga's religious processions, one before Easter in Holy Week and the other on St. John's day, June 24 *should* merit his attention, both in themselves and in booking hotel accommodation well ahead. I was there on Maundy Thursday in 1979 to witness an extraordinary night pageant as the burghers of Braga – clerics and counsellors, choirs, nurses, doctors, lawyers – every form of civic life marched with bands and banners in procession through the old town taking from 10 pm till midnight, crowds from all over North Portugal coming in to line the streets.

When they do so again on June 24, King David – the part always taken from the same family – dances with his courtiers around the Ark.

Braga has yet another *romaria* on August 6 (the Transfiguration) when the grapes are blessed, a custom likely to have originated in Burgundy.

The large modern Hotel Turismo Dom Pedro, with parking space, is at the point where the ring road (Immaculate Conception Avenue, what street names they do conceive!) meets the Avenida da Liberdade, the wide main shopping street. From here, by the shortest route, the old town is 10–15 minutes' walk.

THE OLD TOWN ON FOOT

A walk round it can begin in the Praça da Republica at the top of the 600 yard long Avenida da Liberdade. The Tourist Office is on the S.E. corner and cars may be parked to the east of the Praça. Take the Rua do Souto, the main street running westwards past the Torre de Menagem on the right, the tower being all that is left of a 14c. palace. On the left in the Rua Sao Marcos, the house with windows covered by latticed shutters is the 16c. Casa dos Crivos. 250 yards on the right we reach: **The Former Episcopal Palace.** (Antigo Paço Episcopal). This huge building begun in the 14c. with additions in the 17c. and 18c. is renowned for its library said to contain 300,000 volumes and 10,000 manuscripts going back a thousand years, collected from many convents, though part of the episcopal library was destroyed by fire in

1866. The fountain we see *en passant* in the courtyard (Largo de Paço) is 1723.

Sé (Cathedral.) A turn left should now bring us to the Cathedral on our own side of the street. Only part of the main west door (obscured by the Gothic porch added in 1532) and the whole southern portal remain of the original Romanesque building. Inside, perhaps its finest features are the twin organs (one now restored) which Sir Sacheverell described as a 'golden riot of tritons, dolphins, mermen, satyrs or devils'. Their date is 1733–38 when the Cathedral organist, Carlos Seixas, was a former pupil of Domenico Scarlatti. Son of Alessandro Scarlatti, exponent of the harpsichord and keyboard composer, Domenico had been a court musician in Lisbon from 1720–29. **Treasury and King's Chapel.** Admission on payment is by guided tour. 0800–1130; 1400–1900. Entrance to the Treasury is from the 18c. cloister across the nave from the south door. The great wealth of treasures, comparable to those in the Albert Sampaio museum in Guimarães, include vestments, plate, chalices and chasubles from the 10c. to 18c. On request the guided tour can also include the 14c. King's Chapel on the entrance side of the cloister containing the tombs of Count Henry of Burgundy (1095–1114) and his wife Teresa, the parents of Alfonso I, first King of Portugal.

Town Hall. Returning to our walk the Rua do Souto has now become Rua Dom Diogo de Sousa. Across it on the far side, the 18c. Town Hall facing the western side of the former Episcopal Palace across the Praça Municipal, has a staircase with azulejos worth a glance. The church, a hundred yards north of the Town Hall is the N.S. do Pópolo, c.1600 but rebuilt in 1775–80. Its only rival in Braga for figures galore in blue azulejos is the Palacio do Raio. **Casa dos Biscainhos.** 100 yards north-west of the Town Hall by the market place and where the Rua da Vista goes out towards N201 and Ponte de Lima, the charming 17c. Casa dos Biscainhos has been turned into a museum of fine furniture, glass, porcelain, fans and jewellery. Ethnographical extensions are being added. Much of its charm, however, lies as before in the fountains, statues and clipped hedges of its gardens.

Turning right coming out of the Casa brings us back to the Rua Dom Diogo de Sousa at the pinnacled 18c. church, Arco da Porta Nova. Once again the street name changes continuing westwards as Rua Andrade Corvo. Should it now be lunch time the excellent small **Restaurant Inácio** lies close at hand off this street in the Campo das Hortas.

Palácio do Raio. We can now find the way back to our starting point by taking Rua de Paio Mendes leading downhill to the west front of the Cathedral, which we pass on our left, then curving right so as to pass two churches and two pleasing little squares. First on our left is S. João do Souto, with the early 16c. chapel **N.S. da Conceição** attached to it; secondly on our right a hundred yards beyond in the Largo Carlos Amarante is **Santa Cruz,** 17c. baroque with azulejos and gilded woodwork inside.

Our principal object in coming this way is the Palácio do Raio also called do Mexicano, a 1750 baroque mansion in the street leading out of the south-east corner of the square. It also has a third name which really ought to be Gershwin for the stone may be granite but the façade is a Rhapsody in Blue.

Walking away from the front brings us to the Avenue da Liberdade by the Post Office, five minutes walk from the Praça da Republica where we began.

Bom Jesus do Monte. On a wooded hill about three miles south-east of Braga stands this celebrated sanctuary with a great granite staircase (as at Lamego) leading to it. Both can be seen from the Praça da Republica.

There are three ways of reaching the church at the top which in itself is of no consequence. A road winds upwards through the woods to Sameiro a little higher up where there are fine views and on to the **Citânia de Briteiros** where the Celtiberians had their settlement. This in fact can become a 44 km./27 mile circular tour taking about three hours. A plan is given in the *Michelin Green Guide*. With sufficient time coming from Guimarães, a turn right off N101 at Caldas das Taipas leads to the Citânia and Bom Jesus and thence into Braga.

The second means of ascent is the ancient looking hydraulic funicular which starts near the gates leading to the staircase at the bottom of the hill. The third is to emulate the pilgrims and walk the Holy Way through the gates, up the path and then up the staircase, step by step on your knees if in penitent mood. The total climb is 116 metres/381 feet.

The pathway leading to the staircase is a Way of the Cross with a chapel and a fountain at each station, each scene presented by life size terracotta figures. The steps were built in 1723, the landings being embellished later. **The Stairway of the Five Senses** is ornamented with fountains of the Five Plagues and statues of Old Testament persons. **The Stairway of the Three Virtues** follows, its fountains and chapels contriving to represent Faith, Hope and Charity.

ACCOMMODATION, FOOD, WINE

For two nights on a short fly/drive I would prefer to be in Braga rather than out at Bom Jesus, except perhaps in hot weather. During our two night 1979 Easter visit, we were comfortable at the modern Hotel Turismo except that the bath water was barely warm and not hot. Hotel food usually being dull and monotonous, we enjoyed *Inácio*, Senhor Macedo's little restaurant where dinner with plenty of table wine and a glass or two of wood port came to about £4 each then. His sweet soufflé, served with two spirit lights in egg shells, was in great demand before the Maundy Thursday procession.

At the Bom Jesus the hotel at the top by the church is the Do Elevador with only 25 rooms, each with private bath. Omitted in guide books but commended by David Wright and Patrick Swift in *Minho* (1968) is the old fashioned Parque Hotel half hidden in the woods not far from the lake, where boats can be hired. Sitting on the terrace at the top of the staircase, a glass of Portuguese brandy in hand, the view seemed incomparable and there is a café at the bottom of the stairs where *al fresco* lunches can be taken.

DAY 8

Barcelos, Viana do Castelo and the Arcadian Lima valley

km.			Total
0	Braga	N103	0
19	Barcelos	N103	19
32	Viana do Castelo	N103/N13	51
23	Ponte de Lima	N202	74
17	Ponte da Barca	N203	91
30	Braga	N101	121 = 76 m.

This day is a rural ride through the sort of green countryside, particularly along the Lima valley, that might have inspired Beethoven's Pastoral symphony. With stops to look around Barcelos and Viana (the best place for lunch) the day soon passes and to see more of Braga than may have been possible yesterday, Ponte da Barca could be omitted. There is no great climbing, road surfaces are generally good though there are long stretches of *pavé*; in fact the entire 30 kms. from Ponte de Lima to Braga are all *pavé*.

BARCELOS (Ba-say-los) (Pop. 4000). After a pleasant country run the 15c. bridge over the Cávado leads into this ancient market town, seat of the first Duchy of Bragança (1442) and capital of Portugal's first county.

The Cávado, only 73 miles from its source in the Serra do Larouco almost in Spain, reaches the Atlantic at Esposende. Its upper valley was dammed 30 years ago, three hydro-electric stations, with two more on its tributaries the Rabagão and Homen, generating 900 million kilowatts, around a fifth of Portugal's harnessed water power in 1980.

'Another of those beautiful small Portuguese towns which, if it were in Italy would have been the subject for English raptures for a century and a half', wrote Ann Bridge and Susan Lowndes of Barcelos.

Those fond of markets should go on a Thursday. The celebrated market where one can buy anything from a gaily painted cock to a pair of lyre-horned oxen occupies the entire Campo de Feira República. A pity perhaps because one cannot see this very large open square – one of the finest in the land – for a fair.

The Cock of Barcelos is based on a 14c. 'Fowl play' legend of an innocent pilgrim bound for Santiago de Compostela accused of some

Barcelos. Fruit and vegetable stocks almost exhausted at the market.

crime and sentenced to death. Protesting his innocence he declared that a cock would crow to prove it.

When the roasted bird that the judge was about to carve for his dinner stood up and let forth a formidable 'Cock-a-doodle-do', the astonished legal eagle dashed to the jail just in time to save the poor fellow from the gallows. The grateful victim erected the Crucifix do Senhor do Galo, the Cross of the Lord of the Cock that now forms part of the free, open-air Archaeological and Ceramic Museum in the former Ducal Palace. The cock is seen above at the foot of the cross, the victim dangling below and St. James of Compostela at the base.

The gaily painted pottery cocks, now almost a national emblem, are to be seen all over Barcelos among the clay dolls, crockery and numerous other rustic arts and crafts. Though much pottery is for sale in Barcelos, very little achieves the standard of Rosa Ramalho, dubbed 'The Grandma Moses' of Portugal who died recently when over 85.

Archaeological and Ceramic Museum. The ruined palace now housing the open air museum was built by Alfonso, an illegitimate son of João, first of the Avis monarchs (1385–1433), married to Philippa of Lancaster, John of Gaunt's daughter. Alfonso marrying Brites, daughter of Nun'Alvares Pereira, Holy Constable and hero of Albjubarrota was given the entire county of Barcelos by his father, the King, thus becoming Count of Barcelos, his predecessor having been killed in the battle. (Soon afterwards Queen Philippa managed to marry off her husband's illegitimate daughter, Beatriz, to Thomas Fitzalan, Earl of Arundel.)

The site of the Palace belonged to the Holy Constable, a gift made to him in 1385 by João I after the battle. The museum exhibits include heraldic ornaments and an 18c. lavabo.

Close by is the Parish Church (*Igreja Matrix*) with a rose window above its 13c. door and to the north of the Town Hall is an 18c. palace. A 14c. house used by the Holy Constable stands in a small square.

Walking north along the main street from these buildings by the bridge there is the Craft Work Centre and the Baroque Municipal gardens, in which the municipal gardeners' topiary 'statues' bid fair to outnumber the fountains and obelisks. The gardens lead into the Campo da República, site of the Thursday market.

The three churches on different sides of the Campo are all early 18c. The most interesting, **Bom Jesus da Cruz,** in the midst of the topiary and pinnacles, Myhill describes as 'an unusual Baroque compromise between a cross and a rotunda, with a granite dome rising above its white walls.' Inside the wooden furniture is all of the highest quality.

On the east side the Joanino façade gives distinction to the originally 14c. Misericordia. At the north end Igreja N.S. do Terco has ceilings

Viana do Castelo, Rua Gaga Coutinho with the facade of the Capela dos Malheiros Reimões and azulejos dated 1713 illustrating the life of S. Bernard. Barcelos annual *romaria* is from May 1–3.

ACCOMMODATION, FOOD, WINE

The modern three-star Albergaria Condes de Barcelos in the Alcaides de Feria near the centre is in the Red Michelin and has 30 rooms each with bath. There are at least two restaurants, The Café do Turismo, next to the Tourist Office is in the main street; the Pensão Bagoeira is next to the Post Office, the restaurant being upstairs.

The Minho rivers are renowned for their lampreys which go so well with the Vinho Verde; none more so than Barcelos lampreys from Cávado tanks. Spring is the season for them.

VIANA DO CASTELO (Pop. 16,000). Five miles south of Viana the Oporto road N13 merges on the left as we move through fine woods to cross the Lima on Eiffel's 1895 bridge. The town lies to our left at the foot of the 650 foot Santa Luzia slope, with the Hotel Santa Luzia at the top and an ugly 20c. neo-Byzantine Basilica just below it.

'Diana' in Roman times had become 'Viana' by the 16c. when the fishermen were bringing back cod from Newfoundland to be dried into *bacalhau* and a sprinkling of Britons had founded a colony to ship Minho wines to England. Though disbanded from 1580–1640 during the Spanish dynasty, another generation returned to form the first British Factory, moving to Oporto when the port trade had developed in the 18c.

The prosperity of Viana, thus founded on maritime trade, enabled Portuguese families such as the Velho and Távora to build themselves delightful 16c. mansions, which are to be found in the old town around the Misericordia.

PARKING

Having crossed Eiffel's bridge, immediately make a U-turn to the left past the Alfonso III hotel keeping to the road that goes down stream with the Jardim Marginal on your left (there are plans in the Michelin Red and Green guides but none in the town's leaflet). Park the car in the shade anywhere along this 600 metre strip of garden between the road and the river.

THE OLD TOWN

Viana's charms are conveniently grouped close to the Misericordia and Praça da Republica 250 metres up the Rua Gago Coutinho, the street *before* the garden ends. 100 metres up it we cross the Rua San Pedro, a narrow street in which the old families mostly lived and their handsome houses are worth a passing glance. Another 70 metres in a fork between two streets the Capela dos Malheiros Reimões, its twin pillars surmounted by a cross forming a lofty arrowhead, is meant to point straight on and it does. A beautiful façade, there are lots of sea shells in the detail of the Rococo window and the main doorway underneath. The interior is of no consequence.

Bearing left leads into the main square, the almost triangular Praça da República where, in April sunshine, the tables will be outside the café. The Misericordia in the north-east corner was begun in 1520 and continued until 1598. It is an extraordinary edifice of three storeys, two open loggias, the upper storeys supported by caryatids (sculpted female figures used as supporting pillars). 'The Lion of Viana, yet heavy and muddled', said Sitwell.

Unmentioned in other books, Wright and Swift enthuse in *Minho* over 'some of the most magnificent azulejos in Portugal painted in Lisbon in 1714 with just a hint of the obscene in the antics of the demons', which are inside the church. Alas the church custodian was taking a long lunch hour from 1200–1500 and we were unable to see them.

Outside the Misericordia the 1553 fountain with falcons and leaves supported by the armillary sphere and a cross by João Lopes, the elder, became the model for many fountains all over North Portugal. On the southern side of the square above an arcade is the 1502 Paços do Concelho, now restored as the Town Hall.

If we continue northwards along the Rua Candido dos Reis there are more houses with Manueline façades, culminating on the corner at the end near the railway station in the Palace of the Távoras or Condes da Carreira, now the Tourist Office. Rebuilt early 17c. it has a good painted ceiling and azulejos.

In precisely the opposite direction the Rua de Sacadura Cabral takes us back from the square to the Jardim on the water front. It leads first to a small square with 16c. houses and then past the Parish Church (*Igreja Matrix*) which has two Romanesque towers and a 15c. Gothic west door carved with figures of the 24 Elders of the Apocalypse on its archivolts. **The Municipal Museum** 1930–1230; 1400–1730. 600 metres west of the old town the 18c. palace of Barbosa Macieis has good early 18c. azulejos of hunting and fishing.

Starting again in the car from the Jardim Marginal, we can continue along the circular road passing on the left the dock and the Castilo, an old fort that Philip II of Spain had built when King of Portugal as well as Spain to guard against the likes of Drake in the future.

Circling the town completely brings us back on the north side along Avenida 25 de Abril from which both the funicular and a twisting road ascend Monte Santa Luzia. The view from the top over the town and the Lima estuary is certainly worth the ride with its hairpin bends. Near the Pousada is Citânia, a Celtic settlement like that near Bom Jesus at Braga, but better preserved.

Festivals. Viana's *romaria* centred on N.S. da Agonia, occupies three days and nights around the third Sunday in August. There is a procession, a bull running around the barricaded streets, fireworks on the Lima and much singing and dancing in traditional Minho dresses.

The Minho is a great province for dressing up. There are wedding dresses in black, in scarlet and in white, glittering with tinsel and sequins and in many other combinations of colour. Wright and Swift went to the trouble of naming some of the village *romarias* where they can also be seen.

February 5. São Bras – Serveleis.

Easter Sunday. Nazarefes – Senhora das Boas Vistas.

Ascension Thursday. Perre – Senhora das Dôres.

May, last Sunday. Cardielos – Senhora do Ampero.

ACCOMMODATION, FOOD, WINE

Six kms. out, the Santa Luzia, is not strictly a Pousada but a 48-room hotel with terraced gardens and a fine view out to sea over the town and the Lima estuary. Though recently refurbished, its former *Which?* recommendation seems to have gone north to the Pousada at Valença. In Viana itself both the three Turret hotels are close to the river by the Jardim Marginal; the 89-room Alfonso III already mentioned, on the western side of the bridge; Do Parque 100 metres to the east of it.

Among restaurants I have enjoyed a sole at Alambique in the R. Manuel Espregueira. This street runs westwards out of the Praça da Republica towards the Museum. Alambique is about 300 yards from the Praça on the right. Local Cakes and Biscuits: *Torta de Viana, meia lua, fidalguinhas, Vianas, Santa Luzia or delicias.*

Just off the Praça is **Os 3 Potes** (The Three Jars) a typical Minho restaurant patronised by Blackheath Travel Tours for dinner and its good *fado*.

PONTE DE LIMA (Pop. 3000). Market Day – Monday. Rising quite close to the Tamega in the mountains of Galicia, south of Orense, within 40 kms. of the frontier and only 60 more to the sea, the Lima is much loved for its rural beauty.

Seeing the Lima for the first time at Ponte da Barca, where it flows out of the mountains into the open green plain, the Roman legions

Still seen in the Minho, the picturesque bullock cart becomes increasingly rare. With spoked wheels, this is a bit of a fancy model. The real ones have solid wooden wheels, unchanged since those of the Roman chariot.

c. 135 AD decided the river must be the Lethe ('Oblivion' in Greek mythology) from which those who crossed would lose their memories. To prove they had not reached the Elysian Fields, the officer commanding, himself crossed on horseback returning to recite the names of the legions to show his memory was unimpaired.

Of the two roads, one on either bank, going upstream from Viana, N202 on the north side is much the prettier, taking one into the town – on the southern bank – across the long, low 14c. bridge that has 31 arches alternately wide and narrow.

The Monday market, said to be the oldest in Portugal and 200 years older than the bridge, spreads itself down the river bank shaded by plane trees. Last time we forgot it was Monday; the cars and the crowds made parking impossible so the quiet walk around this charming place, even though it has no outstanding works of art, had to be abandoned.

The return to Braga along the cobbled N201 is through pleasant wooded country with vines growing up trees here and trellises there. Tibães, on Michelin Map 37 4 kms. north-west of Braga has a large ruined monastery with a derelict water staircase that may have inspired the Bom Jesus architect.

PONTE DA BARCA (Pop. 1500). Narrower here, the Lima's much restored 1543 bridge needed a span of only ten arches. By the bridge is a Manueline granite pillory. N101 running north through the village to Moncão was a Pilgrim's Way between the holy places of Braga and Santiago de Compostela. The 16c. Matríz church, a side tower destroyed by lightning, was rebuilt c. 1714 by Vilalobos, the architect of Viana's Misericordia.

Wright and Swift describe the villagers' custom of midnight baptism of children yet to be born. If the godparents are the first to cross the bridge after the bell tolls midnight, the child will be a healthy specimen. **Bravães.** On N203 6 kms. west of Ponte da Barça the carvings of birds, griffons and animals on the south and west portals of the Romanesque church are exceptionally good. See too the rose window and murals, Virgin and Child and St. Sebastian (the key should be obtained from the house at the north end of the apse.)

DEPARTURE. BRAGA – OPORTO AEROPORTO

N14, Braga to Oporto, is 50 kms.; to the airport about 40. The surface is good, the road becoming fast through wooded country after Vila Nova de Familicão. Follow 'Aeroporto' signs after Mura.

Madrid – Oporto

km	m			Total km	Total m
0	0	Madrid	A6 (to Escorial)	0	0
79	49	Villacastin	A6/N501	79	49
29	18	Avila	N501	108	67
99	62	Salamanca	N501	207	129

This is just a matter of going to Salamanca and following the Sea/ Drive route that enters Portugal from there.

The day can be combined with seeing Philip II's vast monastery – palace, El Escorial, only 5 miles from the motorway. Segovia, where the Roman aqueduct can be admired from Méson de Cándido, arguably Spain's best restaurant, entails a 20 mile detour. Avila's 11c. walls and Cathedral are right on the route.

Salamanca. Casa de las Conchas SPANISH NATIONAL TOURIST OFFICE

Traveller's Notes

Traveller's Notes

Part 4
FLY/DRIVE FROM LISBON

INTRODUCTION

Summary of Fly/Drive. Doing it by Motorcoach.

		Night at:
Day 1	Arrival. Finding the hotel. The City on foot.	Lisbon
Day 2	South West by Car. Meet Manueline. North West and West by Car.	Lisbon
Day 3	Queluz and Sintra returning via Cascais and the Coast.	Lisbon
Day 4	The Arrábida to Evora or Estremoz.	Evora or Estremoz
Day 5	Round Tour from Evora or Estremoz.	Evora or Estremoz
Day 6	Estremoz to Tomar.	Tomar
Day 7	Tomar to Óbidos, Alcobaça and Batalha.	Leiria
Day 8	Departure.	—

This tour spends the first 2½ days (3 nights) based in Lisbon seeing the city's sights, the Royal Palaces at Queluz and Sintra, the coast resorts, Cascais and Estoril and the Arrábida mountain and coast across the Tagus.

Day 4. From the Arrábida for the fourth and fifth nights we go across the Alentejo plain either to Evora's 28-room 3-turret Pousada or to the Estalagem (17 rooms) 5 kms. out in the country or to the 4-turret 23-room Pousada at Estremoz. Of the latter's 23 rooms three are suites at prodigious extra cost to be avoided. Otherwise room and meal prices should be much the same at either and in line with the *Michelin Red Guide*.

Get your Lisbon hotel porter to book in advance by telephone; should all the above be full, Evora has three 2-turret hotels and should be better than Estremoz.

Day 5. Evora needs at least a morning or afternoon on foot. Estremoz much less, the essentials being the Pousada and its associated buildings of the Upper Town. Motoring on this fifth day can be limited to the 75 mile circuit: Evora–Estremoz–Vila Viçosa and back.

If you wish to rush things, Elvas in addition involves a 35 mile detour there and back. Unfortunately although Elvas is included in this guide, our hired Mini broke down completely as we reached the outskirts and by the time telephone calls to the hire company in Lisbon to arrange a replacement were completed, late afternoon had turned to dusk as we hired a taxi to take us back to Estremoz, the town of Elvas unexplored.

Replacement of broken-down hired cars appeared to be more efficient than their routine maintenance, for at 8 am the following morning a small car carrier duly arrived with a second Mini, the driver going on to Elvas to collect the first.

Originally we had intended to spend the fifth night at the Pousada at Marvão or at the hotel at Castelo de Vide a few miles from it. Marvão, 50 miles north-west of Estremoz, is a white mediaeval fortified town on the top of its own little mountain nearly 3000 feet up in the wilds, close to the Spanish border. Given the usual clear weather its views over Spain and the Alentejo are spectacular. Without it the town could be in mist or cloud.

Unfortunately the Pousada serves no lunches and has only eight rooms. Nevertheless it is usually booked well in advance, especially at weekends, and the 2-turret hotel Albergaria Jardim at Castelo de Vide though clean, seemed a little dismal when we stopped there for lunch.

Although metalled the roads of the Alentejo can be in poor repair making speeds over 40 mph bumpy and uncomfortable in a Mini. Failing accommodation in Marvão in good weather, we concluded that visiting Portalgre, Castelo de Vide and Marvão needs an extra day based on Estremoz, Elvas or Evora. Omitting Marvão mediaeval towns are still well represented on our seventh day by Óbidos, less dramatically sited but with more to see.

Day 6. A morning cross country drive from Evora or Estremoz via Ponte de Sor and Abrantes reaches Tomar comfortably in three hours. This leaves the afternoon and evening in which to see the famous convent and walk round this pleasant town. With the large modern Templários hotel in Tomar and the cool Pousada by the lake nine miles out on our route in, accommodation should present no problems.

Day 7. A 9.30 am start should give time for a walk round Óbidos before lunching there. The afternoon visits are to the monasteries of Alcobaça and Batalha, direct mileage from Óbidos being only 35 miles. Either Batalha or Leiria have suitable hotels for the last night and a two hour drive down the main Lisbon–Oporto road reaches the Lisbon Airport next morning.

Day 8. Report in good time at the airport, with other people hiring or returning cars formalities at hire firms' desks can take quite a few minutes.

Doing it by motorcoach

From Lisbon there are many tours by motorcoach which provide an alternative means of seeing many of the places in this fly/drive.

They start from Praça Marqués de Pombal, a pick-up service calling at all the leading hotels, in which leaflets giving full details of dates, times, itineraries and fares are obtainable from the Hall Porter.

Such is the popularity of Lisbon that many of the city tours operate daily throughout the year. Those going further afield run several days a week, maximum frequency being from April to October inclusive. A summary is as follows:

Excursion	*Start*	*Hours duration*
Lisbon	0945	3
Lisbon and Casino Estoril with dinner	2030	5
Touristic Lisbon	1430	3
Artistic Lisbon	0930	3
Old Lisbon	0930	3
Panoramic Lisbon	0930	3
Lisbon by night with dinner	2100	4
Alcobaça, Batalha, Nazaré, Fatima	0830	12
Fatima, Tomar	0830	12
Evora	0830	10
Mafra, Sintra, Estoril	0930	9
Óbidos–Nazaré	1430	5
Arrábida	1430	5

DAY 1

Arrival. Finding the Hotel. The City on foot

ARRIVAL

The first attraction of Portugal's capital city is the proximity of the airport, seven kms. from the central Praça de Marquis Pombal and barely two more down the magnificent Avenida da Liberdade to the Tagus estuary where the big ships berth and the ferry boats cross to Cacilhas on the southern side.

From the airport Rotunda, take the Avenida Marechal Craveiro-Lopes, an outer ring road leading westwards to Sintra. For the city, after two kms. turn left by the Stadium down the wide Avenida Campo Grande with the University buildings conspicuous on the right. After two roundabouts and 2.5 kms. bear half right in the Praça Duc de Saldanha. You are now in the Avenida Fontes Pereira de Melo, which in 800 metres ends in the Praça de Marquês Pombal, his statue in the centre. From here the tree-lined ten-lane Avenida da Liberdade slopes down to the centre of Lisbon with the Tagus beyond, much as the Champs Elysées slopes down from the Arc de Triomphe to the Place de la Concorde in Paris.

Many of the hotels are in this locality; some on the western side of the great avenue between the Praça de Pombal and the Botanical Gardens; others on either side of the Parque Edward VII, the much larger green space to the north.

WALK: 2–3 HOURS

There are few car parks and the city is best explored on foot, easing the strain as needs be with public transport – trains, double-decker buses, the underground and taxis, which are cheap.

Lisbon's underground system is virtually a letter V with a shorter third line in the middle. The base of the V is Rossio Station at the foot of the Avenida da Liberdade. The north western arm, with stations roughly 500 metres apart, runs up the western side of the Avenida, through the Praça de Marquês Pombal, past the Parque Edouardo VII and the Gulbenkian museum to a terminus at the Zoo, all three being tourist attractions. The other two arms, one from Rossio to the Avalade district and the other from the Pombal Praça to Entre Campos, near the University, are less useful to visitors.

Like the Inner Circle in London the Metro is only a few feet below street level; a fixed fare is charged irrespective of distance.

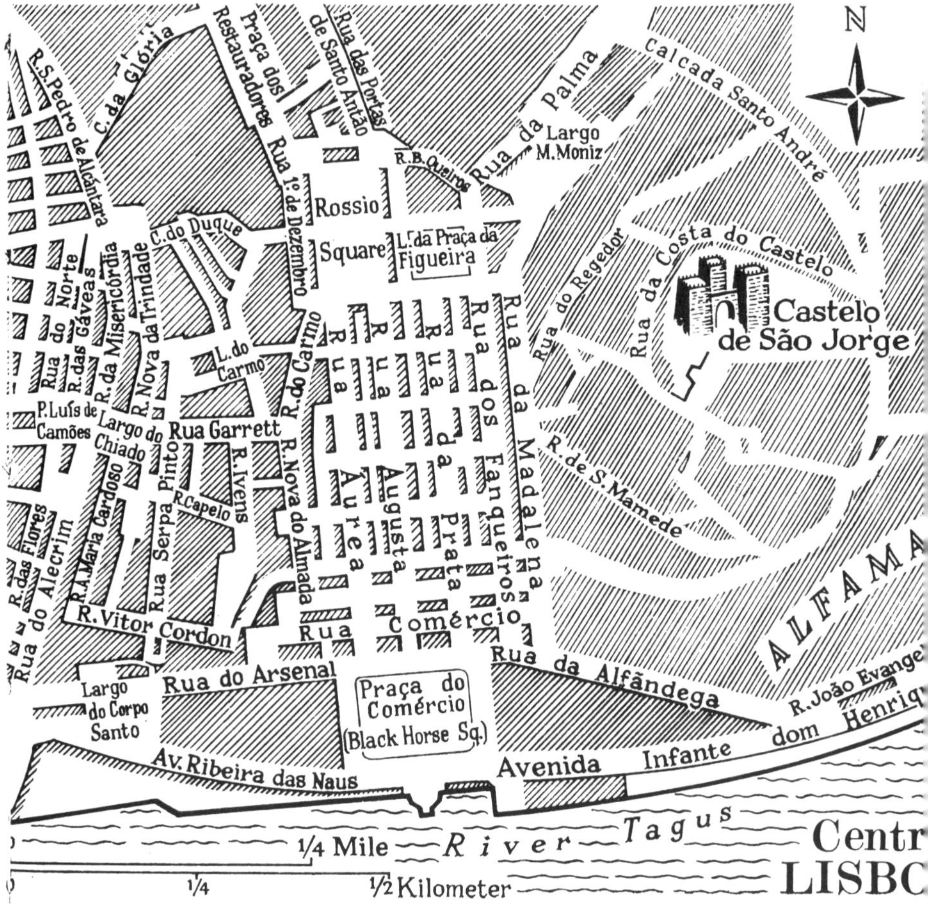

A walk down the mile long Avenida da Liberdade ends in a square, the Restauradores. The Post Office is on the left, the main railway station opposite with the Tourist Office close to the entrance. Almost immediately we are in the central square known as the Rossio, the National Theatre on its northern flank. This is Pombal's Lisbon, rebuilt after the earthquake and its accompanying tidal wave on 1 November, 1755, which destroyed most of the existing city and some 40,000 of its inhabitants. (History also records the birth of Marie Antoinette, herald of yet another disaster, on this same day.)

Pombal (1699–1782) Principal Minister to the King, D. José I had been Portuguese ambassador in London from 1739 to 1745 and in

Lisbon he received powers which Christopher Wren would have envied after The Great Fire. Perhaps the colour-washed façades broken only by the regular line of plain, stone-framed windows owe something to Adam's influence, but the black and white tessellated pavements so comfortable to walk on must surely be wholly Portuguese.

Two main streets, Aurea and Auguste, each half a mile long, join the Rossio to the Tagus. Aurea is full of banks. Take Auguste in order to enter, through its triumphal arch, one of Europe's finest squares – the Terreiro do Paço, known to the English as 'Black Horse Square'. This the Baixa (lower) part of Lisbon, its five parallel streets with others intersecting them at intervals, has been called New York in miniature.

Away to the South, the distant hills of the Serra da Arrábida can be seen across the Tagus from the square. Upstream in the lagoon the commercial quays spread eastwards from Sacavém, industrial buildings such as cement works, oil refineries, cork factories and refrigeration plants creep upstream towards Vila Franca de Xira, twenty miles along the new motorway completed towards Oporto from Lisbon. On the southern side of the lagoon the world's largest tankers now have their own exclusive repair yards. Lisbon is a major port; yet standing in Black Horse Square tourists may make more use of the small ferries that will take them to lunch in the fish restaurants of Cacilhas on the far side, or, in summer, make trips up and down the Tagus giving delightful views of the city. The cruise liners berth alongside only three kms. downstream from the Square. Best known of the Cacilhas fish restaurants is Floresta, which has a big room upstairs with a splendid view across the water of Lisbon on its seven hills, particularly on a warm summer evening as darkness falls and the lights come on. I still recall my first visit in 1952 drinking a rosé wine called Mateus quite unknown then outside Portugal.

Back in Black Horse Square the three sides not open to the river have uniform arcaded buildings. José I (1750–77), the monarch who gave Pombal a free rein, cast in bronze astride his horse by Machado de Castro, the 18c. sculptor, surveys the august scene from the centre, a bas-relief medallion of Pombal on the pedestal below. The square witnessed the deed that was to end the monarchy in Portugal, when in 1908, King Carlos and the Crown Prince D. Luis Filipo were assassinated; the ensuing revolution leading to the deposing of Manuel II, his successor, and the proclamation of the Republic in 1910. The square today is a car park, marked on maps by its official name Praça do Comércio.

Sir Sacheverell Sitwell, as good an authority on Baroque as any living, regards Dom José, riding forward proudly as befits an 18c.

monarch with a Hapsburg mother, as perhaps the most beautiful equestrian statue of that century, but the square he won't allow as being comparable to the Piazza San Marco in Venice, nor the Place Stanislas in Nancy: nor, perhaps, dare I add, the Plaza Mayor in Salamanca, built by Philip V just before Lisbon's earthquake?

MEDIEVAL EAST LISBON

That Lisbon is built on a series of hills and ridges becomes apparent on either side of the square. To the east the Alfama, the rocky mediaeval Moorish quarter that escaped the earthquake, is a maze of steep alley ways, steps and cobbles leading upwards past bars and birds, people and plants to the Castle of St. George (free and open daily). This moated Castelo de São Jorge looks down upon Pombal's Lisbon much as Edinburgh Castle dominates the New Town.

Cars can in fact be parked; on foot it is not much more than a ten minute climb following the Castelo signs through the narrow streets from the Praĉa de Figueira, adjacent to Rossio. Below the ramparts there are stone tablets and seats under olive trees and evergreen oaks; within its ivy and creeper clad walls a fountain plays in every corner and the birds roaming around include white peacocks and at least one golden cock pheasant.

The view of the Tagus lagoon westwards to the bridge and of Lisbon below (the empty shell of the Carmo church looking very weird) is well worth the climb.

Igreja São Vicente de Fora. This church 500 metres east of the Castle was built about 1600 and is of historical interest in that since João IV, the first Bragança king (1640–1656), it has become a mausoleum for Portugal's last Royal House.

Igreja da Madre de Deus. (A mile east of Alfama.) A fine Manueline doorway leads to a church rebuilt after the earthquake, which is now an exhibition of *azulejos* from 14c. to 20c.

Among other places of interest in this eastern quarter of the city are: **Museu-Escola de Artes Decoratives** in a 17c. palace with tiles, tapestries and Portuguese furniture. 1000–1300: 1400–1630. Sunday free. 1300–1600. **Museu de Artilharia.** Weapons and military relics in former arsenal. 1000–1620: Sunday 1100–1640. Closed Monday and holidays. Not free. **Cathedral (Sé)**. Rather a dull cathedral with some Gothic cloisters. 0900–1800.

MANUELINE WEST LISBON

To the west of Black Horse Square the steepness of the Bairro Alta (High Quarter) comes as another surprise unless a look has been taken already at the stairs necessary to ascend from the entrance to the main railway station in the Restauradores to the platforms on a higher level altogether, whence the trains come and go through a mile long tunnel. Human legs can be saved by using either Eiffel's steel lift, which goes up to the Carmo church, or the tramcar-funicular from the Restauradores to the Miradouro de São Pedro de Alcantara, which we shall come to shortly if still walking.

Just down stream from the square, Rua do Arsenal leads into the Praĉa do Municipio. Turning north (backs to the Tagus) from there, take the Rua Nova d'Almeda, turning left into the Rua Garrett, also known as the Chiado, a street for window shopping and a 'dish of char' in one of the cafés. Sad to relate Lisbon's bars and cafés are rather dull and dreary, with few outside tables *à la Français*, but the seafarers were the first to bring *cha* (tea) to Europe from the Far East.

Igreja São Roque. A right turn now takes us climbing northwards (Tagus again astern) up the Rua Misericordia, with a passing glance perhaps to see the menu outside No. 37, Tavares restaurant. In less than 300 metres the aforesaid rack and pinion tramcar (fare 5 esc.) deposits people from the Restauradores below, close to the Misericordia and its exquisite little church of São Roque, a miraculous survival of the earthquake built by the Italian, Felipe Terzi (architect of São Vincente church), about 1600.

Ann Bridge and Susan Lowndes in their admirably detailed 1949 book, *The Selective Traveller in Portugal*, record how Padre Antonio Vieira in 1642 preached a sermon that went on for two days and a night. (Whether Savonarola in Florence was longer-winded or Fidel Castro has since beaten them both, *The Guinness Book of Records* might tell us.)

The fourth chapel on the left is that of St. John the Baptist, built in Rome in 1742 at a cost of £225,000, which was certainly a record then for so small a sacred edifice. Vanvittelli of Caserta, near Naples, made it of agate, lapis lazuli, alabaster and verde antica with mosaics and paintings. Having done so, he and his team dismantled their creation for the voyage to Lisbon in three ships.

Buried upright near the pulpit is a Cornishman, Sir Francis Tregian, a Catholic whom Lisbon came to regard as a saint. His last 20 years were spent here after being imprisoned in England for his faith by Queen Elizabeth.

Somewhere among Anglican hymns *Ancient and Modern* is the line 'All my silver all my gold, not a mite will I withhold' often sung at Confirmation services by 'sable-bodied' mothers who would be very cross if they really did have to hand it over to the Lord. Here, on the other hand, in this rich rococo church, the craftsmen really did do Him proud.

São Roque is one of the many chapels of the Misericordia, *The Pity from the Heart* organisation that raised money, freely given, for almshouses. It still does. Alongside the church every Friday at midday the weekly lottery in aid of Portuguese hospitals is drawn, the tickets being sold all over Lisbon, chiefly so it appears – by blind people with white sticks. There is still a Misericordia in almost every Portuguese town. A high proportion of these buildings rank among the country's major architectural achievements worth looking for, that at Bragança, started in 1418, being perhaps the oldest.

Outside, the street's name changes to S. Pedro de Alcântara. On the left in a 17c. palace the Port Wine Institute has a comfortable bar where anybody is welcome (on payment) to sample every style and type of port. The narrow street opens into a pleasant *miradouro* with benches under the trees and a fine view of Pombal's Lisbon spreading east and north below.

This street, which has about six names before it ends, sweeps left for the Botanical Gardens, becoming the Rua da Escola Politécnica. After a dull half mile, passing the Academy of Science at the south west corner of the gardens, the next turning right, the Rua Nova de S. Mamede, descends steeply past the Hotel Altis to join the Avenida de Liberdade a short way below the Praça Marquis de Pombal, and just above the Tivoli and Tivoli Jardim hotels.

The region south-west of the Praça Marquis de Pombal, surmounted by the huge basilica of the Estrêla church (conspicuous from most parts of the city) and running down to the Tagus below Black Horse Square, is mainly residential and apt to be too hilly for easy walking. Most of the British institutions – perhaps to exercise their inhabitants going out in the midday sun – have been established here; they include the Anglican church, the British club, Hospital and the helpful office of the British Chamber of Commerce. The Embassy is further on in the Lapa district between the Estrêla and the river.

DAY 2

South West by car. Meet Manueline. North West and West by car

SOUTH WEST BY CAR

From Black Horse Square, Belém (pronounced Belem) is nearly 7 kms. downstream requiring a car or a taxi. The attractions are the Abbey, the Coach Museum and the Tower. The road (N6) runs alongside the Tagus by the quays past the second railway station – which is the terminus for the coast line to Estoril and Cascais – and then under the Ponte 25 de Abril, the great road bridge completed in 1966, connecting Lisbon and the north with the Arrábida peninsula and the south.

National Gallery. 1000–1700 (1900 Th. and Sun.). Closed Monday and holidays. Free Saturday and Sunday.

A first stop can be made at the Museu de Arte Antiga, the National Art Gallery. It contains the famous triptych, The Temptation of St. Anthony by Hieronymous Bosch, which once belonged to Philip II of Spain, the Armada monarch.

The Portuguese themselves, other than Grão Vasco and his Viseu school were not great painters. Better, advises Sacheverell Sitwell, to dally – if at all – among the pottery, china and French silver rather than among acres of poor Portuguese primitives. To be sure of getting to this art gallery in the first place, say 'Janelas Verdes' to the taxi driver. Every place and street in Lisbon seems to have two names and the gallery is better known by that of its street, Janelas Verdes (Green Shutters). **Coach Museum.** 1000–1700. 1830 June to September. Closed Monday. Free Saturday and Sunday. The golden coaches of the 18c. in the former Riding School of the Belém Palace are acclaimed as the finest collection in Europe. The earliest model is the red velvet coach in which Philip III of Spain rode to Portugal in 1619; the latest, the 1903 model, built in Lisbon for the State Visit of King Edward VII and Queen Alexandra when they were rowed ashore in the Royal Barge by 80 sailors. Spanning three centuries there are carriages and cabriolets of unsurpassed splendour, matched upstairs by a collection of slippers, saddles, liveries and uniforms of powdered and bewigged Royal bodyguards.

Monasteiro dos Jerónimos. Across the road the Mosteiro dos Jerónimos, begun in 1502, has been described as one of the most original and beautiful places of worship in the world. It is the apotheosis of Manueline architecture, born of an exuberant age when the Portuguese navigators were enlarging man's world, the nation's sculptors commemorating their feats with ropes, anchors, sea-beasts and sextants hewn from stone. In its Santa Maria church only six huge octagonal pillars hold up the vaulted roof of the high and wide transept. Boytac, the architect, is thought to have come from that 'ac – land', the Languedoc or the Dordogne. Though Western Europe abounds with cloisters, Boytac's works here and at Batalha are unique. Sacheverell Sitwell explains that the Manueline was an *art nouveau*, more extreme than any that came later in the age of Baroque. In 16c. Catholic Italy it never would have been allowed; only here, hard by the Tower of Belém, built in the Tagus where the first voyagers set sail to discover Africa and India, could it possibly have happened.

Maritime Museum. 1000–1700. Closed Monday and holidays. Free Wednesday. The Museu de Marinha in the west wing of the Monastery has models of 15c to 20c. ships and galleys.

The Tower. 1000–1900 (1700 winter). Closed Monday and holidays. Downstream the white limestone tower, built in 1515 with its knotted stone cables and look-out towers, still greets every mariner entering Lisbon by sea. Francisco de Arruda, the architect, had worked on fortifications along the African coast. The style is Moorish, inspired perhaps by the Koutoubia Moroccan mosque in Marrakesh.

Museu de Arte Popular. A few hundred yards eastwards along the quay from the Torreo de Belém, this small and well arranged display of provincial necessities – agricultural tools, fishing gear, cooking utensils and hand woven clothing illustrates Portuguese country life. There is also an Overseas Agricultural Museum with gardens at the eastern end of the Jerónimos.

HOTELS

Of some 40 Lisbon hotels in the *Michelin Guide* only the five turret Ritz Continental near the Parque Edward VII and the two turret York House (Residencia Inglesia) are printed in red indicating 'particularly pleasing.' The latter with some 50 rooms usually gets a good notice in the *Which Good Hotel Guide.* In Rua des Janelas Verdes, 32–1–2 Tel. Lisbon (01) 66.24.35., it is close to the National Gallery away from the centre.

NORTH WEST BY CAR (OR METRO)

Parque Edouardo VII. 0900–Sunset. After the huge Monsanto Parque, this is Lisbon's second largest green space sloping upwards from the Praça Marquês de Pombal and opened by Britain's Edward

The Tower of Belém.

VII himself in April sunshine during his 1903 State visit. A landscaped garden with trees, bushes, plants, ponds and streams it makes a cool spot in which to spend a hot afternoon. The Estufa Fria (cold house) is a show place for horticulturists and the highest part gives good views over the city. Some parking is allowed in roads around it.

Museu Calouste Gulbenkian. Closed Monday. 1000–1700 Tuesday, Thursday, Friday. 1400–1930 Wednesday, Saturday free. 1000–1900 Sunday free. Half a mile north of the park (metro station Palhava) this admirable modern building with its remarkable collection of Chinese porcelain, Egyptian jewellery, Japanese furniture and European paintings owes its existence to the Gulbenkian Foundaton.

Born in 1869 at Scutari, opposite Istanbul, where Florence Nightingale had her hospital in 1857, the poor Armenian boy became a much respected international oil broker known as 'Mr Five per cent'. Much of his fortune was given to Portugal, the Foundation sponsoring its own orchestra, choir and ballet and much artistic and scientific research. You may even meet its mobile library vans that take a wide selection of books to the remotest villages.

Jardim Zoológico. Daily 0900–Sunset. A mile north west of the Gulbenkian museum, served by the Metro terminus station Sete Riós, the Lisbon Zoo is aptly named in that the animals really do live in a large park with trees, shrubberies and notable rose beds. The children's Zoo is particularly attractive.

WEST BY CAR

Parque Monsanto. This huge open park to the west of the city, 4 kms. by 3 kms., catering for tennis and outdoor activities, includes a luxurious camping and caravan site.

RESTAURANTS AND NIGHT LIFE

Many restaurants and taverns are to be found in the Bairro Alto said to be the original home of the *fado*, though some say this far from bright and cheerful entertainment was imported from Brazil. Derived from mediaeval sea songs sung by troubadours, *fado* is accompanied by guitars. Entertainment in the night spots of the Bairro Alta and Alfama starts late and may go on into the small hours.

The three good restaurants, close together in the Bairro Alta, **Aviz,** Rua Serpa Pinto 12B. Ornate Edwardian decor. **Tagide,** Largo de Biblioteca Pública 18. **Tavares,** Rua da Misericordia 37. With red carpet, red velvet curtains, red pseudo Chippendale chairs, 19th c. mirrors and chandeliers and a solitary carnation in a metal vase on each table, Tavares is an Edwardian delight, reminiscent of London's Café

Royal pre-war. Though Portuguese cuisine rarely reaches French standards, Lisbon food can be superb and I can commend the Dressed Crab, a speciality of the maison. **Tagide,** with a Michelin gastronomic star, is a first floor restaurant with a balcony overlooking the city. *Crèpes de Fromage à l'Oriental* is a hot cheese rissole, the cheese having the melt-in-the-mouth texture of a *Quenelle.* After it *Crabe farci façon du Chef* can follow as the main course. Bill for two with a bottle of table wine and a glass of port; £45.35. **Conventual Praça das Flores,** opened in 1981, this is a Portuguese restaurant near the National Assembly patronised by delegates usually dining late. Bill for two; £30.25.

Gambrinus, Rua das Portas de Sto, Antão 25. Informal with tables and a bar counter this is a sea food restaurant in an incredible street of fish shops off the Restauradores on the eastern side of and parallel with the Avenida da Liberdade. **Michel,** Largo de Sta. Cruz do Castelos. Best restaurant in the Alfama, close to the castle. French restaurant to which Michelin awards a star.* **Tivoli Hotel Roof Restaurant,** Rua Julio César Machado. The Tivoli and the Tivoli Jardim are two separate modern hotels with garages, at the top of the Avenida da Liberdade on the right going down. I have enjoyed an excellent dinner on the 9th floor roof restaurant of the former finding on the wine list a Colares 1967, the colour of old claret, with a good nose and a lovely aftertaste. The **Tivoli Jardim** has a ground floor restaurant that serves light lunches (egg dishes and mixed salads). Among the charms of our oldest ally an Englishman derives pleasure from the red pillar boxes, double decker buses, replicas of Georgian silver candlesticks and, at the Tivoli, a lemon covered with muslin to prevent the pips coming out.

*The 1987 Michelin recommends 45 hotels and 53 restaurants in Lisbon. Three of the latter are awarded *bonne table* stars. Michel's has been withdrawn; Conventual Praça da Flores gains its first; Tagide invariably gets one. The other newcomer is **Casa da Comida**, due North of the Largo de Rato and only ten minutes walk from the Praça de Marquês Pombal. It has a pretty patio of plants – not edible presumably.

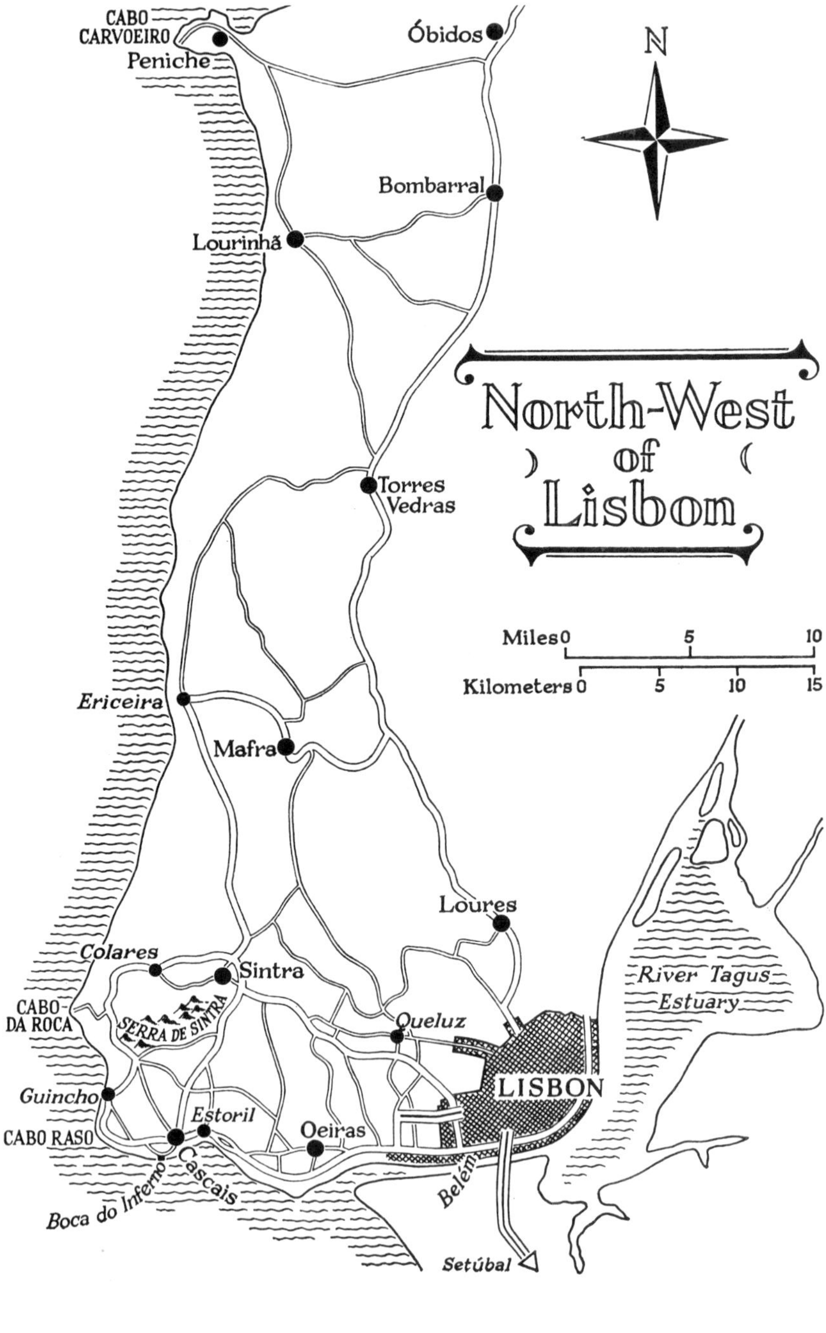
North-West of Lisbon
N
Miles 0 5 10
Kilometers 0 5 10 15
CABO CARVOEIRO
Peniche
Óbidos
Bombarral
Lourinhã
Torres Vedras
Ericeira
Mafra
Loures
Colares
Sintra
SERRA DE SINTRA
CABO DA ROCA
Queluz
Guincho
Estoril
Oeiras
CABO RASO
Cascais
Boca do Inferno
Belém
LISBON
River Tagus Estuary
Setúbal

DAY 3

Queluz and Sintra, returning via Cascais and the coast

km			Total
0	Lisbon		0
12	Queluz	N117	12
15	Sintra	N249	27
15	Cabo da Roca	N247.4	42
16	Cascais	N247	58
3	Estoril	N9	61
28	Lisbon	N6	89 = 55m

QUELUZ. Starting from the Praça Marquês de Pombal a wide road leads in three kms. over the fly-over complex associated with the big Tagus bridge into the Auto-Estrada for Estoril and Cascais that splits the Monsanto Park in half. In another three kms. N117 goes off north west for Queluz and Sintra, two small towns 12 and 27 kms. from Lisbon respectively, each with its own 18c. royal palace.

O Palácio Real. Guided tour about one hour. Closed Tuesday and Public Holidays. Begun in 1758, the pink washed palace at Queluz is a piece of rococo perfection in the same class as the Petit Trianon at Versailles and the Casa del Labrador, the Labourers' Cottage in the Prince's Garden at Aranjuez south of Madrid. Its semi-circular wings spreading from the main block on to the gravel square, combine with the houses across the square, the Town Hall and the clock tower to delight the eye like a well designed architect's model.

The architect was Mateus Vicente de Oliveira, joined later by the French, Jean Baptiste Robillon, who also laid out the gardens. It was built for D. Pedro, second son of King João V, whose eldest son, Joseph had become King on his father's death in 1750. D. Pedro married Joseph's daughter, ie. his own niece, who, on her brother Joseph's death in 1777, became Queen Maria I. She and her husband were extremely devout. Living with a man who heard three or four masses in the morning in the utmost ecstasy and went to evening prayers as well, perhaps it is not surprising that she developed religious mania and by 1788, two years after her husband's death, was so insane that her second son, D. João became Regent. But in choosing to live here her taste was admirable.

The interior was superbly restored after a fire in 1934. The rooms are small with beautifully painted walls and ceilings. The dining room has yellow azulejos and Hepplewhite chairs. Whilst the marble mirrors and magnificent Venetian chandeliers in the Music and Throne rooms are superb, the simple panels in the bedrooms of royal picnics and children dressing up have an endearing charm.

Robillon's gardens with their formal balustrades, topiary and statues are delightful. Coming to the Dutch canal with blue and white azulejos, we can imagine that eccentric dilettante, William Beckford, his overriding ambition to meet the Queen fulfilled here at last in 1795, being made by the sad, dotty old girl sitting cooling her legs in a fountain, to play hide and seek among the hedges and alleys with her Maids of Honour.

A luxurious restaurant, Cozinha Velha, open at 1230 daily has been established in the Palace.

SINTRA. (Pop. 21,000). After Queluz N117 becomes N249 to Sintra, 28 km. from Lisbon. *Sierra* in Spain, *Serra* in Portugal, can mean anything from a mountainous massif such as the Serra da Estrêla, over 6,500 feet in mid-Portugal to the Sintra, an isolated damp misty ridge 1500–2000 feet high, north of the Tagus estuary and a few miles inland from Cabo da Roca, Europe's most westerly point. There are three separate villages on the north side. São Pedro, the highest, attracts tourists to its fairs on the second and fourth Sundays of each month. Santa Maria is half way up on another escarpment and Sintra, the lowest, is where the Kings of Portugal as early as the 14c. chose to build a summer palace. The Palace, the Misericordia Hospital, the two turret Hotel Central are grouped round the small square with shops close by. **O Palácio Nacional.** 1000–1700. Closed Tuesday. The palace is still the most Moorish building in Iberia after Granada's Alhambra in spite of Manueline windows and a pair of conical chimneys added later. The interior has been heavily restored but the guided tour (about an hour) does reveal some pleasing swans and magpies on painted ceilings and some beautiful *azulejos*.

For Englishmen Sintra owes its fame largely to Southey and Byron (*Childe Harold*). The Serra rising from the plain by the sea amid its crags, convent and luxuriant foliage does give an impression of romantic grandeur.

> 'The vine on high, the willow branch below
> Mixed in one mighty scene, with varied beauty glow.'

Much of the 'varied beauty' is to be found in the Parques of Pena and Monserrate, forming one green space 5 miles by 3 roughly the shape of Sicily, with Sintra itself in the position of Messina.

To camellias in spring, purple bougainvillea, pink geraniums and intensely blue plumbago in summer, the warm Atlantic rains certainly impart a glow. **Palace, Castle and Cork Convent.** Before descending

Robillon's gardens at the Royal Palace of Queluz.

through flora to the coast, there are superb views of country, coast and estuary from the terraces of Pena, the 1840 Moorish-Scottish-baronial Palace built by Fernando II, a cousin of our Queen Victoria's husband, Prince Albert. (1000–1700, closed Monday.) The Palace festooned with balustrades and minarets, its domed tower, looking like an aerial torpedo about to be shot into space, is an architectural joke that might be some Russian health hydro for dissidents.

Looking down upon Sintra a few hundred feet below, the Castelo dos Moros 0900–1800 (0800–1700 winter) also gives a fine view from its royal tower, on clear days as far south as Cabo Espichel jutting out of the Arrábida Peninsula.

Taking N375 through the Parque to Colares passes the Quinta da Monserrate, now a state school of forestry, but long owned by the Cookes of Doughty House Richmond, who c. 1850 planted an English garden in this steep valley with ample water.

Away on the other side of N375 lies the 'Cork Convent' or Convento dos Capuchos (0900–1800. 0800–1700 October–April) where 8–12 friars lived from 1560 to 1834. Their tiny cells hewn from the rock are lined with cork in this peaceful place where birds sing to the tinkle of running water and the wild flowers bloom in the spring tra-la!

COLARES AND ITS WINE

Being a wine trade man I wished to visit Colares on the edge of the Parque, making wine by royal charter since 1255. The region is interesting because the vines are grown in two parishes of wind-swept sandy soil between the *Serra* and the Atlantic. To plant a vine the sand is dug away to a depth of perhaps ten feet till the Ramisco vine's roots can be anchored in the clay below that has to be penetrated with an iron bar. To save such slow intensive labour the vines are spread by 'layering', a technique well known to gardeners. As the vine shoots extend laterally they are pegged down, each given an elongated slit from which a 'layer' makes roots, that in their turn grow down to the clay, forming a new plant.

Between 1860 and 1900 when European vineyards were destroyed by the root-eating phylloxera and had to be replanted with every vine grafted on to an American root-stock which is too tough for the red bug to take, the vineyard of Colares was unharmed. The phylloxera is unable to penetrate such a depth of sand, so Colares vines are now unique in being on their own roots. Bottles of red Colares are on sale in Lisbon leaving little if any for export. The white Colares tends to become straw coloured and maderised in a few years and has not the balanced acidity of a white Dão.

Only wines made in the regional cellars in the village qualify for the Colares seal of origin. But production – tending to decrease – is little more than 2200 hectolitres (1 hectolitre = 22 gallons) and quite insufficient to export. The *Armazem* (lodge) where visitors are welcome (no English spoken) Monday to Friday has some impressive tonels of Memel oak holding from 6365 litres to 16,000. Two years there and at least four in bottle bring Portugal's greatest red wine to maturity. In 1980 in the Tivoli Hotel restaurant I was lucky to find a Colares 1967 with the charm of an old claret.

Cabo da Roca. About four miles beyond Colares, a right turn reaches the western tip of Europe, 'Cape of Rock', the Atlantic pounding 500 feet below. Though 'the Atlantic isn't romantic' and I've rolled, pitched and felt sick upon it too often in my time, the view from the Cabo must, in the minds of good British Europeans, now replace that from Land's End, so I went to pay it my respects.

Along this coast northwards the beaches are storm-swept, with a strong undertow making bathing dangerous in many places. Back on the coast road, turning south for Cascais on N247, the fury of the sea can be seen along the long beach, Praia do Guincho, and heard in the Boca do Inferno (Mouth of Hell), an abyss at Cascais formed by marine erosion.

CASCAIS AND ESTORIL. Cascais, once a charming fishing port, is now a resort that reminds one of Paignton; Torquay (Estoril) merging with it. The 20 miles of Costa do Sol into Lisbon are now a mass of villas inhabited by rich, sun-seeking Europeans. In the Holy Ghost and Commercial Bank a specially selected young lady helps with their problems. The Tourist Office has a reading room with European newspapers.

I stopped there for a few minutes alongside a small supermarket buying very foolishly, a bottle of Gordon's gin instead of a Portuguese brand. The Gordons at £10 cost me twice as much.

Carcavelos – a vineyard that was. Carcavelos once made a strong, sweet white wine; in the days of the Marquis of Pombal the wine from his Oesiras property in 1752 got as far as the Court of Pekin. Since the region was demarcated in 1908 urban encroachment has reduced the average annual output to a trickle of 273 hectolitres and Carcavelos no longer gets anywhere at all.

Mafra: Palace and Monastery. 1 hour guided tours. From Sintra those who have not had enough of Portuguese palaces can wind northwards for 15 miles to Mafra where John V on the birth of his son and heir in 1714 commissioned a palace-monastery required to be more imposing than Philip II's giant, the Escorial.

50,000 workers, paid from the riches of Brazil, gave it no less than

4500 doors and windows. German, Italian and Portuguese architects contributed their individual styles over 13 years. Sacheverell Sitwell commends the local marbles, the embroidered vestments, the bronze grilles and lamps and the magnificent Baroque library, which has 36,000 volumes. Otherwise his summary is 'a monument to the monotony of Royal Palaces'.

ACCOMMODATION, FOOD, WINE

There are over a dozen hotels at Cascais ranging down from the luxury 400 rooms Estoril Equador to the 17 room Estalagem near the Boca do Inferno. There are several more at Oitavos 5 kms. towards Lisbon.

Estoril is much the same as you would expect from a fashionable international resort. Cascais has a dozen restaurants and at Estoril the English Bar is one too. The best hotels have heated swimming pools.

Of the two resorts Cascais is the more attractive and lively, with gaily painted boats, a fish market and fish restaurants.

Estoril's hotels are on the hilly ground above the crowded beaches and the coast railway. Reports say the Casino is dull in spite of roulette and a room full of one-armed bandits.

For the tourist preferring sea breeze to city life the ample accommodation is at least ideal for exploring elsewhere. Many 7 and 14 night tour operators offer hotels here as an alternative to those in Lisbon, easily reached using the coast railway.

At Sintra close to the 13-room Hotel Central, the 75-room Hotel Tivoli Sintra, is under the same management as the Tivoli and Tivoli Jardim in Lisbon. On the Colares road 1.5 kms. away, the 4-turret Palácio dos Seteais has only 18 rooms in a former 18c. palace. There is also the Estalagem Quinta dos Lobos with about 20 beautifully furnished rooms but no restaurant. Swimming pool, English spoken and lovely views.

DAY 4

The Arrábida to Evora or Estremoz

After three nights in Lisbon it is time to move on for the remainder of the week having booked two nights at either Evora or Estremoz and one each at Tomar and Leiria. This itinerary takes in some of the charming, shining-white little towns of the flat dry Alentejo, then almost reaches the Atlantic at Obidos, a gem of a medieval walled town, and ends with the two great abbeys, Alcobaça and Batalha, Portugal's national monuments comparable as shrines to Westminster Abbey and – though much later – St Paul's. Leiria, under two hours from Lisbon Airport with a large modern hotel has been chosen for the last night.

The fourth day is worth a 9 am start. Though the distances round the Arrábida are short, a day soon passes exploring places like Sesimbra, Portinho da Arrábida, Azeitão, Palmela and possibly Setúbal. Lunch at Portinho is recommended or, if not posh enough, at Palmela's Pousada. From this locality Evora may take 1½ to 2 hours and Estremoz half an hour more.

The distance table as described is:

km.			Total
0	Lisbon (Motorway)	E4	0
43	Sesimbra	N378	43
15	Portinho	N379-1	58
14	Azeitão	N379	72
14	Palmela (P)	N379	86
8	Setúbal (P)	N252	94
34	Atalho X-roads	N10	128
37	Montemor-o-Nova	N4	165
30	Evora (P)	N114	195 = 121 m

Estremoz (N4) is 67 kms. from Montemor-o-Nova making Lisbon–Estremoz 232 kms. = 144 m.

For the inhabitants of a capital city this glorious combination of Arrábida country and coast forms an Arcadian recreation ground on their doorstep, with walks over the hills, unsurpassed views and boats in which to mess about. Let us hope that it will be made a national park unsullied by litter. If the Portuguese have not yet learnt to preserve their beauty spots, it is perhaps because few have had the money to see and care for them.

The Great Bridge. The 1½ mile long Ponte 25 de Abril spanning

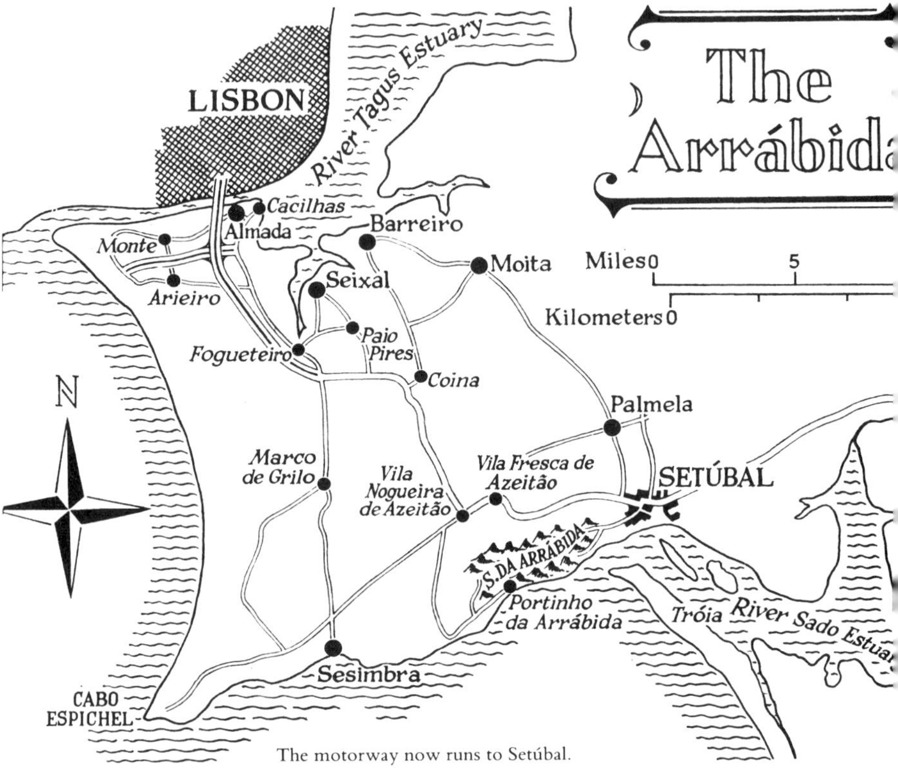

The motorway now runs to Setúbal.

the Tagus took four years (1962–1966) to build and is 23 feet longer than the Forth Bridge. Britain and America supplied much of the steel. The foundations penetrate 79 metres/259 feet below the river bed into basalt rock, the road bridge itself being 230 metres/753 feet above the surface of the Tagus. The name was changed from 'Salazar' to **'Ponte 25 Abril'** when, in 1974, the Dictatorship was overthrown. Going north across the bridge there is a fine view of Lisbon on its various hills, the Tower of Belém almost a toy tower far below on the left. Yet another view – over the estuary and south to Setúbal is from the top of the Cristo Rei (Christ in Majesty) statue south-east of the bridge.

On the southern side the road becomes the N252/E4 toll motorway crossing the Arrábida peninsula to Setúbal in 40 kms./25 miles. The toll may be avoided by taking the old N10 road via Vila Nogueira de Azeitão through fields, orchards and pinewoods. The climate here becomes distinctly Mediterranean, with winter temperatures of 14° C/57° F., similar to those of the Algarve a hundred miles further south. This is because, on the far side the gentle green slopes of the Serra da Arrábida seen to our left, descend in a series of cliffs 500 to 1500 metres high to a sheltered bay that turns the 30 kms. of coast, facing south-east from Setúbal to Cape Espichel, into a riviera.

To start at the seaward end branch right a dozen kms. from the bridge on to N378 for Sesimbra. A 10 kms. detour (N379) reaches the lighthouse on Europe's south-western point where, on September 26, people foregather around the little chapel and the handful of dwellings for a fishermen's festival 700 years old. The great sweep of coastline 25 miles north to Cascais and another 45 miles south as the crow flies across the bay to Cape Sines is majestic, though on a lovely late autumn day sea mist prevented us from seeing it.

SESIMBRA. Still a fishing port with plenty of shell fish, whiting and scabbard from these well protected Atlantic waters and a reputation for excellent swordfish angling further out, Sesimbra becomes more of a seaside resort too as time passes. Not only for sea and sun worshippers either; in my home town the Chichester Travel Agency combined with the *Chichester and West Sussex Gazette* to organise for over a hundred *avant garde* travellers a spring tour from Lisbon, such as I am describing. Within four hours of leaving Gatwick they had reached Sesimbra's modern 4 star hotel, Do Mar, built into the cliff side, its reception rooms on the top of the building, with bedrooms and balconies below looking out across the bay.

Not only the location but this hotel with 119 rooms proved an excellent base for a week in which their daily excursions included Batalha, Fatima and Tomar on one day, Estoril, Sintra and Mafra on another, Evora on a third, with Lisbon by night as well as day at other times. Arthur Treagust who runs the Chichester Travel Agency assisted by Margaret Evans, whose family built Reid's Hotel in Madeira, described this holiday as the best the Society had done.

Close to the beach at the other end of the Esplanade, the one star Espardate hotel (80 rooms) is simpler. On the hill, above the Moorish castle, Sesimbra has an old church with a numismatic (coins and medals) museum.

THE ARRÁBIDA CIRCUIT

From Sesimbra N379 climbs briefly to Santana (Restaurant Angelus) before heading east towards Azeitão and Palmela on the north side of the Serra, a right fork after six miles returning to the coast. A narrow lane off it descends to an almost white sand beach at Portinho da

Portinho da Arrábida, the white sand beach. The structure like a bandstand is the Galeão re

Arrábida. Green hills fall sharply to a series of beaches, where the sea is a translucent blue. 1200 feet up, the weathered walls and the faded red roofs of the 'new' convent set among pines and cypresses, though very Portuguese, may evoke Mediterranean memories.

The 33-room Santa Maria Estalagem (closed from late October to April) has no restaurant, the patrons presumably eating at the Galeão restaurant bar, a structure on wooden piles where dangling a minnow from your table you could easily catch your own fish. Galeão is none the less a well run restaurant serving all manner of fish from the bay, £3 a good sized grilled sole being the most expensive.

One of several caves, the Lapa de Santa Margarida, so thrilled Hans Andersen that he almost made a fairy tale out of its 'veritable church hewn out of the living rock, with a fantastic vault, organ pipes, columns and altars'. A festival is held here on July 20, which must be linked to Setúbal's St. James's fair, a holiday with bull fights and folk dancing from July 25 to August 8.

Before reaching Setúbal, only three miles away, it is a relief to find the Arrábida circuit does almost a U-turn at a point where a number of cement factories have been built and the distant view of Setúbal has been marred by four tall ugly blocks of flats at the tip of the Troia Peninsula and a pair of chimneys across the Sada lagoon belching forth.

The mountain is now on the left, the circuit road rejoining N10 between Setúbal and Vila Presca de Azeitão, a small village by-passed by N10 before coming to Azeitão a mile or so further on.

In the village, surrounded by a wall and unseen is the **Quinta de Bacalhoa,** 'a lovely half caste of East and West' that pleased Sir Sacheverell as echoing an early Renaissance villa in Florence. Artists fared better at the hands of medieval monarchs than dukes and bishops; while King João II was planning to dispatch his powerful rivals, Andrea Sansovino, the Florentine architect and sculptor, was his invited guest.

Sansovino left some statues in Coimbra and is thought to have had a hand in the pavilions here with their melon domes, the great water tank, the house itself and the layout of clipped box, orange and lemon trees. Sir Sacheverell also mentions the azure-winged magpies (*Cyanopica ciganus*) found only here and in China. Once too there were della Robbia medallions, which not even the admirable American lady, restoring the long-abandoned quinta in 1930 was able to trace.

Since the American owners are often in residence, this early Portuguese dwelling house is not open to the public. The gardens are however; Monday to Friday 1 pm to 5 pm. Ring the bell at the gate hidden in a spinney opposite the bus repair garage on N10. An elegant pavilion contains the earliest dated tiled panel in Portugal, Susannah and the Elders, 1565.

Azeitão (a-zay-ee-tah-ung). Literally the 'little place of olives', the groves, vineyards, orchards and woods continue almost all the way back along the old Lisbon road to Cacilhas, where the ferries cross to Black Horse Square. The town too is charming with its disused palaces, alley ways and fountains. It is also the best starting point for walks up the Arrábida mountain.

Almost opposite though not in all the guide books the Quinta das Torres I have seen described as 'an inn with restaurant service'. In fact it is a 16c. country house turned into an hotel the rooms being round its courtyard. There are delightful azulejos; a cupola set in a lake with swans forming part of the garden. Details in the *Good Hotel Guide 1987*; the food is excellent and the owners, two elderly ladies, speak French, English and German. The nearest alternative accommodation is at the Palmela and Setúbal Pousadas.

A Wine Establishment. Azeitão has its own vin rosé, Faisca and the region between it and Setúbal, demarcated in 1907, makes the one and only Moscatel de Setúbal, a sweet dessert wine of the highest class. As with port, fermentation is checked with brandy, but fresh grape skins are macerated with the wine to impart an intensely fresh fragrance. Maturing in wood continues for at least six and perhaps 20 years.

All this can be seen and sampled free by those who care to call on José Maria de Fonseca's 1834 establishment in Azeitão. The company (not to be confused with the other Fonseca in Oporto) makes many of Portugal's best table wines and brandies, which they export not least to America. Except in August (closed for holidays) tourists are welcome during working hours, first here and secondly, time permitting, at the modern premises on the N10 towards Vila Nogueira de Azeitão.

Urban development has virtually ended commercial vineyards nearer Lisbon, leaving J. M. Fonseca – 17 miles from the bridge – to show the flag for Bacchus in the south of Portugal.

PALMELA. Having completed the Arrábida circuit at Azeitão we can go back eastwards for barely ten miles to the hump at the end on which stands the pretty little white town of Palmela. Leave N10 at Vila Presca de Azeitão taking the left fork N379 and drive right up to the top following the signs to the Pousada. The buildings there are the Castle, the Church and the 17 room Pousada itself, formerly the convent.

In 1484 King João II, having disposed of the Duke of Bragança the year before, stabbed the Duke of Viseu to death in the royal bedroom of the castle, condemning the Bishop of Evora to the dungeon below

Azeitão. Quinta das Torres. 'A cupola set in a lake'. JAN READ

where he died, probably poisoned.

The Pousada is beautifully arranged around the cloister, where guests can sit at tables under brightly-coloured umbrellas. The day we lunched there service was slow, the staff's full attention being given to a formal lunch party of 14, in which the eight guests were Chinese generals in plain green uniforms with no badge of rank; their plain caps, each with its red star, had been placed by the door in the neatest line abreast as if to advance on a broad front.

The 15c. church just outside is good plain Gothic with a fine west front, built by the Knights of San Tiago (St. James), one of the military orders which lasted until the earthquake of 1755.

It is well worth climbing up to the castle keep in clear weather for a superb view in all directions – westwards over the Serra, south over Setúbal and across the Troia spit to the Atlantic, east over the Alentejo plain and north over Lisbon and the Tagus, sometimes as far as the Serra de Sintra.

St. Peter's, the 18c. church in the town below is lined with *azulejos* showing the miracle of the fishes, Christ walking on the water and the crucifixion of the fisherman saint. Being wine country, early in September the vintage is celebrated both here and in Setúbal with music, dancing and fireworks. Here, in Palmela, a wine press is actually built in front of the church.

SETÚBAL. With 97,000 people this busy port, 50 kms. from Lisbon, is Portugal's fourth largest city, placed after Lisbon, Oporto and Coimbra. Braga and Evora come fifth and sixth. Commercial activities include fish-canning, salt from the river Sado pans, cement and wood pulp manufacture and a number of automobile assembly plants. Visits to sardine canning factories can be arranged, but the smell all around the town should be more than enough for most people. **Church of Jesus.** Being the earliest work of Boytac, creator of the Manueline style, the interior of this church is of great historical interest. It was even begun in 1491 seven years before Dom Manuel became king lending his name to this unique architecture, whose spiral columns of twisted ropes – as much the emblem of *Manoelino* as the pointed arch is Gothic – are illustrated in every guide book.

Nautical embellishments were Portugal's contribution to Gothic evolution just as Perpendicular fan-vaulting (Henry VII Chapel in Westminster Abbey and St. George's Chapel Windsor) were England's. And when in the late 17c. classical architecture came to be much more adorned, a Portuguese word *barroco,* meaning an irregular pearl, evolved into *baroque* to describe the innovation.

St. Philip's Castle. Built in 1590 partly to protect the inhabitants should Drake and his friends take to singeing beards other than the

King of Spain's, part of this castle is now Setúbal's 15 room Pousada. To the north west it looks at Palmela's castle and Pousada; then, sweeping seawards, across the huge Sado estuary and the long thin Troia spit, a view sadly impaired by the ugly blocks of flats already seen from the corniche road that runs along the ridge of the Serra between Portinho and Setúbal.

Troia. The tip of this extraordinary promontory is only five minutes across the harbour by hydrofoil and 15–20 by launch or car ferry. For ten miles it has double beaches facing the Atlantic on one side and the calmer, almost land-locked estuary on the other. The river Sado has its source in the Serra do Caldeirão, which protects the Faro end of the Algarve from the northerly blasts.

In spring this sandy spit is even more of a garden of wild flowers than the Arrábida. Keen archaeological interest centres on the buried town of Cetóbriga, in which foundations of Roman villas can be seen at low tide and where Roman coins and pottery are still found.

Troia's superb 18-hole course, recently finished, closely approaches 'links golf'. Golfers crossing on the motorboat ferry are picked up free by the Club's mini-bus if they telephone from the hotel near the landing place.

WINE AND FOOD

Setúbal is the centre for the Portuguese oyster (a different species to our European or flat oyster though no less enjoyable) found mainly on S.W. European and N.W. African coasts. The Portuguese prefer them cooked, that is to say those that remain for local consumption after 5000 tons have been exported to France. Dão Branco and Vinho Verde suit them well.

Arrábida marmalade is also excellent.

SETÚBAL – EVORA

Rice fields soon give way to orchards and olive groves, the last 55 kms. being across the open Alentejo plain. Turning eastwards along N4 at the Atalho crossroads the going is reasonably fast until Montemor-o-Nova, where N4 continues towards Estremoz, Elvas, Badajoz and Madrid while N114 for Evora branches south-east.

Having left Estremadura, the maritime province of Lisbon and Setúbal extending northwards beyond Leiria, we enter the Alentejo (from Alem Tejo 'beyond the Tagus'). An area nearly one third that of Portugal, with only one tenth of her ten million people, the Alentejo stretches from the Ribatejo (the land either side of the Tagus north-east of Lisbon) to the Algarve.

Long the national granary from the Lusitania of the Romans, the Visigoths and the Moors, there is little natural vegetation except the olive tree and the cork oak; moreover 20c. mechanisation while reducing employment has substantially added to the number of Portuguese men going overseas for years in order to earn a living wage with which to support their families at home.

Burning hot all summer and fiercely cold in winter, this flat plain with the occasional hump could well be Spain, never much more than an hour's drive away to the east. Driving along straight roads we see the shepherds in their hooded winter coats standing motionless watching their flocks by day accompanied only by their dogs, all curs of lowest degree. The sparkling white hill towns and villages, each with its castle and church, can be seen miles away, looking like white sails in a sea of reddish brown soil and greyish-green corkwoods.

Alentejo villages have long had the reputation of being spotlessly clean. Wellington's troops liked them as billets in spite of the summer heat. Later, in 1835, that majestic looking tramp and travelling Bible salesman, George Borrow, passed this way from Lisbon to Evora and on to Spain, stopping to ask a goat herd carrying otters and wolf cubs if he believed in Jesus Christ. The man looked as mystified as I did having inadvertently read the phrase as 'blotters and golf clubs'. George Borrow's book *The Bible in Spain* describing these travels made his name.

Vendas Novas. This is where in 1729 D. João V employed two thousand workmen to build a palace in nine months, not as one might imagine to provide a royal nursery for some unexpected brat, but to lodge for two nights two royal honeymoon couples. His daughter had married Philip V of Spain's eldest son; his own heir-apparent a Spanish princess. Of no great architectural merit, the place has long been an army barracks.

Montemor-o-Nova. Nothing much here except a Great Fair on May 1. Birthplace of St. John of God (1495–1550), an uninteresting saint canonized 140 years after his death, who is depicted in the main square carrying a beggar to hospital.

DAY 5

Round Tour from Evora or Estremoz

km.			Total
0	Evora (P)		0
46	Estremoz (P)	N18	46
13	Borba	N4	59
5	Vila Viçosa	N255	64
19	Redondo	N254	83
34	Evora (P)	N254	117 = 73 m.

Evora is the day's most important place, needing a good half day on foot. Those staying there could move on to a late lunch at the palatial Pousada at Estremoz looking at its associated buildings afterwards. Those staying at Estremoz will find at Evora an equally interesting Pousada and some pleasant small restaurants.

The guided tour of the Ducal Palace at Vila Viçosa lasting 1½ hours is long and unlikely to appeal to people other than the Portuguese unless they are particularly interested in the personal possessions of deceased royalty. An additional visit to Elvas involves a quick (for Portugal) 35 mile detour there and back that might appeal to the energetic.

EVORA (Pop. 35,000). The Praça do Geraldo is the centre of Evora marked by a 1570 vase-shaped fountain with the Tourist Office close by. Motorists on reaching the outer walls should follow the signs marked Pousada, which is by the Cathedral at the summit of the town where cars can be parked. A short street, Rua 5 de Outobro, with wrought iron balconies leads down to the Praça do Geraldo from the Cathedral. The town leaflet has a plan with three coloured routes for a brief, full day and longer visit respectively.

With 35,000 people this walled hill town 300 metres up, is the capital of the Alentejo, Moorish roots and royal associations making it one of the most interesting places in Portugal, needing at least a morning pottering through the narrow streets peering at old palaces and churches. Arriving at the Pousada, converted after World War II from part of the 16c. convent, the Corinthian 'Temple of Diana' by the entrance is Roman, believed to be 2c. or 3c. AD. Excavation during the last century revealed its light and graceful granite pillars with bosses and capitals of Estremoz marble.

From the 12c. to 1580, when Portugal was annexed by Spain, the Court preferred Evora and the town came to be renowned in Europe as a seat of culture. Painters and sculptors, writers and intellectuals

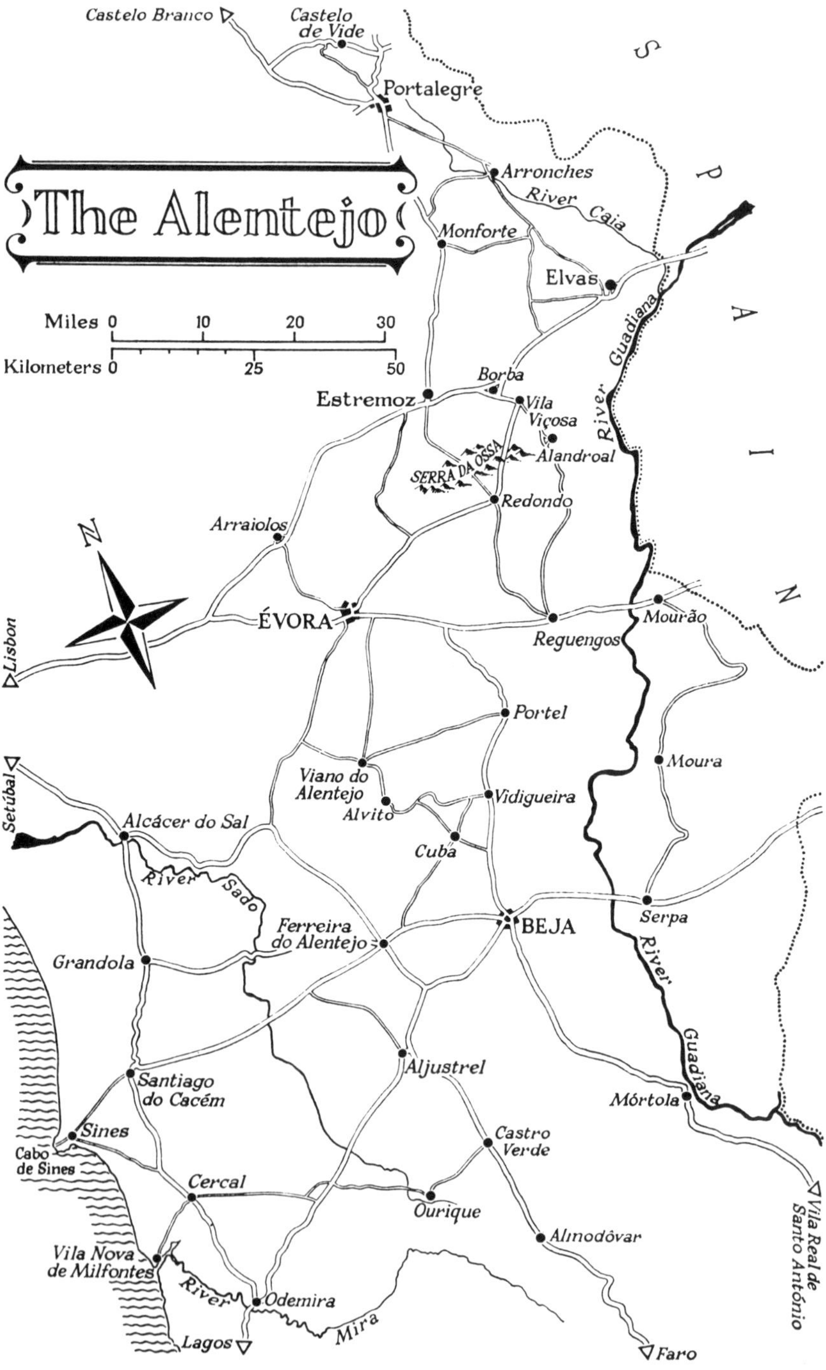
The Alentejo
Miles 0 10 20 30
Kilometers 0 25 50
N
Castelo Branco
Castelo de Vide
Portalegre
Arronches
River Caia
Monforte
Elvas
SPAIN
River Guadiana
Borba
Estremoz
Vila Viçosa
Alandroal
SERRA DA OSSA
Redondo
Arraiolos
ÉVORA
Lisbon
Reguengos
Mourão
Portel
Viano do Alentejo
Alvito
Vidigueira
Moura
Setúbal
Alcácer do Sal
River Sado
Cuba
Ferreira do Alentejo
BEJA
Serpa
Grandola
Aljustrel
Santiago do Cacém
Sines
Cabo de Sines
Castro Verde
Mórtola
Cercal
Ourique
Almodôvar
Vila Real de Santo António
Vila Nova de Milfontes
River Mira
Odemira
Lagos
Faro

foregathered here much as they did in Italian towns such as Urbino under Montefeltro. In the 17c. gold from Brazil stimulated a mild renaissance, ending in 1759, when Pombal's expulsion of the Jesuits suppressed the University.

The Cathedral. A massive rather than beautiful piece of many periods, the façade with its two different towers over an arched porch and large central lantern with pepperpots dating from the 13c. makes an unusual start. The cloister is 14c., the choir and pulpit 16c., the sacristy and side chapels 17c. and the chancel and High Altar by Ludwig, architect of Mafra, 18c. **The Palace of the Dukes of Cadaval** (Paço dos Duques de Cadaval). Now used as local government offices this Palace, across the two squares from the Cathedral, was for King John III (1521–57) and John V (1706–50) the Royal Palace where they liked to live best. The Gallery housing Cadaval family documents and two 15c. Flemish plaques in bronze is open to the public, except Mondays and holidays. **Convent of Lóios** (Convento dos Lóios). 1000–12.30: 1400–1700. Closed Monday and holidays. The church of this convent (the rest is the Pousada) founded in the 15c. but heavily restored after the earthquake in the 18c., has some Gothic tombs and two renaissance ones of Estremoz marble. The walls are lined with large 17c. azulejos panels depicting the life of St. Laurence Justinian who was a 15c. Venetian, not the Christian martyr best known for his death by burning on a grid iron (a fable not in fact proven) who lived in 2c. Rome. **Museum of Ancient Art** (Museu de Evora) 1000–1200: 1400–1700. Closed Monday and holidays. Free Saturday and Sunday. In the Palacio Amaral, close to the Cathedral, this has one of the best Flemish pictures in Portugal, the Virgin in Glory crowned by Angels, moved from the Cathedral where it was part of the High Altar.

Mr Billingham's Spirited Pupil. Quarter of a mile west of the Cadaval Palace the Convent and church of Calvario in the Largo de Joaquim António de Aguiar once harboured a Dona Isabel Juliana de Sousa Coutinho, aged 14, forced against her will by Pombal to marry his second son. A spirited young lady, for three years the marriage remained unconsummated and when annulled, her angry father-in-law confined her here.

But in 1777, when Pombal was disgraced, she was able to marry her true love, Don Alexandre de Sousa Holstein, with whom she had shared an English tutor, Mr Billingham, as a child. Portuguese minister in London from 1812–1819, Don Alexandre represented Portugal at the Congress of Vienna in 1814–5.

City of Azulejos, another fine 16, 17 and 18c. collection can be seen in the Largo do Colegio, where the Liceu and an orphanage occupy the former Jesuit university disbanded by Pombal. There is a vast

Evora, the Roman Temple of Diana. The Pousada in the former convent is on the right.

classical cloister and inside some good painted ceilings in theatre and church, notably the life of St. Ignatius in the latter.

Evora also abounds with fine 15 and 17c. buildings. Among them the Condes de Basto palace in the Pátio de S. Miguel, where Charles II's widow, Catherine de Bragança stayed on her return, has 16c. frescoes; the palace of the Cordovils by the Portas de Moura can be recognised by its Moorish capitals and horse-shoe arches. Close by in the Rua Misericordia the 15c. Casa Soure has a delightful balcony, and the Misericordia church yet more azulejos.

The towers of the Largo das Portas de Moura were part of the mediaeval fortifications; in the centre of the square in the form of a globe from the emblem of King Manuel is another of Evora's Renaissance fountains. **Church of Our Lady of Grace** (Igreja Nossa Senhora da Graça). Diego de Torralva, the architect, had studied Italian Renaissance and his granite façade of this 16c. church is universally admired as 'Michael Angelo Baroque'. The interior is a ruin. **Church of St. Francis** (Igreja de São Francisco). The larger 16c. Moorish–Gothic church 200 yards away to the south west has a Manueline doorway surmounted by a globe as well as the Pelican, emblem of João II. Its Ossuary Chapel – *graffiti* a few thousand skulls and bones of Franciscan friars – was built, with others elsewhere, to encourage monastic meditation. **St. Blaise's Chapel** (Ermida de São Brás). From the Graça church a 500-yard walk down the Rua da República past the Public Garden and through the city wall reaches another curious sacred edifice. Built in 1482 when Christians still needed battlements from which to pour boiling oil on infidels or brothers of like faith, this church of S. Bras must have been quite a formidable toy when its battlements and all the pepperpot turrets were manned.

ACCOMMODATION, FOOD, WINE

The 32 rooms at the Pousada dos Lóios are arranged on the four outer sides of the old convent's cloister. The cloister's centre piece is a garden, its sides glassed in to allow the restaurant tables to be arranged under cover around it. On the first floor above there is a gallery with some fine Arraiolos carpets on the walls. The setting within and without is attractive, the place popular with tourists.

In the town there are several good hotels and pensions with double rooms at £12–£15 a night. Only 5 kms. out the rather better, Estalagem Monte das Flores has 17 rooms with tennis and swimming pool.

Close to the Pousada on the Rua 5 de Outobro the restaurant Portalegre looks pleasant. On a corner of a narrow street at the eastern end of the Graça Church we have lunched satisfactorily at the little restaurant Giãno.

Pork fried with clams is among the local dishes and local wines from Redondo and Reguengos de Monsaraz are potable. Monsaraz is a walled village overlooking the Guadiana river 52 kms. from Evora; Mary Chalmers (*Guardian* 16.8.81) reported its small inn (7 rooms) as comfortable, with strings of onions and scented melons hanging from the ceiling.

SHOPPING

Inspired by azulejos and being with our own car on one visit, we found a local builder outside the city walls from whom we bought an assortment of coloured tiles intending to give a Lusitanian touch to our veranda or bathroom wall at home. Other matters distracted us but 'bathroom azulejos' remains a feasible project.

The cork bowl with lid and strap which we bought back is on the other hand, still in constant use. Fitted with a plastic bowl inside it makes a practical and handsome ice bowl.

EVORA TO ESTREMOZ

The town plan and others fail to show the exit road for N18 via Evora Monte. Care should be taken to find it unless N18 is reported as being in bad condition in which case proceed via Arraiolos.

Environs Evora. With more time to spare, journeys by car could take us to the Charterhouse outside the Porto da Lagoa, a 17c. work begun by Felipe Terzi, architect of San Roque in Lisbon. Three kms. away is the São Bento de Castris monastery with 16c. cloister, 17c. paintings in the refectory and 18c. azulejos of St. Bernard's life.

Five kms. to the north west is the convent of Espinheiro where Don John of Austria (1629–1679) lived when commanding Spanish troops against the Portuguese trying to throw off the Spanish dynasty until defeated by an English/Portuguese force at Estremoz in 1663. (This is not the Don John, victor of Lepanto in 1571, the last oar-propelled naval battle.)

Evora Monte on N18 is yet another little white Alentejo hill town with a castle and a room with a view at the top.

ESTREMOZ (Pop. 9500). From the open squares of the main town, one way 'Pousada' signs easily missed, lead up through narrow cobbled streets to the old town over 400 metres high. The main building is the luxurious 23-room Pousada da Rainha Santa Isabel, a four-sided palace built round a central garden started in 1281 by King Dinis for his court. On the ground floor the reception rooms are palatial, the dining room holds over a hundred people, the corridors above being so long that the hotel hot water system appears to be severely taxed. **The Keep.** Famous for its marble quarries, which helped build the Escorial, there is no question in this region of *dreaming* of dwelling in marble halls, one just does. The famous castle keep is an ancient white marble tower about 90 feet high by the front door, with the key at the reception desk should it be locked.

I climbed up, compass in hand but without binoculars, one cloudless sunny morning trying to identify Palmela to the west, Spain eastwards and to the north that other rocky eminence Marvão, all doubtless as clear as crystal to any wizard of Estremoz, though not so easy for a stranger, content nevertheless with the landscape. To see the other palace buildings of this old upper town grouped around the Pousada, apply to the Curator of the Museum which is one of them.

Chapel of the Queen Saint. King Dinis's widow Isabel, surviving him by 11 years, died in 1336 in this room on the north side below the Keep, later transformed by the mother of our English Queen, Catherine of Bragança, into a tiny chapel, with charming blue azulejos depicting the life of this Holy Queen canonized in the 16c. The fable that the forbidden loaves for the poor hidden in her apron turned to roses when her husband challenged her is included.

In German and Italian art this legend is associated with St. Elizabeth of Hungary (1207–1231). Piero della Francesca's Madonna and Child with Four Saints in the Predella (Perugia Gallery) shows her with Louis IV of Thuringia, who was converted by the miracle.

Church of St. Mary (Igreja de Santa Maria). This square 16c. church, once a Mosque, is entirely marble. The primitives in the sacristy are of less report than the marble lavabo. **King Dinis's Audience Chamber.** A charming little edifice at the southern corner of the *largo* with star vaulting and a Gothic colonnade.

The one way route allows us to descend to the trees and palaces surrounding the Rossio of the main town rather more quickly than we came up.

The Town Hall is in a beautiful 1698 convent; the Misericordia Church and Hospital in another, founded by the Knights of Malta in 1539. Yet another, that of San Francisco is an army barracks, its long corridor lined with shields of battle honours, many of them battles in which British troops took part. The Convent's church has a tomb of a gentleman with his head on three pillows and his feet on two dogs; not a member of Brooks's Club in London evidently where, since Charles James Fox, *four* pillows have been placed daily on a sofa for post-prandial *siestas*.

ACCOMMODATION, FOOD, WINE

With 4 turrets in the Michelin Guide the Estremoz Pousada, being the best Portuguese hotel on the road between Madrid and Lisbon, keeps busy, though its standard could be improved. During our two-night stay, the hot water supply was not hot, the dining room service was slow at times and the food only average by Pousada standards, which are not high, table d'hote menus costing only 500/600 escudos then.

The leaflet of the *Pousadas of the Alentejo* says 'In this Pousada's elegant dining-room the visitor will find waiters only too happy to unravel to him the intricacies of its superb cuisine and to describe in detail such specialities and regional dishes as: *Açorda Alentejana, Ensopado de Borrego, Carne de Porco, Migas com entrecosto, Bacalhau à Moda da Pousada, Sopa Dourada* and *Bolo Pôdre,*' a liaison more likely to leave the visitor all tied up trying to unravel the waiter's Portuguese.

Outside guests arriving and departing in cars were molested by a group of begging urchins, who did not look impoverished. Since there was nothing to stop them entering by the front door and climbing the main staircase to the bedrooms, the staircase approach had been locked on the first floor leaving only one lift for guests. There appear to be no Fire instructions in these pousadas or direction signs to Emergency exits. Of the 23 rooms three are suites with sitting rooms, at twice the price of one double and bath. Staying in such an oasis of luxury in a desert of humble old town dwellings one would gladly contribute to any local fund to improve the lot of the neighbours; a playing field that got rid of the little beggars preferrably.

In the main town below, the Hotel Alentejano (with restaurant) in the Rossio Marqués de Pombal seems to have been overlooked by the Michelin Guide. There are also four Pensãos, the best (with restaurant) being the Carvalho in the Largo de Republica. Aguias d'Ouro (Golden Eagles) gets a 2 knife/fork symbol in the Michelin.

Though not a demarcated region, there are plenty of vineyards making good red and white table wines spread about the Alentejo. Local wines to try are labelled Portalegre, Redondo and Borba, where there is a modern Adega Cooperativa. Guadiana (the river) appears as a label, likewise Monsaraz on the river and Vidigueira.

Borba. 13 kms. towards Elvas from Estremoz, even the window frames and cottage doorsteps are made of marble in this little town. The 1781 fountain in the main square is white marble and the Convento das Servas has a large double renaissance cloister with fountain, azulejos and polychrome tiles. For those tiring of sight-seeing and feeling like a large double *without any cloister,* a bottle of Borba's red wine could be the prescription.

Vila Viçosa (Vila Viss-co-sa). 5 kms. east of Borba the Bragança Palace in its 2000 hectare (4950 acre) *tapada* or hunting park was the favourite residence of a family who gave England a Queen and Portugal a dynasty that lasted from 1640 to 1908.

In the 15c. the 2nd Duke of Bragança chose this 'town of shade' for his family's principal residence. The 3rd Duke was executed at Evora in 1484 by the Avis King, João II on a charge of plotting. The 4th Duke began this great palace in 1501, the 16c. voyages of discovery endowing his successors with wealth more than sufficient to finish it a century later.

From 1580 to 1640, 'The Sixty Year Captivity', Portugal was ruled by Philip II of Spain and his two successors. The 8th Duke, leading the coup in 1640 that regained independence, set out from here that December to be proclaimed King João IV in Lisbon. Thus by dint of being Dukes of Guimarães, Counts of Barcelos, Ourem and Arraiolos, all places contributing either castles or palaces to the royal portfolio, the Braganças were well off for real estate with enough Brazilian gold for its maintenance.

But Vila Viçosa the original home, a country retreat with a charming garden in the largest private property (the circumference of the wall is 18 kms.) had a special place in their affections comparable to Sandringham in those of the British royal family.

The dynasty ended tragically on February 1, 1908. King Carlos and his eldest son travelled by train to Lisbon on the new line from Vila Viçosa. After crossing the Tagus they climbed into a carriage and were assassinated before it had even left Black Horse Square. His French Queen, Maria-Amelia, could not bear ever to return to this happy home. Their son, Manuel II reigned until 1910 when an Armed Services coup turned Portugal into a republic.

In 1932 he died in exile at Twickenham, a British warship taking his body to Lisbon for a state funeral. Both he and his mother left their considerable fortunes to Portugal, the Foundation maintaining this estate and employing guides and others. **The Ducal Palace** (Paço Ducal). 0930–1300: 1400–1800. Closed April 25, May 1, December 25. Guided tours 1½ hours. The three storey palace built between 1501 and 1601 is on one side of an immense square empty but for the large bronze statue of João IV (1640–1656) on his horse. Faced with marble on this side only, the interior is now a museum with Flemish tapestries, Portuguese carpets made at Arraiolos and many personal possessions of King Manuel and Queen Amelia. The 17c. azulejos are by a Dutchman called Ian van Bogaets, not a Portuguese. **Convent of the Wounds of Christ** (Convento das Chages). Formerly a convent the delightful group of white buildings with red low-pitched roofs and a fine classical doorway is now a mausoleum for the Duchesses of Bragança. **The Augustine Church** (Convento dos Agostinhos). On the other side of the palace entrance, this church rebuilt in the 17c. by King João, is the mausoleum of the Dukes. Its 17c. tombs of black and white marble, the coffins resting on the backs of black lions couchant, include an empty one awaiting the next King.

The Knot Gate (Porta dos Nós). Clearly seen on the north side of the Lisbon road by the Palace square, this is the gate leading to the Church, which was part of the 16c. wall, Incredibly Manoeline, with four rope grommets in stone it looks like a surrealist bow tie above an iron grille shirt front that is the gate itself.

Vila Viçosa. The Knot Gate.

DAY 6

Estremoz to Tomar

km.			Total
0	Estremoz (P)	N245	0
17	Sousel	N372	17
12	Casa Branca	—	29
14	Avis	N244	43
21	Galveias	N244	64
10	Ponte de Sor	N2	74
21	Bemposta	N2	95
12	Abrantes	N3	107
13	Constancia Turn R.	N358.2	120
7	Castelo do Bode (P)	N358	127
15	Tomar	N110	142 = 88m

This route which appears to be as good as any on the map took three hours in our Mini from Estremoz to the Pousada at Castelo do Bode. For most of the way the uneven surface made over 40 mph uncomfortable both for passengers and car. From Casa Branca to Avis it was very bad for a kilometre or so. Then quite unexpectedly at Galveias for 30 refreshing kilometres it had been transformed, a perfect surface ending as unexpectedly as it had begun.

This in brief is motoring in Portugal. Allow no more than 30 mph and you won't be far wrong. If starting from Evora take the road to Arraiolos, thence N370 to Avis. The distance to Avis is 83 kms., making the total journey 40 kms. longer than from Estremoz. Arraiolos is famous for its hand made carpets, old and new. The Mateus reception centre at Avintes near Oporto has a large beautiful example of the latter.

Abrantes. Spread across a hill above the Tagus, Abrantes is not of great interest except, perhaps to the military student, because it is where any northern invaders would cross the river. The Portuguese armies assembled here before Aljubarrota; the French under Junot occupied it in 1807; Wellington expelled them in 1809 advancing northwards to Talavera. Cobbled alleyways lined with flowers lead up to the castle but, after castles in the Alentejo, views from 246 feet are an anti-climax.

Abrantes Straw (*Palha de Abrantes*) is a local confectionery, the eggs making it a streaky yellow.

At Constancia, where the Zezere joins the Tagus, the pretty castle on the island in the middle is Almourol, built by the 12c. Knights Templars, whose original round church of about the same date is the pride of Tomar. A boat can be hired to visit Almourol, which needs no guide since it has no history.

For Tomar turn right along the pretty little N358.2 northwards along the Zezere. The Barragem do Castelo do Bode is about 7 kms., the Pousada sited close by below the huge artificial lake.

TOMAR (Pop. 15,000). *The Knights Templars* or *Poor Knights of Christ and of the Temple of Solomon* was a military order founded in the 12c. by a few French knights with the declared aim of protecting pilgrims in transit to visit the Holy Land after the first Crusade. In this they were supported by the powerful Abbot of Clairvaux, who deplored the unruly rabble of rogues, impious men, robbers and committers of sacrilege, murderers, perjurors and adulterers streaming to the Holy Land in the hope of plunder and salvation. A condemnation he would doubtless reserve for their counterparts among some European football club supporters today.

It was not long therefore before this order of warrior monks became enriched by true and grateful pilgrims, not the least of their gifts coming from Baldwin I, King of Jerusalem, who gave them the Temple of Solomon, part of his palace. The Order spread across Christian Europe, kings giving them land in England and France. Based in the Paris Temple they became the Bankers of Europe, issuing loans against deposits. Their military power ensured safe transmissions, their calling as monks being their integrity.

In 1306 Philip IV of France plotted their destruction by means still all too familiar in our own times – suspicion, denouncement (to the Inquisition), arrest by civil power, extraction of false confessions under unspeakable tortures. By 1314 Pope Clement V had been persuaded to publish a bull abolishing the Templars, their goods being confiscated except in Spain, Portugal and Malta.

Whether or not the Order became debased, it had checked the advance of Islam and implanted belief in the virtue of chivalrous men. But the method of its destruction in France prolonged man's inhumanity to man, from the persecution of 'witches' to the political trials of our own time.

At least in Portugal its suppression was to have a happier and glorious outcome. In 1319 the good King Dinis (1279–1325) who consolidated the frontier, built castles to defend it and founded Coimbra University, set up a new Order of the Knights of Christ, which took over the former Portuguese knights' property.

At Tomar there was a 12c. (pre–Dinis) castle built by the Grand Master. Already the seat of the old order, by 1356 it had become that of the new. Thirty years later, when João I came to the throne, marrying John of Gaunt's daughter, Philippa of Lancaster, and signing a

The Tagus from the 12c. Castle of Belver, some 15 miles upstream from Abrantes.

Treaty of Alliance with England, events moved rapidly. Their two eldest sons captured Ceuta; the third, Prince Henry the Navigator, became Grand Master using the wealth of the Old Order to build the present monastery and to fund the voyages that were to make it richer still.

Madeira 1419, Azores 1427, Bojador the Western point of Africa 1434. . . . Henry died in 1460 but the seafaring explorers still went on. The Congo 1482, The Cape of Good Hope 1488. The New World 1492 and Brazil 1500. Such a sequence might have inspired Flecker's lines in Hassan:

> We are the pilgrims, master;
> We shall go always a little further:
> It may be beyond that last blue mountain barred with snow
> Across that angry or that glimmering sea.

Unlike France, in Portugal the order ended with the pen not the sword. In 1523 after his predecessor Manuel I had been Grandmaster for forty years, João III merged the office in the Crown, changing it back from knights to monks. The Convent of Christ is not the only measure of Tomar's prosperity. The 14c. synagogue, after the two at Toledo, is the best preserved of any in Spain or Portugal as is the Maria dos Olivais, mother church of the Order where many of the Knights are buried. And in the Convent's 'Sea Window' we find the apotheosis of *Manoelino*.

Tomar was given the status of a city in 1843 but not before its artistic riches had suffered in the Napoleonic invasions in 1810 and from the final end of the religious order in 1834.

Convent of Christ (Convento de Cristo). 0930–1230; 1400–1800 (winter 1700). The great mass of these buildings, which span five centuries and dominate the city, can be seen from afar. The guided tour may take half an hour from parking the car beyond the old 12c. castle walls at the end of a formal garden with box hedges.

The first building is the Templars' 12c. church, sixteen sided with a central Octagon, considered to be the best example of the churches of the Knights Templar, built in the early Byzantine style based on the Temple of Solomon in Jerusalem that Baldwin I had given them. The church now forms the eastern end to which the 16c. nave was added by Grandmaster King Manuel, its lively Manueline decor by Diogo de Arruda completing 'the most curious building in Portugal coming up dripping from the sea'. Diogo de Arruda was the brother of Francis, architect of the Tower of Belém.

The doorway to this church should not pass unnoticed particularly by anybody who has been to Salamanca, where the University façade and the *Casa de las Conchas* are in the Plateresque style. Spanish

Tomar. The famous 'Sea Window' in the Convent of Christ.

architects had by this date seen Florence, returning determined to improve upon the work of the Medici. Plateresque, from *platero* a silversmith, signalled the lighter touch – the delicate decor of the silversmith rather than the chiselling of the mason.

This door is by the Spaniard João de Castilho, who came after Boytac and whose other work embellishes the cloister at Belém and possibly the 'coralline' door of the sacristy at Alcobaça.

The tour moves anti-clockwise from the 12c. Templars' church to the Ablutions Cloister and the Burial Grounds Cloister, both 15c. Gothic sponsored by Henry the Navigator but since rebuilt. Next comes the nave, a 16c. extension of the Templars' 12c. rotunda by Diogo de Arruda and splendidly 'ropey'. **The Sea Window.** At the north-western end of the nave is the famous 'Sea Window', a unique allegorical memorial in stone to the maritime explorers. At the base a mariner supports the root of a cork oak from which rise two ropes, cables and anchors. And why not? 15c. artists recording events were the press correspondents and photographers of our own time. In Venice Gentile Bellini's great processions of the Scuola relic through St. Mark's were painted between 1490 and 1500. Diogo de Arruda's window sculpted in 1510 is no less a masterpiece, the like of which is not seen again, as Sir Sacheverell is at pains to explain, until we meet a Gaudí house in Barcelona or a Rennie Mackintosh *Art Nouveau* tea-room in Glasgow. **The Main Cloister** (Claustro dos Felipes). The adjoining main cloister (there are seven cloisters all told) is by another Diogo, also from Evora, Diogo de Torralva. Starting it between 1557 and 1562, this Diogo had been inspired by the work of Palladio (1518–1580) in Venice and Vicenza. Completion in 1587 is said to have been by Filippo Terzi. The ground floor has Tuscan columns, the upper floor Ionic pillars, contrasting in their simplicity with the Manueline embellishments of the nave.

Philip II of Spain was proclaimed King of Portugal here in 1581. All these dates, contemporary with Queen Elizabeth of England are interesting in that the Queen's House at Greenwich, the first building by Inigo Jones, 'the English Palladio', was not built until the reign of Charles I, a good 40 years later. **Missionary College.** The Guided Tour fortunately does not enter every cloister and cell of this vast convent built by João III who had to house an awful lot of friars when he turned the Order of Christ from a military to a holy membership. The great T-shaped dormitory built for them now accommodates the pupils of a Missionary college.

Chapel of Our Lady of the Immaculate Conception (Capela de Nossa Senhora da Conceicão). The Venetian architect, Andrea Sansovino (1460–1529) spent from 1494 to 1500 in Portugal designing for

King Manuel I. Half way down to the town from the monastery stands this lovely little chapel credited to Diogo (Main Cloister) de Torralva, so perfect in its classical proportions that Sansovino might well have had a hand in it too.

Writing in 1954 Sitwell deplored the restoration that had taken place here and elsewhere since his first visit in 1926 when the monastery was incomparably more beautiful in spite of the damage in, and subsequent neglect after, the Peninsular War.

'Herein lay the history and poetry of this little country risen to greatness on the Atlantic wave'! Tomar, in its mingled solemnity and exuberance is an extraordinary monument to their sea-faring'.

The City. At the foot of the monastery hill Tomar gains much from its own little river, the Nabão, which ultimately joins the Zezere. The Tomar leaflet which, like the red and green Michelin guides would be better for a map or town plan, mentions several more churches, the 15c. Parish Church of S. João Baptista in a pretty square by the 18c. hospital having a Manueline belfry and a beautiful carved door. In the old town, the synagogue dating from Prince Henry, the only Jewish medieval temple in Portugal is now a Jewish museum.
Water Wheels. The water wheels along the Nabão are known as Moorish wheels or 'Tardo Romanos', such is their antiquity. Today, of course, they are museum pieces. Two, however, are installed in Tomar, one at the entrance to Mouchão park and the other in the grounds of the Templars' Hotel, where the current of the Nabão suffices to fill their 50 porcelain buckets and keep these giant wheels turning.

Tabuleiros Fair. First 14 days of July in alternate years, the prettiest girls of Tomar dressed in white proceed with tall columns of new bread and paper flowers upon their heads followed by clergy, a brass band and a herd of bullocks. The beasts are killed, beef and bread making a feast for the poor.

ROUTE TO LISBON

For the best route between Tomar and Lisbon take N110 and N365 to Golega and cross the Tagus on N243 to join N118. N118 now follows the left bank through Alpiarca, Almeirim and Benavente joining N10 and re-crossing the Tagus to join the Lisbon motorway at Vila Franca de Xira.

From Almeirim this is a fast route on an excellent surface through Ribatejo vineyards. Total distance to Lisbon Airport 145 kms. Time 2½ hours or less.

Tomar. The Tabuleiros Fair.

SHOPPING

A variety of sweets and cakes: ask for Bolos de Cama, Fatias de Tomar, Estrelas de Tomar, Pasteis dos Templários and Queijinhos doces, which are sweet cheese cakes.

ORIENTEERING

Portugal with its woods, rivers and lakes is a fine country for this growing sport of competitive cross country navigation with map and compass. Antonio Manuela Cameira Martins, Bairro de Albertino 50–B, Carvalhus de Figuieredo, 2300 Tomar is (says the British Orienteer) the driving force in Portuguese Orienteering. Henry the Navigator sailing some Elysian sea must approve of this address as the national headquarters of a new form of exploration.

ACCOMMODATION, FOOD, WINE

Given the status of 'city' in 1834, Tomar is an attractive town with two nice clean cafés by the bridge and a dozen inexpensive restaurants. Its direction signs to places such as 'Camping Site' are exceptionally clear.

Dos Templários is a comfortable modern hotel with 84 rooms, swimming bath and tennis courts at the north western end of the Mouchão park. Though its bedrooms are not twice as good as the Pousada's they cost almost twice as much. The food is also more expensive but a good deal better.

Nearby in the middle of the park, which is the city's 7 acre island of weirs, willows, wisteria and water-wheels, is the 10 room Estalagem de Santa Iria, which serves a better meal than might be expected.

A second 15 room Estalagem is on the Ilha do Lombo, an island 16 kms. from Tomar on the lake above Castelo do Bode. A Canadian and his wife said they had booked there but the ferry that takes guests and baggage from shore to island was so slow in coming they thought that with a 'plane to catch from Lisbon to Canada the following day it might be wiser to spend the night in Tomar.

At Castelo do Bode, 14 kms. out, the 15-room Pousada just below the dam 377 feet high and 440 yards long is pleasant and peaceful. When necessary a giant nozzle discharges surplus water in a spectacular shower of spray, full of rainbows, as high as the dam. Far from keeping one awake, the noise, drowning the sound of one's partner's snoring can be welcome and soothing.

Converted from buildings used during the construction of the dam from 1946 to 1952, better fare should surely be possible with a fish supply in so large a lake close by.

Óbidos. The main square with 15c. pillory.

DAY 7

Tomar to Óbidos, Alcobaça and Batalha

AM. TOMAR TO ÓBIDOS

km.			Total
0	Castelo do Bode (P)		0
7	Constancia	N358.2	7
20	Torres Novas	N3	27
12	Alcanena	N361	39
32	Rio Maior	N114	71
14	Caldas da Rainha	N114	85
7	Óbidos (P)	N8	92= 57 m.

This day is based on a fly/drive in April, 1979, leaving the Pousada about 10 am with the object of reaching for lunch the extraordinary little town of Óbidos, almost on the Atlantic coast.

In the late afternoon we looked for sardines at Nazaré, enjoyed the monks' kitchen with a trout stream running through it at Alcobaça, admired Batalha lazily without getting out of the car and were delighted to find the hotel at Leiria, where we had booked by telephone from the Pousada, had a bar in each bedroom's refrigerator.

At that time some stretches of road, particularly approaching Lisbon, were said to be in a dreadful state and sure enough some miles short of Caldas da Rainha we proceeded at less than a walking pace through holes that suggested a Flanders battlefield of World War I.

It is as well to be prepared for this sort of delay when touring Portugal, particularly off the major roads.

Torres Novas has narrow bridges across its little river Almonda and a beautiful Misericordia church with a renaissance door and early azulejos inside. We did not stop here nor to investigate a village announcing itself boldly as Bottonequim.

Caldas da Rainha (Hot baths of the Queen), is one of Portugal's many spas, where the good 15c. Queen Leonor took hot baths for her arthritis. Though the baths (and arthritis) still exist, non-sufferers are better advised to try sea bathing at S. Martinho up the coast; its land-locked port vies with San Sebastian and S. Jean de Luz in providing calm and safe water for Atlantic swimmers.

A cool and clean resort, Caldas da Rainha has a dozen cheap restaurants and three simple hotels. The parish church, Nossa Senhora do Populo, is worth a look at its open-arched Manueline belfry, some

16c. azulejos around the side altars and a painting of the Crucifixion above the unusually curved chancel.

During World War II many refugees from Europe, hoping to get visas to America or Mexico settled into a cosmopolitan colony here. The town remains an inexpensive centre for touring the Holy Places and others in the vicinity, which have relatively poor accommodation.

SHOPPING

Caldas makes a lot of ugly green and yellow pottery, more interesting from under the counter where they are apt to keep the phallic shapes. In Amarante on the first Sunday of June they bake *testicles de S. Gonçalo*, adding novel gastronomic interest to the Oporto fly/drive.

Cavacas, the Caldas meringue-like cakes like the *Yemas* of Seville are much better. Many of these sorts of delicacies were originally monastery recipes and in a long footnote Sir Sacheverell embarks on a world tour describing all the frightful sweets, cakes and dishes invented by nuns for the delectation of visiting bishops.

ÓBIDOS (Pop. 1000). Like Marvão Óbidos is a little fortified hill town unmarred by a single modern building. Shaped like a bird its white walls and narrow cobbled streets give it the same appeal as Hydra or Poros, Positano or Sidi Bou Säid, albeit without their Mediterranean views. The Lagoon (Lagoa de Óbidos) caused by silting on the coast at Foz do Arelho was once part of the Atlantic, the town then being a watch-tower against sea-borne invaders.

Like Sidi-Bou-Säid in Tunisia its origins were Moorish, the town being rebuilt after their expulsion in 1148. Paying a Royal visit in 1228, Queen Isabella loved it so much that King Dinis gave it to her and it remained the Queen's town until 1833, entitled – like Bognor Regis – to call itself Óbidos Rainha.

We drank the local wine, Gaeiras, lunching in the one restaurant, Alcaide in the market square, where a few cars can be parked, rather on our best behaviour because, at the only other table occupied, the English Head of the Salvation Army in Portugal was entertaining three ladies. (We thought he was breaking the pledge by trying the wine too; but honi soit . . . it turned out to be water.)

Entering through the main gate (at the bird's tail) past the nicely furnished 13-room Estalagem do Convento, a U turn leads up the steep main street ending by the Pousada in the old Castle (the bird's head), which has the views but only nine bedrooms.

The Main Street (Rua Direita). This, along the bird's back, is bright with bougainvilleas, pelargoniums and the local cotton carpets, an industry bequeathed by Josefa de Ayala (1634–1684) the woman painter who spent most of her life here though born in Seville.

There are so few Portuguese painters of merit that her pictures in Lisbon's Janelas Verdes Art Gallery claim attention, even though her versatility as painter, etcher, modeller in *terra cotta*, silver work and calligraphist is more admired than her talent.

St. Mary's Church (Igreja de Santa Maria). There being no less than four churches off this main street, we had better see Josefa de Ayala's 'Mystic Marriage of St. Catherine' as well as the fine early 16c. tomb of D. João de Noronha attributed to Jean de Rouen, a French sculptor of altar pieces and low reliefs. **Misericordia Church** (Igreja da Misericordia). Near the South-West corner of the square, this was founded by Leonor, the rheumatic Queen. In the square there is also a 15c. pillory that bears her arms on the fountain. These stone columns (*pelourinhos*) were erected in many towns of Portugal as emblems of *pelouro*, the local authority, not as in Britain, for the purpose of exposing a malefactor to ridicule.

Wellington on the Ramparts. On these ramparts one can well imagine Wellington, or Arthur Wellesley as he then was, arriving here in 1808 at the beginning of his campaign, having been landed at the mouth of the Mondego. Marching south well ahead of his troops he saw, for the first time, Junot's army encamped eight miles to the south at Rolica. Battle was joined further south at Vimiero on August 21. The French were defeated but Burrard and Dalrymple, his seniors commanding the sea-borne troops which had landed there, failed to pursue them. At the end of the month the Convention of Sintra, negotiated in Lisbon and signed at Torres Vedras, sent Junot's army home in British ships with their arms and baggage, an arrangement as displeasing to the Portuguese as to the British, including Wellington. It did, however, leave Lisbon and Torres Vedras free to serve his purpose later in the campaign of 1810–11.

Sanctuary of Senhor da Pedra (Sanctuário do Senhor da Pedra). Retracing steps northwards on N8 towards Caldas da Rainha this is an unusual hexagonal Baroque church built between 1740 and 1747. Inside is of no great interest except for the coach that on September 8 takes the Virgin in St. Mary's church for her annual outing to Nazaré.

PM. ÓBIDOS TO LEIRIA

km.			Total
0	Óbidos (P)		0
7	Caldas da Rainha	N8	7
12	Alfeizerão	N8	19
14.5	Alcobaça	N8	33.5
6.5	Aljubarrota	N8	40
14	Batalha	N8, N1	54
12	Leiria	N1	66 = 41 m.

Alcobaça and Batalha are the two great monasteries of Portugal, both inspired by kings in gratitude for victory in battles. The first led to a Portugal freed from the Moors; the second to independence from Spain and the long alliance with England that formed a friendship and helped to maintain it.

The towns themselves are as small as their monasteries are vast, but a pleasant hour or so can be given to each; Alcobaça being the older foundation, Batalha architecturally the better.

ALCOBAÇA. A market town of 5000 people, Alcobaça is surrounded by good agricultural land growing soft fruit – pears, melons, peaches – which now go mainly to the markets in Lisbon. For tourists the shops display dreary pottery made at Caldas da Rainha and – far more attractive – brightly coloured cottons and chinzes.

The Santa Maria Monastery. Founded by the first King of Portugal, Alfonso I (1112–1185) to fulfil a vow made to St. Bernard after expelling the Moors from Santarem in 1147, with Lisbon to follow soon afterwards, his father, a grandson of the first Duke of Burgundy, had already spent most of his life fighting the Moors and the Castilians. The latter in 1443 by conceding Portugal's independence as far south as the Mondego river gave Alfonso the chance to extend southwards to the Tagus against the Moors alone.

With his Burgundian roots it was natural for him to make any vow to St. Bernard because in 1098 a group of Burgundians had founded the Cistercian Order for the purpose of following his teaching. Dedicated and skilled farmers, the first settlers were already familiar in their grey and white habits at Alcobaça where Alfonso had given them his domain. Thus they began the Monastery in 1178 on the lines of Clairvaux in Burgundy, founded by St. Bernard in 1115.

In the Peninsular War the interior was much damaged in 1811 by Napoleon's soldiery. Greater vandals than these, declared Sir Sacheverell Sitwell, have been the restorers of this century removing and destroying pottery statues, golden woodwork and rococo plaster in order to restore this abbey church (and many other such works in Portugal) to their original Cistercian simplicity. Others not so

Alcobaça. Tomb of Pedro I (died 1367) in the South transept of the Abbey.

addicted to the Baroque, it is proper to add, do not share this view. **The King's Hall** (Sala dos Reis). Outside, the original Gothic doorway and the rose window above it are none the worse for a pair of 18c. towers that rise above the imposing entrance. On the left of the nave the Hall still has some pottery statues of different Portuguese monarchs. We move on past the great white pillars that support the white nave to the two white tombs in the north and south transepts which Sir Sacheverell, in happier mood, suggests are 'the most beautiful sepulchres in all Spain and Portugal after the tombs in the Carta de Miraflores in Burgos by Gil de Siloée'. The Burgos tombs are a hundred years later. **Dom Pedro and Inês de Castro.** Historically Portugal's most famous pair of lovers, Pedro was the King's son and heir, who dutifully married the Aragon Princess chosen for him but fell in love with Inês, her lady-in-waiting. When his wife died early, Pedro went to live with Inês and after ten years they had had four children. His father's counsellors – even though Pedro claimed they had been legally married at Bragança – advised the King, Alfonso IV (1325–1357) that the Aragon lady was politically an embarrassment who must be disposed of.

The next scene has had the attention of Portuguese poets, painters and playwrights. Camões (1525–1580), poet of The Great Discoveries, wove it into *The Lusiads* of 1572. It is almost Verdi's *Traviata* Act II.

The King (Padré Germont) arriving at the couple's country house near Coimbra to tell Inêz the worst is so moved by her tears that he decides she should be spared. Later, however, renewed pressure from the counsellors forces him to give way.

The rest is nearer *Macbetto* than *Traviata*. Inêz was murdered in 1355. Two years later Pedro, succeeding to the throne on the death of his father, had the corpse dug up, dressed it as Queen and made the Court kneel and kiss a decaying hand before having the hearts of the guilty counsellors torn out live below the window where his banquet was in progress. Perhaps they were needed for the next course.

On the tombs, each attended by six angelic maids of honour, the lovers lie feet to feet on either side of the transept as if to symbolise a resurrection in which they would rise to meet again face to face. But in real life Pedro took another, wholly Portuguese, mistress. Their son, John I was to be victor of that other battle, Aljubarrota (q.v.) which routed the invading Castilians and gave rise to Batalha, the abbey 'up the road'.

Death of St. Bernard. In this transept too is the lovely 17c. life size terra-cotta group of the Death of St. Bernard, some monks around the Saint made headless by Marshal Junot's soldiers in 1811. **Chapel of Our Lady of the Entombing.** The pair of Manueline doors, much admired, one leading into the Sacristy and the other opposite, their coral as white as Atlantic breakers, are 16c. Another door leads out of the Sacristy into a quiet little cemetery garden where roses bloom and a stream bubbles by along a stone channel. In it stands a very charming 18c. chapel, *Nossa Senhora do Destêrro* (Our Lady of the Entombing) but, if tiring of holy places by now, on a wall close at hand there are some jolly azulejos of stags being lassoed and a gentleman up a tree with a bear (no, not bare) behind.

Distinguished Temple of Gluttony. The handsome 14c. cloisters with a 16c. upper storey on the left of the nave lead on to the kitchen and, adjoining it, Beckford's 'most distinguished temple of gluttony in Europe', the refectory. In its heyday around 1587, when Drake was passing down the coast 20 miles away raiding Cadiz, Alcobaça had become the head monastery of the Cistercian Order. Nine hundred monks, ravenous after hard work in the huge gardens of flowers, orange groves, fruit and vegetables that surrounded the place then, or just hungry after righteousness in celebrating mass unceasingly night and day, ate in the refectory. They would have been well served from this kitchen, its running water a stream diverted from the local river, its fish tank teeming and a stag or two roasting under a monumental chimney 60 foot tall. Should you be unable to squeeze through the narrow passage that leads out of the refectory, then, like the monks that failed, you must be too fat and will have to diet.

William Beckford's 12-day trip described in his *Recollections to the Monasteries of Alcobaça and Batalha* was made in June 1774 but the book was not published until 1835, as it happened one year after the monks had been disbanded. If their own fare included, as his did, swallows' nest soup and sharks' fins prepared by a Chinese lay brother from Macão, the monks had done well to keep 'out of the red' for so long.

ALJUBARROTA

Decisive battle ground. A few miles along the road to Batalha, this is the village where on 14 August 1385 the second decisive battle in Portugal's history took place, giving the country two centuries of independence without which the pioneer spirit and the ship building skills that brought about the Voyages of Discovery might never have developed.

King João I, first of the Avis line, having vowed to raise a great church given victory, Batalha began three years later.

Bowmen of England in Support. As to the battle, the contestants were 1) the invading Castilians supporting the Spanish pretender Juan, a nephew of the last Portuguese king and 2) João I of Avis, already mentioned as the illegitimate son of Pedro lying in his tomb at Alcobaça. The Castilians were allegedly far superior to the handful of knights and peasants under Nuno Alvares Pereira, known to history later as The Holy Constable. A religious general, in 1423 towards the end of his life he became a Carmelite brother, dying in 1431 in the convent alongside the now roofless Carmo church in Lisbon that he himself had erected.

Yet there seems no doubt that a detachment of 500 English archers (sent by John of Gaunt planning to make João I his son-in-law and thus a supporter of his own bid for the Castille throne) took part with, I fancy, the descendants of the many northerners who had stayed, instead of going on to, or after returning from, the Crusades.

The Holy Constable. That the archers played a greater part in this victory than the baker's wife who dashed out and slew a dozen Spaniards with her long handled bread-shovel does seem probable. A few miles to the north of the village a St. George's chapel marks the spot where Nuno Alvares Pereira raised his standard; outside a pitcher of water, still freshly filled for travellers daily, has commemorated the hero's thirst upon the battlefield from almost that day to this.

His thirst could well have been formidable. An intelligent nobleman, the Holy Constable chose to dismount and fight on foot with his men, a position in which, protected by the bowmen, he was far less likely to be killed than mounted conspicuously upon a charger. Thus, at Batalha in front of the monastery his statue is equestrian, while in Lisbon a plinth in the Praça de Figueira exists to present him as a foot soldier.

Philippa – Portugal's English Queen. From this victory there followed in 1386 the Treaty of Windsor, an alliance that was successively ratified by Henrys IV, V and VI of England. A year later John of Gaunt's daughter, Philippa, married the King, João I, who in 1400 was made a Knight of the Garter, the Order having been founded by Edward III, Philippa's grandfather and father of John of Gaunt.

BATALHA. This great Dominican Monastery of Our Lady of Victory, is a Portuguese national shrine that has also been described as a monument of English influence prevalent at the time. Lying close to the main Lisbon–Oporto road, rounding a bend in the hills going towards Lisbon, the sudden sight of all its honey-coloured stone spires, towers, pinnacles and buttresses is dramatic. Building went on from 1388 to 1533 by which time the voyages of discovery being complete, exuberant Manueline decor had been added to the original Gothic, as seen, for example, on the huge doorway dividing the church from the Unfinished Chapels.

The Dominicans (founded by the Saint near Toulouse and known as the Black Friars in England) lived the austere life – no meat, fasting,

Batalha. The Abbey.

no money, silences and hence no belfries, yet they did permit, a rarity in Portugal, fine 16c. stained glass windows here, showing scenes from the life of the Virgin and Jesus Christ.

The Founder's Chapel. Admired more for its octagonal chamber and eight pointed star roof vaulting than for the sculpture of the Royal tombs, King João I (d. 1433) and Queen Philippa (d. 1415) lie hand in hand. Missing among their sons is the eldest, Edward, who died in 1438, only five years after succeeding his father, but Henry the Navigator (d. 1460) is there.

The Unfinished Chapels (Capelas Imperfeitas). Edward, a writer of distinction, instigated the seven Unfinished Chapels in the octagonal space at the east end of the Church, intending to be entombed in one of them; but work only started in 1435, three years before he died. Not until Manuel I (1495–1521) three monarchs later was the money available from the discovered lands to embellish them with the new decor that bears his name. They still stand roofless because he became absorbed in another project, the Jerońimos church at Belém. Possibly too, even though Boytac is buried with his wife at Batalha, the ageing master architect had enough work already, superintending the building of cloisters in two places 75 miles apart.

The tomb of the unknown soldier. Batalha being a national shrine the tomb of the Unknown Soldier was placed in the Chapter House soon after World War I. With it there goes the national legend that at the unveiling ceremony the Guest of Honour was the Unknown Soldier's Mother. A second soldier killed in Africa has since been added. Other casualties could have occurred; the single span roof being so dangerous to build that condemned prisoners were used to complete it.

Artistically the position is not ideal, impeding the view from the centre of the Chapter House to the finest part of the Abbey, the Royal Cloister, which experts think the architect intended.

The Royal Cloister. It is here, notably in the window traceries added later probably by Boytac – that Manueline blends so delightfully with the original Gothic, the work perhaps of English architects sent for by Queen Philippa. To all the trappings of seamanship there are added the flora of Africa and the Orient, poppies, globe artichokes and lotus blossoms brought back by the voyagers.

In the north west corner stands the well house or lavabo with three basins one above the other, the light, if sunny, shining through the stone tracery of the arches to give the stone and the water a golden touch.

Damaged by the earthquake of 1755, sacked by the French in 1810, denuded of monks in 1834, excessively restored in our own times, few can be oblivious of Batalha and its associations. As the English girl, quoted by Henry Myhill as hitch-hiking from Coimbra to Lisbon most week-ends, said: 'I sweep past it so often and feel I owe it a deeper obeisance'.

ACCOMMODATION, FOOD, WINE

The Estalagem do Mestre Afonso Domingues close to the monastery had pretty little flags of many countries in the dining room when we last had a final steak in April 1980 before catching a 5 pm flight home from Lisbon. Agreeable decor and staff. Only 21 rooms. Book early if you wish to stay.

Pousadas This *Estalagem* became Government-run as a Pousada in 1985. The word *Pousada* is derived from the verb *pousar,* to rest. *Portugal's Pousadas** by Stuart Ross, a comprehensive guide published in June 1986, lists all thirty of them in three classes: CH (Châteaux), B, C; equating respectively to 5 star, 4 star and 3 star hotels. Prices vary in each class according to seasons – Low, Middle and High. In 1987, with 225 escudos to £1, those of double rooms with bed and breakfast ranged between £53 and £20.

Pousadas are run by ENATUR, Av: Santa Joana Princesa 10A 1700 Lisbon, whose Central Reservation Dept for all Pousadas is Lisbon 881221, Telex 13609 or 63475 ENATUR.

DAY 8

Only seven miles north of Batalha, Leiria's modern Euro-Sol hotel, conspicuous on a hill above the town, has 92 rooms, each with a mini-bar refrigerator, making it suitable for a last night after a long day.

Continental cookery having no great appeal, we found our way to the Acquário restaurant in the town. Dinner was adequate if a little primitive, but the bill of 1600 esc. (about £16 then) for four did include six glasses of port and two of Aguardente Bagaceira.

Nowadays this big hotel may be booked for conferences and there is a second small restaurant called Reis in the town, where our sort of bill for four (1979) could hardly be less than £50.

DEPARTURE. LEIRIA TO LISBON AIRPORT

From Leiria the distance to Lisbon Airport along N1 is about 75 miles/120 kms. The last 30 miles/50 kms. being motorway.

*Available in UK by post price £5.80 from APN Publications, 5 Watling Street, Leintwardine, Craven Arms, Shropshire.

The Estremadura Coast

A NOTE FOR THOSE WITH MORE TIME

Those with more time to spare can investigate the coast southwards from S. Pedro de Moel to Nazaré and beyond or go inland to Fatima, joining if they wish the 100,000 people who assemble there on 13th of each month from May to October inclusive.

The water off Portugal's 500 miles of coast is not as warm as British people might reasonably expect of a region so much nearer the Equator. The Canaries current – cold water from the North Atlantic – curves south east, south and then, off the Portuguese coast, south west, dissipating the warm Gulf Stream that makes British Isles bathing bearable. The strong prevailing south west winds battering Western European shores make matters worse.

South facing beaches – the Algarve, the Arrábida and the brief Lisbon stretch are relatively protected, but north of Cabo da Roca, Europe's most westerly cape only one out of the following five resorts offers safe sea (as opposed to pool) bathing, a Portuguese brochure giving the temperatures as Max. 16°C/60°F and average 14.5°C/ 57.5°F.

Ericeira. 32 miles from Lisbon and 15 from Sintra, until recently this was a small village with two Estalagems and three simple restaurants. Completion of the large Hotel Turismo with two salt water swimming pools, two paddling pools, three bars, night clubs and disco dancing makes Ericeira a new attraction with package holidays offered from Manchester and Gatwick.

Peniche. N114, the road we took to Óbidos ends on the coast 15 miles beyond at Peniche, a fishing port at the foot of the rocky peninsula of Cape Carvoeiro, runner up to Cabo da Roca as Europe's most westerly spot.

Peniche has a sheltered bay, low sand dunes and some sandy beaches. Narrow access across a small bridge can cause overcrowding in summer. From the port a ferry service, June to September, takes an hour to Berlenga Island, seven miles out from Cape Carvoeiro.

A rocky island nearly 300 feet high, half a mile wide but less than a mile long, Berlinga is the largest of the group shown on Admiralty charts as the Berlings. On passage south from Portsmouth or Plymouth in January storms, it was always off the Berlings that visibility improved and the sun usually appeared. The island's Pousada is now an inn, from which boats can be hired to explore the blue grotto and the caves of the other islands. Inquiries to Tourist Office.

Nazaré.

Latest attractions are the hotel Praia Norte two miles out on N114 and a sea food restaurant called Gaivota in Peniche itself.

S. Martinho do Porto. This little place is a perfect – almost land-locked – salt water bay with safe bathing from a sheltered beach. The Parque is a comfortable two-turret hotel with 36 rooms; no restaurant, but for meals there is also the 27 room Estalagem Concha. There are four hotels altogether with over 100 rooms between them and a luscious local pastry cake called *pão de ló* (paio is a sausage). With Nazaré only eight miles up the coast, S. Martinho's attractions tend to be overlooked.

North from Óbidos N8 passes through a hilly countryside of vines, pines and olive groves through Alcobaça and Aljubarrota to join the main Lisbon–Oporto road south of Batalha. Turning left at Alfeizerão on to N242 we can return to the coast at S. Martinho do Porto in a few kilometres.

NAZARÉ (Pop. 10,500). The primary object of our own visit to Nazaré when driving northwards from Óbidos was not to discover whether the fishermen there are of Phoenician descent (they probably are as in Malaga and Cadiz), nor to see if their multi-coloured, tartan-pattern shirts and trousers relate them to Scots; nor yet to study their sardine fishing boats, shaped to ride the Atlantic swell, familiar from every other travel poster about Portugal. None of these – we just wanted to eat a fresh sardine and even though the next day we inspected every menu in every restaurant as far north as Figuera da Foz, there was not one to be had.

Yet at Nazaré along the mile long *praia*, where the boats are launched over rollers and hauled up by winches, powered by women and oxen when they return with the catch, there were sardines by the million laid out to dry.

What can be the explanation? I am told there is a close season, not for canning but for eating. Nobody seems to know how long it lasts. This was in April; in summer Nazaré becomes very crowded – with people playing sardines as it were.

The modern town with most of the inhabitants is **A Praia** 'on the beach' at the northern end, nestling under the conspicuous rock escarpment. A funicular goes up to Sitio, the old town 360 feet above.

The hotels and restaurants are all in the modern town. The *Michelin Guide* gives five hotels and there are as many restaurants which – close season permitting – should save you bringing your own fish.

São Pedro de Moel. Some 12 miles up the coast from Nazaré and much the same distance westwards of Leiria, São Pedro de Moel makes the fourth fishing port northwards of Cabo da Roca. Sited among rocky cliffs and sand dunes, the small shelving beach is sandy and the Atlantic swell so strong that a modern salt-water swimming pool has been built by the beach.

The resin-scented air is not just due to any old pines; the forest stretching northwards is said to be the oldest of artificial woodlands, planted by King Dinis about 700 years ago to arrest the inland march of sand dunes, just as the French contrived to do 200 years later in the Landes. Queen Isabel of Aragon, wife of Dinis, is said to have scattered an apron full of pine seed.

(If this is so, Hayling Island in Hampshire had better twin with São Pedro de Moel. The banks of wild yellow lupins that scent the celebrated Hayling golf links in May were created in the early days by a Secretary who collected and broadcast the seed whenever he played. The wind and the birds now do the rest.)*

The bungalow development is in fact very 'Hayling'. Of the resort's two two-turret hotels the Mar e Sol is modern with 33 rooms and near enough to the sea for a view of the Atlantic rollers. The São Pedro (60 rooms) is nearer the woods in which many of the pine trees look as dead as King Dinis and his saintly Queen.

*Sad to relate, in a recent summer a plague of greenfly destroyed the lupins. They should grow again in time.

An Alentejo shepherd wearing his straw overcoat brings his rams to market.

Linking fly/drive Faro to Evora

No time is specified. The aim is to join the Lisbon fly/drive at Evora returning perhaps via Lisbon and the Arrábida.

In the Algarve the winter population living in rented villas increases rapidly and the golf courses are becoming too crowded.

A golfer myself, I believe that taking to the road with the clubs left behind for a few days will certainly refresh the mind and the rest might even improve the game.

Telling a friend I was writing a *Travellers' Guide to Portugal*, he said, 'I spend January and February each year playing golf in the Algarve to escape the English winter; playing every day gets rather boring, but there's not much else to do. Perhaps it's time we took an interest in the country'.

Self-drive cars can be hired at Faro airport just as well as in Lisbon. Those with the time and the money are well placed on the Algarve to join my 7-day Fly/Drive from Lisbon at Evora, going on to Tomar, Óbidos, Alcobaça and Batalha before completing it along the Arrábida coast.

The return to the Algarve could be made from Setúbal along the coastal road N120 to Lagos and Faro or, more directly, through the centre of the southern Alentejo along N2, retracing steps to some extent.

Purposely no time has been suggested. The 190 miles between Faro and Lisbon could be done in four hours when in a hurry or four days if content to potter around the small white towns of the Alentejo staying at the Pousadas that are well sited in pretty places for that purpose. South of Lisbon and Evora there is little alternative accommodation that I would recommend inland from the Algarve.

km.			Total
0	Faro (P) at São Bras		0
76	Almadovar	N2	76
41	Mértola	N267	117
53	Serpa (P)	N265	170
29	Moura	N255	199
35	Vidigueira	N258	234
16	Portel	N18	250
52	Evora (P)	N18	302 = 188 m.

From Faro at sea level N2 climbs 900 feet to São Bras de Alportel in 17 kms. crossing the East/West N270, the short cut inland from the coast that avoids the town of Faro. The Pousada de São Bras 2 kms. north has 23 rooms; staffed by women, except for the Manager, it is very well run and should have a swimming pool soon.

The climb through the Serra do Caldeirão reaches its peak at Barranco do Velho (1685 feet) descending sharply with a number of hairpin bends.

At Almodovar, while the direct route to Evora and to Lisbon continues northwards, we can branch eastwards to meet the Guadiana at Mértola, where it becomes navigable for the last 42 miles to its mouth between Portugal's Vila Real de Santo António and Spain's Ayamonte, the two frontier towns. 510 miles long the Guadiana rises east of Spain's La Mancha, flowing westwards near Ciudad Real to reach Portugal six miles south west of Badajoz. It forms the boundary for some miles near Monsaraz and again from a point less than 20 miles below Mértola to the sea.

Mértola. Interest in this Roman village *Myrtilis*, above the point where the Oeiras tributary joins the Guadiana, lies not so much in its 13c. fortified castle as in the only church in Portugal that is a converted mosque. Visitors familiar with Cordoba or Granada will notice the similarity – low and square with four rows of pillars.

Walking down from the castle to the town, Henry Myhill relates how he was hailed from a low-barred window in a building that turned out to be the local prison. Humanely the Portuguese permit prisoners in their jails to talk to people on the street, resulting in an engaging conversation between Mr Myhill and half a dozen of the inmates. This was his first experience of Portugal's semi-open prison system, reminding me that I first met it when asked to pass a few cigarettes through the bars at Ponte de Lima in the north, where the luckless captives at least have a glorious view of freedom across a beautiful bridge and the wide Lima river.

Serpa. Ten miles east of Mértola almost on the Spanish border, where the road turns north towards Serpa, the name Mina de Sandomingo tells the sad story of a formerly British owned copper mine, which happened to be at the western end of the Rio Tinto and Tharses hill mines across the border in Spain.

Though never a rich seam, the mine did maintain a village of some 7000 people until a take-over bid brought a new and inexperienced ownership. The company went broke and the village has diminished to a mere 1500.

Mértola, Serpa, Moura, Mourão, Monsaraz and, of course, Elvas are all frontier towns, their castles mostly built in the 13c. by King Dinis. Serpa, on the direct Lisbon–Seville road, has the advantage of a simple 17 room Pousada out in the country amid corn and cork oaks from which to explore the locality. Serpa's convent of S. António has a tiny cloister and some 18c. azulejos of the life of St. Francis.

Moura. Quite a large agricultural town with 12,000 people the

Guadiana is close enough to be seen from its castle. A spa with springs and medicinal waters, Moura– like Evora – has some fine buildings.

The date of the marble fountain in the main square is that of Waterloo, 1815, its medallion and description relating to King John VI, who at that date was still with the entire court in Brazil and did not return till 1821. Since 1792 he had been Regent in place of mad Queen Maria acceding on her death in Brazil in 1816. The parish church of John the Baptist has a fine Manueline doorway, a marble pulpit and polychrome azulejos.

On the outskirts the Convento do Carmo circa 1250 was the first of its kind in Portugal. The tombs include one of a man who, according to its inscription, died of laughing.

BEJA (Pop. 20,000). Off my selected route the capital town of the lower Alentejo is only 17½ miles west of Serpa along the main road and could be fitted in between Moura and Vidigueira.

From many directions Beja's white buildings, tightly grouped on the hill, can be seen across the white dusty plain that becomes burning gold at harvest time, from as much as fifteen miles away. The only shade along the pair of roads that meet here, Lisbon–Seville and Evora to the Algarve–Spanish frontier, is from the eucalyptus trees, where the storks nest high up in spring.

Pax Julia to the Romans, their Porta de Evora still stands and a good view of it can be had from the castle's marble tower and keep, yet another King Dinis (1310) model, taller and thinner yet similar to that at Estremoz.

Architecturally overshadowed by Evora, Beja nevertheless has in Santa Maria an interesting 15c. church whose façade has been plastered in the adobe manner met in Mexico and the arid western parts of America. A similar curiosity is the fortified Hermitage of S. André whose dozen 'tubular Gothic' towers make the Ermida de São Bras at Evora almost an 'also ran'.

Regional Museum formerly **Convent of Conception.** Guided Tours. 0900–1700 (closed Sunday).

But it is a book rather than a battlement that has focussed much attention upon Beja. Nobody knows for certain if Sister Marianne did write *Love Letters of a Portuguese Nun* because the original has never been found. A French translation, published in France in 1669, was widely read later in many languages. The nun is presumed to have been Mariana Alcoforado of the Convent of Conceição, who ended a long life here as Portress or Doorkeeper. Her supposed lover, the Chevalier de Chamilly, to whom she wrote so passionately was one of many French soldiers stationed in Beja to support the Portuguese in the long wars that eventually brought independence from Spain in

1668. The 15c. convent, closed with all the others in 1834, is now a regional museum, the grille through which the lovers communicated being the most popular exhibit. A Gothic building with wide Arabic arches, the interior includes a pointed arch (ogival) door to the chapter house, a beautiful Manueline altar-piece of Carrara marble and a vaulted chapter house rich with 18c. azulejos.

Beja is the garrison town in which General Humbero Delgado, a former supporter turned opponent of Salazar, led an abortive uprising catching the headlines in 1962. Escaping to exile he was murdered near Badajoz, aged 59, in 1965, five years before the death of Salazar.

Vidigueira. The body of Vasco da Gama, brought back from Cochin some years after his death there in 1524, lay in the 16c. church of the Quinta do Carmo just north of this village until moved in 1898 to the Jeronimos Church in Lisbon, near the site of the Chapel at Belém, where a service was held before the first expedition sailed on July 9 1497 to discover the Cape of Good Hope. Later, between voyages, the great man lived at Evora.

Portel. Worth a final word before reaching Evora for its carpet and azulejos, which decorate the walls of the former church of S. António, now the local record office.

ACCOMMODATION, FOOD, WINE

Mértola has nowhere to stay but there are some restaurants, notably Alengarve in Rua Dr Alfonso Costa. South of Serpa however, on a hill off N265, is a nice 17-room Pousada with a 14c. chapel worth a look in its car park. Windows, water mills and wells are among the little town's charms and at Sandomingo, the local lake has brought about some recovery through tourism. Beja, having only Pensions is no place to stay, but the attractive Pousada de Vale do Gaio at Torrâo (Page 231) is only 34 miles away along N121 and N2.

Vidiguera gives its name to the dry white wine of the locality made principally at its own co-operative. Twenty miles to the north east Reguengos de Monsaraz has a red wine also ranking in the 'pleasant drinking' class.

EVORA See page 191.

RETURN ROUTES FROM LISBON TO THE ALGARVE

km			Total
0	Lisbon	E4	0
50	Setúbal (P)	N10	50
21	Marateca	N10/N5	71
31	Alcácer do Sal (P)	N120	102
52	Santiago do Cacém (P)	N120	154
18	Sines	N261	172
19	Tanganheira	N120	191
30	Odemira (P)	N120	221
42	Aljezur	N120	263
6	Alfambras	N120	269
24	Lagos	N120	293 = 182 m.

For Sagres take N268 at Alfambras distance 37 kms.

Setúbal. From Setúbal the first 20 kms. are eastwards through rice fields, salt marshes and cork oaks, the signs being to 'Evora' and 'Espagne'. The Algarve road branches south just before Marateca crossing the river Sado at Alcácer do Sal. (The adventurous can, of course, save 20 miles by crossing the Sado on the car ferry from Setúbal to Cetóbriga, then running down the long sandy Troia spit to Grandola, Santiago do Cacem or Sines on N261.) There is now an 18 hole golf course at Troia, see page 189.

Alcácer do Sal. Colonised first by the Romans and then for three centuries by the Moors, who were expelled finally in 1217, this region is full of architectural remains.

Among the rivers south of the Tagus, the Sado, Mira and Guadiana are navigable, so the bridge of this 'town of salt' (the best salt in Portugal) can be raised to allow small ships to pass. A sleepy town in a once malarial region the white buildings and steep narrow streets leading upwards from the river retain its Moorish air. A castle with salty views over rice and river, an Archaeological Museum, the S. Tiago church close to it with blue and white azulejos are worth a glance. Within the castle walls Sta. Maria do Castelo is a Romanesque church seldom seen in the south of Portugal. **The Convent of S. António** below the castle was founded in 1524. There is a fine renaissance doorway and a marble chapel of the Eleven Thousand Virgins, cold marble clearly being the right material. The church on the outskirts at one end of the castle hill formerly belonging to the Knights of S. Tiago (James) was 13c., the earliest part now being the octagonal chapel.

Pousada de Vale de Gaio. Many tributaries of the Sado have been dammed creating large lakes for hydro-electricity and agricultural

Sines, birthplace of Vasco da Gama, where new tanker installations and oil refineries lessen its charms for the tourist.

irrigation. One dam lies 12 kms. to the north-east of Alcácer do Sal and another 25 kms. along N5 to the south-east.

The brochure of this 7-room Pousada on the lake near this *barragem*, waters the mouth with woodcock, wild duck and partridge prepared in the delicious Alentejo fashion in a land of wild flowers and sweet-smelling herbs. Alas only a French chef will be lacking!

20 kms. from the Pousada along N2 north-east towards Evora, the palace of the Counts, Condes das Alcáçovas, in the little town of that name, has much of its 15c. Gothic remaining and the inside of its little chapel de Conceição is prettily decorated with scallop shells.

ALCÁCER DO SAL – FARO

18 kms. south of Alcácer a fork inland before Grandola joins N2 at Ferreria do Alentejo to form the shortest route to Faro, 187 kms. from Grandola. South of Ferreria do Alentejo the road skirts westwards to avoid a huge artificial lake near Erdivel where Beja may be seen to the eastwards, fully fifteen miles away across the plains.

Castro Verde, the most interesting town on this route, has a parish church, S. da Conceição with baroque altars and azulejos dated 1713 depicting the battle of Ourique which took place at Ourique near Santarem (not the other Ourique near here) in 1139 when Alfonso Henriques defeated the Moors.

Much improved this is now the fastest route to the Western Algarve.

ALCÁCER DO SAL – LAGOS

At the same point short of Grandola mentioned above, the coastal route N120 branches right to give an undulating 50 mile run through wooded hills and valleys to Odemira. Then, on the last stage to Lagos through the Serra de Monchique (2963 feet), there is a climb to 820 feet with views of the sea on the right.

Santiago do Cacém. A small town of 6000 people, the *Michelin Red Guide* rates the 7-room Pousada de São Cacém as a two knife and fork restaurant with rooms. It stands on the slopes below the castle in which the cypress trees seen from a distance jutting up above the walls are part of the cemetry also inside the walls.

A path round this Templars' castle gives fine views over the coast and there are some old houses on the Praça do Conde de Bracial.

Sines. The only place of any size along the west-facing coast south of Setúbal, Sines was the birth place of Vasco da Gama. The house built on the spot since and the chapel he had built above the little port can be seen. A pretty town but remote, a growing industrial zone has made Sines more commercial, the 20 kms. stretch of motorway leading nowhere on the map being associated with the Petro Sul depot. Whether the great exploring sailor would approve of today's steel monsters discharging their strange, foul smelling means of propulsion at his birth place is another matter. The iron ore mined far up the Douro will also come here for export. River barges bringing it downstream will enter a sea-going mother ship at Oporto for the passage to Sines.

Though Sines is 17 kms. from Santiago do Cacém, the detour to it, rejoining the N120 at Tanganheira, adds only 10 kms. North and South of Sines the coast is one long expanse of deserted sandy beach, mild as the Mediterranean in summer.

Odemira. Both the Sado and the Mira rise close to each other in the Serra do Caldeirão, the range of low hills immediately north of Faro. The Mira has a relatively short run to the Atlantic via the Marcello Caetano, the largest reservoir in these parts. Emerging from the *barragem* it runs on to Odemira in a series of Mosel-like loops straightening out to reach the coast at Vila Nova de Milfontes. Nicely sited in woods above the lake, the 6-room Pousada Sta Clara-a-Velha is a conversion of the Chief Engineer's house when building c. 1970. There is swimming in its small pool or in the lake, with sailing, fishing and walking in peaceful country. The road south leads through the hills to Monchique (33 kms.) passing a cork establishment at Nave Redonda.

Odemira – Lagos is 71 kms. = 44 miles of undulating road with views of the sea and the hills of Monchique and Espinhaço de Cão. Lagos via Sagres means branching left at Alfambras adding another 40 miles to the journey.

For Lagos and Sagres see the Algarve Coast, pages 257 and 259.

Linking fly/drive Madrid to Lisbon

This Fly/Drive is for those with sufficient time to be touring Spain *and* Portugal. It joins my Lisbon Fly/Drive at Elvas and a return could be made after it from Evora, following the Faro Fly/Drive and Seville – Algarve Fly/Drive in reverse.

				Total	
km	m	Spain		km	m
0	0	Madrid	E4	0	0
117	73	Talavera de la Reina	E4	117	73
32	20	Oropesa (P)	E4	149	93
105	65	Trujillo (P)	E4	254	158
88	55	Mérida (P)	E4	342	213
62	38	Badajoz	E4	404	251
		Portugal			
18	11	Elvas (P)	N4	422	262
41	25	Estremoz (P)	N4	463	287
103	64	Atalho X-rds	N4/N10	566	351
33	21	Setúbal (Motorway) (P)	N10	599	372
49	31	Lisbon (Motorway)		648	403

English speaking visitors from overseas making an extensive tour of Spain and Portugal might first land at Madrid. Making for Lisbon the *Michelin Red, España – Portugal, Guide* and Michelin Map 990 with the same title both show the way, National route E4, running S. W. out of the Spanish capital along the Avenue de Portugal to the frontier town of Badajoz, 251 miles away.

A fast run of 73 miles, through olive and cork oak country, reaches Talavera de la Reina. 20 miles beyond is **Oropesa** where the 44 room Parador in the old restored castle, with a fine view northwards over the Tagus valley to the Gredos mountains, is one of the best in Spain.

The Tagus is crossed after by-passing Navalmoral. Hereabouts it has been heavily dammed for agricultural irrigation, hydro-electricity and nuclear power creating large lakes. The road remains fast even when rising to 2180 feet with fine views to the S.W., before Trujillo is seen on a hill in the far distance.

Mérida, on the river Guadiana, now a town of 40,000 people and once the capital of Roman Lusitania, is still full of Roman remains, including its bridge, theatre and amphi-theatre. In the old town the elegant white Parador, converted from a former convent, would be the best place to stay. The main road sweeps south east round Mérida crossing the Guadiana on a bridge built in 1960.

The next 40 miles to Badajoz run due west through the orchards and farms of a valley made prosperous by irrigation. Upstream at wide intervals, the Guadiana has been dammed in half a dozen places.

Badajoz with over 100,000 people is of more interest for what its citizens have endured over the centuries than from what it has to show for itself. The many sieges of the Peninsular War, with the British losing 5000 out of 15,000 men and then sacking the place in Wellington's attack of 1812, were horrible. Yet in August 1936 the Spaniards surpassed them when Franco's Nationalists forced their Republican opponents into the Bull Ring and massacred them.

The frontier posts are astride the Caia, small tributary of the Guadiana, four miles beyond Badajoz.

In Portugal, Evora , Elvas, Estremoz and Palmela (near Setúbal) all have Pousadas suitable for overnight stops. These four form part of the Lisbon Fly/Drive, which can begin either at Estremoz or Evora. See pages 196 and 191 respectively.

ELVAS (Pop. 14,000). About 1000 feet up Elvas is 41 kms. east of Estremoz and 18 from Badajoz. Fortified with ramparts since the 13c., the Moors were driven out in 1226, but Elvas has seen plenty of action at intervals since. The present ramparts are 17c. and anybody with a passion for fortifications can walk the 5 kms. round them.

Having a 750 mile frontier to defend, with a larger and more powerful neighbour on the other side, the Portuguese were bound to make Elvas a frontier fortress against invaders crossing the Guadiana. Spanish sieges were resisted successfully in 1658 and 1711. The French under Marshal Junot took it in March 1808 evacuating in August after the Convention of Sintra.

Previously, in 1801, Napoleon's ultimatum to Spain had required Portugal to close her ports to British ships. When she refused, Spanish troops under Godoy entered the Alentejo. Olivenca, then part of Portugal, offered no resistance while Godoy besieged Elvas sending two orange trees as a trophy to the Queen of Spain.

This 'War of the Oranges' forced Portugal to cede the territory round Olivenca when the Spanish dictated a peace at Badajoz that September. In 1814 the Treaty of Paris required its return, a clause ignored by the Spaniards even though to some extent they owed their liberation from the French to the Anglo–Portuguese troops. Thus to this day the Portuguese patriot, looking across the Guadiana from Monsarez or Juromenha, regards the land as his. How surprising that the Spanish Government does not seem to be offering it back; after all, Franco and Salazar did sign a Treaty of Friendship in 1939!

Amoreira Aqueduct. Approaching Elvas from Estremoz on the left is the five-tiered Aqueduct that brings water 7.5 kms. across the plain to the town. Built on Roman foundations it was paid for by the citizens and – hardly surprising – took from 1498 to 1622 to build.

Cars can be left outside the wall near the Municipal Gardens and the Pousada in order to see, just inside, the 1622 Misericordia fountain surmounted on his horse by Don Sancho II, the hero who expelled the Moors. **Praça de Sancho.** The main square of the town has a Sé, demoted to Parish church, because there is no longer a Bishop. Manueline with 17c. alterations, the black and white chequered pavement approaching it across the square is delightful. A little way north of the Sé is the Largo Santa Clara, a triangular space with a 16c. marble pillory in the middle. **Church of Our Lady of Consolation** (Nossa Senhora da Consolação). On the south side of the main square this 16c. octagonal church is remarkable for its fine proportions and polychrome azulejos dating from 1659 and lining the interior right up to the lantern of the cupola. Lit by only two windows besides the cupola, the tiles glittering in semi-darkness give a mosque-like effect. **The Castle** 0930–1230: 1400–1600. Closed Monday. At the northern corner, the castle, begun by the Moors, gives a good view over the town and of the Fortress of Our Lady of Grace, said to be an 18c. military masterpiece, some way out on the Portalegre road.

ACCOMMODATION, FOOD, WINE

The two-star hotel Don Sancho II in the middle of the town has 24 rooms; other accommodation is to be found on the N4 going round it outside the walls. The Pousada de Santa Luzia has 11 rooms and a good restaurant. The Don Luis, three turret, is the best hotel and the Estalagem Aqueduto is a restaurant on N4 with four rooms.

Bacalhau dourado, Carne de Porco á Alentejo, Carnes fumades are cod, pork and smoked meats respectively.

Cericaia and *Capitólios* are the best known cakes and there are good olives. Almost too well known are the plums – gorgeous sugar plums the books never fail to mention.

For local wines see Estremoz.

SHOPPING

Besides the plums and olives, Elvas is where the striped blankets – reds and blacks, greens and yellows, blues and crimsons that look so pretty in Lisbon shop windows are woven.

Marvão. Worth a visit given a clear day. This attractive hill village with staggerin
is reluctantly omitted from the itinerary for reasons explained in the text.

Madrid to Lisbon, a second route via Cacéres, Marvão and Abrantes

km	m	Spain		Total km	m
0	0	Madrid	E4	0	0
254	158	Trujillo (P)	E4	254	158
47	29	Cáceres	N521	301	187
100	62	Valencia de Alcántara	N521	401	249
		Portugal			
17	11	Galegos	N246	418	260
17	11	Castelo de Vide	N246	435	270
78	49	Abrantes	N118	513	319
56	35	Almeirim	N118	569	354
39	23	Samora	N10	608	377
8	5	Vila Franca de Xira	N1/E3	616	382
31	19	Lisbon		647	401

This route is the same as far as Trujillo and to Lisbon the distance is much the same – just over 400 miles. The frontier is a relatively minor one, the road surface being generally fair to Lisbon, becoming good, flat and fast from Almeirim. It would enable the Lisbon Fly/Drive to begin at Tomar, returning to Spain via Badajoz. The Serra de São Mamede rising to 3363 feet, with Marvão towering above the main road on the one side and the town of Portalegre away on the other makes an oasis of greenery in the Alentejo, which some may like to explore for a day.

From Trujillo N521 runs west to Cáceres, a large market town with some charm and many moderately priced hotels and restaurants. The Parador marked on some maps has never been completed. The main square's Roman walls, gates and towers are still intact. Some 60 miles of undulating road over open pastures and heath reaches the frontier posts of Valencia de Alcántara and Galegos. Whether in Spain or Portugal this territory is Estremadura (or Extremadura) embracing the basins of the Tagus and the Guadiana, not bad land for sheep and pigs except for its prolonged droughts and even the irrigation schemes since 1950 have not stemmed the tide of emigration.

The route joins the main Lisbon Fly/Drive at Abrantes (page 201).

PORTALEGRE. A town about the size of Elvas nearly 500 metres above sea level, the apex of the Serra de São Mamede triangle, the highest point being almost 1025 metres (3400 feet). By car N246-1-2 makes a 43 mile circuit between Portalegre, Marvão, Castelo de Vide and back, estimated time 2½ hours. The chestnuts, willows, pines and eucalyptus break the monotony of cork, olives and gum cistus.

Portalegre, becoming rich in the 16 and 17c. through silk mills and tapestries, does not lack for baroque houses and azulejos decor. *The Michelin Green Guide* gives a town plan (denied surprisingly for Elvas) naming 17 and 18c. houses in the Rua 19 de Junho and the Sé – all close together – as worth seeing. Visits can also be paid to the tapestry workshop in a former Jesuit monastery and ten minutes' walk from the Sé, worth seeing for its fine 18c. façade, groined painted ceiling and a Sacristy with pleasing blue and white azulejos.

For the Mamede circuit go east on the Reguengo road N246-2. For the direct route to Marvão go north on N246, the Castelo de Vide road, branching right after 4 kms. on to N359.

Marvão (Romaria 8 September). This whole district was well populated by the Romans as can be seen by its many roads and bridges. Many remains have been found near San Salvador-de-Araminha where the 6 kms. climb to Marvão begins.

Almost on the frontier, Marvão's position 865 metres/2820 feet up is described by José Amaro's verse, 'Marvão how lovely you are . . . Portugal at your feet and opening your arms – Spain'. A formidable fortified stronghold in the Middle Ages and, indeed, as late as the civil war of 1833, circle the ramparts before leaving your car in the village square, since you are unlikely to get it through the narrow gate. As in the Alentejo the walled town is bright with flowers, singing goldfinches and canaries on 17c. iron balustrades over Manueline windows. The best view is from the castle, east across the mountains of Spain, west over the plain of Portugal, south to the São Mamede and north to Castelo Branco. At the foot of the hill a small trout stream has been dammed to make a municipal swimming pool.

Castelo de Vide. Henry Myhill rated Castelo de Vide among the most attractive small towns of Portugal. A small spa, there are big fairs on January 15 and August 10. The recipe remains unchanged – charming unspoilt 15 and 15c. streets and squares; a granite fountain c. 1586; 17 and 18c. houses with iron grilles over Manueline windows; castle, church and shining white cottages. The church is dedicated to Senhora da Alegria – Our Lady of Joy – well expressed in the polychrome 17c. azulejos that line it completely. *A-lay-gree-a* means joy, merriment, cheerfulness or, discarding the dictionary, just fun. **Jewish Quarter** (Judiaria). At the northern end below the castle this 13c. Judiaria is the town's most interesting feature, complete with synagogue, Rabbi's house and some fine Gothic doors. Below it there is a baroque granite fountain.

We arrived about 12.30 just in time to find the lady in the Tourism Office locking up for lunch. No illustrated brochure, she provided a duplicated sheet with a rough plan and a note in English and German.

Most of the houses run up the steepest of slopes from the Santa Maria church and the municipality in the town's main street with the Praça D. Pedro II on the other side.

ACCOMMODATION, FOOD, WINE

Portalegre. Rococo houses with good iron work and pleasant azulejos make this town a good choice for an overnight stop in its modern hotel, D. Joâo III, which has 54 rooms. O Tarro and Alprende are two inexpensive restaurants.

Marvâo. The Pousada de Santa Maria, built from two private houses in 1976, seems to have expanded its bedrooms from 8 to 13. The charming little place has a great reputation for trying to make its fare worthy of the glorious views from the dining room, invitingly illustrated in *Portugal's Pousadas*. Should it be full, there is now an Estalgem D. Dinis as well. To summarize, in fine weather without low cloud, Marvâo is undoubtedly worth the 600 metre climb.

Castelo de Vide. On my visit some years ago we lunched simply at the Albergaria Jardin y Estal Sâo Paulo in a quiet spot facing a bit of garden. Now there is a second two star hotel, the Sol e Serra with a pool, and another in the park called the Casa do Parque. With over a hundred rooms between the three of them booking should not normally be necessary.

Local wines are Borba, Redondo, Reguengas de Monsaraz and Vidigueira; Castelo de Vide natural spring water is widely on sale in southern Portugal.

Traveller's Notes

Part 5
FLY/DRIVE FROM SEVILLE THROUGH THE ALGARVE

INTRODUCTION

This is intended to link an Andalusian tour with the Algarve, Seville being 88 miles away through lovely country, two-thirds motorway. It is always fun to slip across a frontier into another country and Andalusia and the Algarve are so close that given 14 days or more, a Moorish holiday divided between the two is feasible and might appeal, particularly to any Americans, Canadians and Australians determined to make the most of a visit to Europe.

Though Spain is outside my province in this book, I can recommend from personal experience a rough Andalusian timetable.
(P) indicates a Parador.

Day	Notes	Kms. approx.	Night at
1	Arr. Seville Airport. Carmona (P) avoids driving in crowded city perhaps after dark.	10 or 22	Seville or Parador at Carmona
2	Seville on foot. Don't miss Barrio de Santa Cruz where at night Mozartians may feel Don Giovanni could appear round the next corner.	Nil or 64	Seville or Parador at Carmona
3	Drive to Cordoba via Montilla to taste the wine at Bodegas J. Cobos, and lunch at their Las Camaches.	160	Cordoba. Book well in advance.
4	am. see the Mosque, Cathedral, Juderia. pm. on to Granada. Parador always booked months ahead.	169 (N432)	Granada. Book well in advance. Hotels Alhambra Palace, Generalife
5	Stay if possible on the wonderful hill near the Alhambra and the terraced water gardens of the Generalife.		Guadeloupe and America well sited on the hill.
6	Granada–Antequera (P) 96 kms. (Ronda 196 kms) Arcos de la Frontera (P) 283 kms. – Jerez 313 kms. Slow through mountain scenery after Antequera.	Jerez 313	Arcos (P) or Jerez at Jerez.
7	Jerez and environs. am. visit a Sherry Bodega eg Domecq, Sandeman, Croft. Lunch El Bosque or Gaitan. pm. San Lucar de Barrameda and coast towards Cadiz.		Arcos (P) or Hotel Jerez at Jerez.
8	Jerez to Algarve; Toll Motorways A4 and A49 for first 160 kms.	231	Parador at Ayamonte or hotel in Algarve.

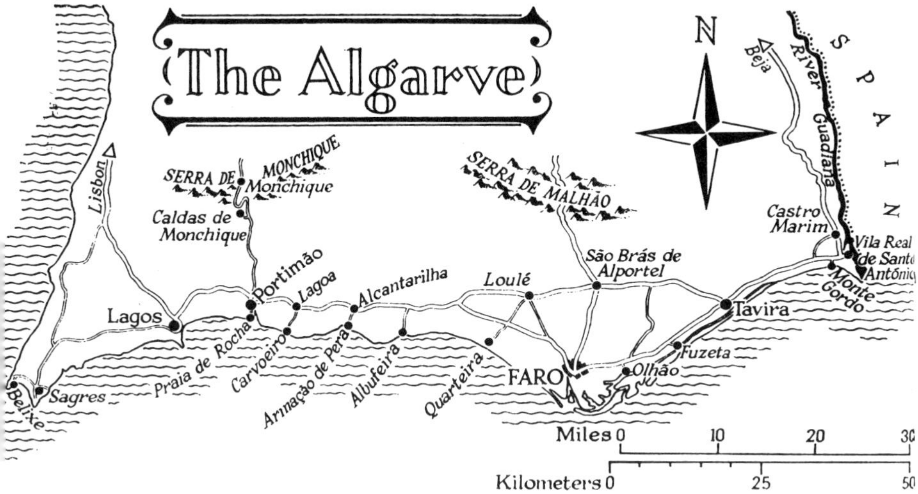

Whereas Lisbon to Lagos, the nearest Algarve resort, is 267 kms./167 miles taking around four hours, Seville to Vila Real de Santa António, the Algarve eastern frontier town on the Guadiana opposite Spain's Ayamonte, is only 141 kms./88 miles, or from Jerez 231 kms./144 miles nearly all on motorways.

Leaving Autopista 49 short of Huelva a flat run of some 60 kms. along N431 through vineyards and orange groves reaches Ayamonte, where the 20-room Parador on the hill gives a first view of the Algarve across the Guadiana. The crossing is short and the service at least hourly, but the car ferries are small and awkward for caravans.

How delighted the ancient Mediterranean seafarers must have been to discover this 150 km. strip of south-facing coast, where the climate was as warm as their own and the Atlantic fish better and more varied! The Cyretes from Andalusia came first, followed by Phoenicians, Greeks and Carthaginians, who established fishing stations. Next the Romans, introducing agriculture through irrigation, and building towns like Ossonoba at Milreu six miles north of Faro. Their occupation, ending in AD 409 when the Visigoths swept south across the Pyrenees, had brought six centuries of peace to what was then Lusitania.

From 711 to 1249 the Arabs held sway, leaving their mark now mainly in place names, even though in Chalb, now called Silves, they built a port and capital city with 30,000 inhabitants barely second to Lisbon. In 1189 a force of Crusaders and Portuguese sailed up the river

Arade (which later silted up) to capture the place. Sixty more years and the Moors had all gone from this province they had named *al Gharb,* 'the land beyond to the west'.

In the next seven centuries in the Algarve, apart from Gothic churches and a little Manueline architecture, the Christian contribution now appears to have been one of well designed golf courses, pseudo-Moorish hotels and self-catering villas. The province, cut off from Spain by the Guadiana and from the rest of Portugal by the two Serras, Monchique and Caldeirão that protect it, did however achieve great distinction through Henry the Navigator's school of navigation at Sagres.

Third surviving son of João I, victor over the Castilians and the Moors, Henry (1394–1460) was half English, his mother, Queen Philippa, being John of Gaunt's daughter. On his return from capturing Ceuta (the African Gibraltar) in 1415, the English made him a knight and the Portuguese, Governor of the Algarve.

The great discoveries which he organised, began with a rediscovery of Madeira by Zarco in 1418. An exploration of the Azores followed in 1427. During the 1430s and 40s his expeditions explored the West African coast beyond Cape Verde, almost as far south as Freetown (Sierra Leone). At Sagres his court became a school for mariners, astronomers and cartographers from many countries, the combination of experience and study making possible the much greater voyages that led to India and the New World after his death in 1460.

He died on November 13 at Sagres, his own town near Cape St. Vincent. A year later the body was moved to the Founders' Chapel in the great monastery at Batalha. His statues can be seen at Belém over the centre column of the side gate of the church, and in Lagos, his principal base where the monument was erected in 1840.

Tucked away south of the mountains the Faro airport has brought the Algarve within three hours of Britain. By road, across the Tagus bridge completed in 1966, four hours suffices from Lisbon. The sea temperature seldom falls below 15° C/59° F and spring can begin in January with the countryside a mass of foaming white almond blossom, soon to be followed in February by 'scrambled eggs' as the mimosa flowers in its place. There are too – as in the Douro valley – many kinds of wild flowers. A legend declares that the almond trees were planted by a Moorish emir married to a homesick Scandinavian princess pining for the snows. One January morning she awoke content at last to see the ground as white as snow from the blossom.

Vast new hotels, some best described architecturally as the unacceptable face of tourism, have arisen in the last 20 years, close to the gently shelving beaches swept clean by Atlantic tides.

Golf course architects like Frank Pennink and Henry Cotton have done better. There are half a dozen new clubs with tennis courts and every amenity, from hiring golf clubs to bars and restaurants; some have a 9 hole course as well as an 18 and the greens and fairways have automatic sprinklers.

Sailing, surfing, water skiing, deep sea or underwater diving and fishing are all there for the asking along this coast, where the people are primarily fishermen. As to straightforward sun bathing and swimming the Algarve is one long series of golden *Praia,* cooled by Atlantic breezes when the heat inland becomes intolerable and even the developments of the past 20 years still leave plenty of open space along them. The swimming pools too, amply provided at hotels, clubs and villas, are a boon for children.

Formerly, as Cedric Salter stresses in his 1970 book, *Portugal,* most of the Algarve was a semi-desert; the water to irrigate it lay so far below the surface that the cost of sinking wells down to a thousand feet required capital that only prospective finance companies possess. Today if the local people still cannot afford to live as luxuriously as their visitors, no longer in the droughts that still plague southern Spain and Portugal will one see water being brought by a string of donkeys all the way from Galicia. The extreme poverty of peasant farmers and tradesmen has gone.

Seeing the lack of planning on the Spanish Mediterranean *costas,* the Portuguese government has restricted the number of luxury hotels while encouraging good second class accommodation such as the state Pousadas and the privately owned and run Estalagems.

FOOD

The hotels – whatever the brochures may say – are seldom the places in which to eat well. The red mullet, sole, sea bass and bream; the fresh tunny, cuttlefish, squid, octopus and, of course, the sardine come hot, well seasoned with marjoram and onions, from a charcoal grill, with a tomato salad in the modest *taberna* or *bistro,* often indicated by a sign *casa de pasto* over a dingy door. The fish will be fresh and when it comes to soup the Algarve version of *bouillabaisse* is called *Caldeirada* (*caldo* being just soup). Traditionally these little restaurants have two prices alongside each item, *dose* indicating a full portion, *meia dose* half.

Pork, goat, kid, sucking pig (very rich), hare, partridge and chicken may be offered but the Algarve is too dry for beef or mutton. Fruits in season abound, notably melons, oranges, apples, quinces, pomegranates, cherries, plums, peaches and strawberries. There are local goat cheeses from the mountains (*queijo da serra*) and the Moors left a legacy of fancy cakes made from almonds, figs and eggs.

WINE

The length of the province may be 100 miles but the depth is barely 30, which does not leave much room between the sea and the mountains for vineyards. Nevertheless some 70,000 hectolitres (1 hectolitre = 100 litres) of light red wine are made and a little white. Though light on the palate they are strong in alcohol (about 13°) with little acidity. Cooperative *Adegas* are at Portimão and Lagoa.

The better Portuguese table wines, such as Dão and Vinho Verde, being nationally distributed should also be easy to find.

Algarve. Almond blossom time.

Vila Real de S. António (Frontier) – Cape St. Vincent

km.			Total
0	Vila Real de S. António		0
23	Tavira	N125	23
22	Olhão	N125	45
8	Faro	N125	53
18	Turning L. Val de Lobo		71
15	Turning L. Albufeira		86
21	Lagoa	N125	107
8	Portimão	N125	115
18	Lagos	N125	133
33	Sagres (P)	N268	166
7	Cape St. Vincent	N268	173 = 108 m.

Coming from the warm south is not, say the Portuguese, the best way to approach their 'balmy Southland'. For full appreciation bear down from the north having suffered the torrid summer heat of the Alentejo or the November rains in the Minho.

Vila Real de S. António. Crossing from Ayamonte on the ferry this is the 'modern' town, which Pombal decided they needed here in 1744. Possibly the first example of pre-fabrication in history, it is said to have been erected in five months, all window and door frames being sent post haste ready-made from Lisbon. Nobody seems to have liked the result except for his *Praça* that has fine houses and tessellated black and white pavements.

On the other hand Monte Gordo, 4 kms. along the coast, is a bright and cheerful holiday resort, where besides tennis courts, bathing pools and a Casino, the shallow water, said to be the warmest along this coast, makes its vast sandy beach ideal for children. There are many hotels, the Vasco da Gama being the best equipped for young people. Three kms. up the Guadiana the fort at Castro Marim was one of many built by King João IV, father of Catherine of Bragança. North east of Castro Marim the new high suspension road bridge should have joined Portugal to Spain by 1990 and the river will be dredged for deeper draught vessels.

Tavira. Thirty years ago along the road to Tavira a botanist counted 40 different species of wild flowers, most of them unfamiliar to British gardeners at home. What with insecticides and petrol fumes one hopes they still survive.

In spite of destruction in the 1755 earthquake, suffered by many

Tavira. 'A handsome 1870 bridge'.

places in the Algarve, the towers and cupolas of Tavira make it the prettiest town, a handsome 1870 bridge crossing its river Ségua, which has become too silted beyond to reach the sea. Good beaches are less than a mile away but the Eurotel hotel is two miles north east of the town on the main road.

The Misericordia church has a particularly good renaissance doorway; at Luz six kms. westwards there is a church with a Manoeline portal.

At Tavira the inland route N270 avoiding Faro branches right rejoining N125 approaching Albufeira.

Olhão. Next stop before Faro, Olhão is, surprisingly, an 18c. fishing and canning town that looks Moorish because the fishermen who first settled here from Aveiro in the north plied their trade from Portugal to Morocco. The cube shaped white houses have flat roofs, the best view being from the Parish Church belfry. Though its angular mazes and miniscule squares are amusing, fishy smells and mud banks make Olhão an olfactory spot.

FARO. Capital of the Algarve, with 28,000 inhabitants, Faro was a Moorish town when Alfonso III captured it in 1249. Regrettably in 1596, when Portugal was ruled by Philip II of Spain, an expedition sent by Queen Elizabeth to 'singe his beard' at Cadiz sacked and burned Faro instead, except for some looted religious books which started the Bodleian Library at Oxford. Two earthquakes, in 1722 and 1755, again destroyed the town. Inspired by Bishop Dom Francisco Gomes, whose Praça contains the hotel Faro with the larger Eva Hotel close by, the people rebuilt Faro, learning much about good husbandry from him in the process, one example being the Manuel Bivar garden in the square.

Faro is also home port for a substantial fishing fleet bringing in sardines and tunny. Canning factories, salt pans, light industries and the thousands of tourists, coming to shop en route to and from the international airport by the beaches seven kms. to the south east, ensure that Faro folk are gainfully employed.

The main shopping street is the Rua de Santo António, a pedestrian precinct leading eastwards from the Manuel Bivar garden, the old town being only 400 yards to the south. In it the mainly 18c. rebuilt Cathedral has a Rosary Chapel with 17c. azulejos. The Arco de Vila is the town's oldest gateway, forming part of the old Alfonso wall in which a niche holds a marble statue of St. Thomas Aquinas, the 13c. Neapolitan theologian. **Archaeological Museum.** Guided tours 1000–1200; 1400–1700. Closed Sunday and holidays. Sited in the Covent of Our Lady of the Assumption the museum has Roman remains from Milreu, Moorish jars and Christian Mudejar azulejos. **Maritime**

Museum. 0930–1230; 1400–1730 (1300 Saturday.) Closed Sunday and holidays. In the Captain of the Port's old office by the dock this museum displays models of ships and fishing vessels. **Carmelite Church.** 0900–1800. Built in 1713 this Baroque church 700 yards north west of the Maritime Museum has a graveyard with an Ossuary Chapel entirely faced with bones and skulls (see also Church of St. Francis at Evora). An annual fair takes place on July 16 outside the church. **Ethnographical Museum.** 1000–1230; 1400–1800. Not Saturday or Sunday. Off the Rua de S. António, this regional museum has paintings, photographs etc. related to the Algarve way of life.

TOURIST INFORMATION

Most towns have one office, Faro has two. The first is by the Cathedral and the second in the Rua Ataide de Oliveira close to where the N125 enters the town from Olhão.

Worth collecting free from them is the little 136 page booklet *Algarve, The Traveler's Paradise.* Updated every few years it is full of information on hotels, restaurants, property, shopping, sports etc. with good colour photography and diagrammatic line maps.

Estói (for Milreu). Close to N2 at Milreu, nine kms. north of Faro, are the remains of Roman baths and fragmented columns discovered in 1876. The Romans called the place Ossonoba.

More delightful is the palace of the Viscount of Estói, set in a magnificent garden with orange trees and other greenery which appear to be growing out of fountains, marble statues, balustrades and staircases. An 18c. delight, some call it the Queluz of the South.

FARO TO PORTIMÃO

The Golfing Algarve. For the next 25 kms. after Faro, N125 leaves some five kms. between itself and the coast which have largely been developed for riding, swimming, tennis and golf among the pine, fig and almond trees, numerous *miradouros* giving glimpses of the bay's blue waters. Nearest to Faro is the **Quinta do Lago** golf club with little surrounding development, its 27 holes designed by William Mitchell of Florida so that 18 holes can be made up of three different combinations of 9; average length of each 9 hole loop is 3500 yards (Ladies 2,800). Accommodation with service and a restaurant is at the Casa Velha, where a 'Studio' comprises a bed-living room with bathroom and a 'Duplec' a living room and two double bedrooms and bathroom.

Further on, now surrounded by villas, the **Club de Golfe Vale do Lobo** designed by Henry Cotton opened in 1968. It too has three nine-hole loops forming Red, Yellow and Green 18-hole courses. There are some spectacular carries over the cliff tops notably at the much photographed short 7th on the yellow nine. The Club House and its restaurant are open to the public.

The Roger Taylor Tennis Centre, run by the star and his wife has twelve courts and the courses for amateurs, including complete novices, are a popular combination of work and play. (Brochure from Caravela Tours).

Only ten miles from Faro Airport this 750 acre/300 hectare development is dominated by the large Hotel Dona Filipa, named after John of Gaunt's daughter, King João's Queen, who, could she return, might make a dash for the riding school on seeing the Moorish dining room and Gothic bar, being neither a golfer nor, one assumes, a swimmer. A grill room has been added to this Trust House Forte group hotel.

Ten km. further on in what one booklet calls 'the most comprehensive tourist urbanization' is **Vilamoura** where 1600 acres were set aside for building. There are numerous hotels and villas, a yacht marina, a casino and again two golf courses with views of the sea, but not really links as known in Britain.

The popularity of golf in the sun has led to over crowded courses in Spain and to a lesser extent, in Portugal. This club no longer accepts players without a handicap certificate, which has led to fewer novices and quicker rounds.

The Vilamoura Club's course opened in 1969. Designed by the English amateur, Frank Pennink, it is 6500 yards Par 73 and the 5th, 9th and 15th greens he arranged to be near the Club House. Restaurant, bar, swimming pool, hard tennis courts, the Casino and the Golf Hotel are other amenities. Vilamoura II (formerly called Dom Pedro) also by Frank Pennink but recently redesigned by Trent Jones is now 6700 yards, Par 72.

For eating out there are simple Portuguese restaurants at Quarteira, the oldest fishing village, which has a fine long beach.

Loulé. On N270 the inland road, and five kms. off N625 abreast the Algarve's Sunningdale-by-the-Sea described above, Loulé lies in unspoilt countryside, cherishing its folk lore, particularly during the Carnival in March.

The craftsmen, descendants of the Moslem community, are great coppersmiths, saddlers, basket makers and potters plying their trade visibly in the streets around the square. A tinsmith in fact actually rebuilt the church of Nossa Senhora da Piedade in 1553.

Apart from being on the list for souvenir hunters, Loulé has some curious houses with pierced Moorish chimneys of mortar or plaster. The fine Parish Church of San Tiago has a melon shaped dome,

Carvoeiro, becoming popular for self-catering villa holidays.

renaissance archways and a side chapel of azulejos showing St. Michael at the Last Judgement.

ALBUFEIRA (Faro Airport 36 kms.) Once the most attractive of Algarve resorts, the white town on the cliff has become the largest and the most popular. Five kms. towards Faro stands the enormous 5-star Hotel da Balaia – its Conference room holding 150–200 people. A short way inland its rival the Montechoro, has rooms for twice the number but no dogs.

The informative *Traveler's Paradise* gives six pages to Albufeira's *estalegem*, pensions, restaurants, bars, night clubs, shops and Rent-a-Car firms. Montinho is a classy French restaurant at Montechoro, but the majority, preferring to 'eat Portuguese', should try A Ruina, Jardim d'Allah Adega do Zé, Borda d'Agua or the 3 Marias, all easily located on the booklet's Albufeira plan. Regrettably, since my first edition, The Sleeping Donkey (English operated) seems to have bitten the dust, but for shaking down the fishy fare of the Algarve we can still take a stroll to Isabel's Beauty Salon or – some holiday – round the Supermarket Marrachino (English spoken).

The Travel Club Upminster, the largest tour operator to the Algarve, has day flights from Gatwick, Heathrow and Birmingham to Faro every Sunday throughout the year.

Armacão de Pera (Faro Airport 44 kms.) Five miles westwards along the beaches this small resort has plenty of beach and three modern hotels, Garbe, do Levante and Viking all close to it. The popular Garbe is on the beach, where sun-tanned tourists can mingle with the weather-beaten fishermen who auction their nightly catch there each morning. Viking's visitors are closer to some rocks and grottoes, worth hiring a boat to see. Despite some high rise development a package holiday here could be less crowded than at Albufeira.

Carvoeiro (Faro Airport 60 kms.) The next resort growing fast is a village on a small cliff five kms. from N125 at Lagõa not frequented by tourists because the one hotel is relatively new. This is the three-star Dom Sancho with 47 rooms. There are two simple restaurants, O Patio and Togi; the latter, in a position on top of the hill overlooking the sea, also rents a few double and single rooms fully furnished next door. Beaches are secluded, some only accessible by boat and there are villas to buy and rent from several local companies. A new 36-hole golf course with large hotel should open in 1988.

Silves (Faro Airport 62 kms.) From Lagão N124.1 gently climbs 6.5 km. to Silves, once the Arabs' capital city of the Algarve called Chelb, lying at the confluence of two rivers, Odelouca and Arade. The 1755 earthquake left only the castle and the Gothic cathedral built of local reddish stone with some good rococo altars. By an orange grove just outside the town there is a remarkable 15c. stone crucifix, the crucifixion on one side and the descent from the Cross on the other.

The Moorish castle has two huge cisterns in which water supplies for a year were kept. Access is on foot from the Cathedral Square.

About ten kms. north east of Silves the Barragem Arade, damming the lake through which the river flows, makes a pleasant trip to a spot with a restaurant and picnic site.

PORTIMÃO (Pop. 27,000. Faro Airport 64 kms.) Chief town of the Algarve because Faro ranks as a city, Portimão splendidly placed on a bend of the Arade estuary is a busy deep water port for the fishing boats.The town is on the right bank; the expanding port, where the catches are unloaded, on the left. Two 250 yard bridges, for N125 and the railway respectively, join the two, the road bridge giving the better view of the town. Good shops are in the Rua Santa Isabel.

Praia da Rocha. Only a 2 km. ride in a horse or mule-drawn *carinha* Praia de Rocha at the mouth of the estuary is the Algarve's best known and longest established resort, its huge red rocks the most photographed. The line of hotels above the beach had a 1930 English South Coast look reminiscent of Littlehampton when I first saw them in 1967.

As at Albufeira huge new hotels stretching westwards at intervals have since been added, the 5-star Algarve, the 5-star Alvor Praia (240 rooms and a Conference room for 400) on the next beach called Tres Irmãos (Three Brothers) and, no distance away, the 4-star Dom João Torralta (214 rooms). All told there would appear to be twenty hotels, pensions and *Conjuntos Turisticos* along a three kilometre front.

The car hire firms, Avis, Hertz and others have representatives in the big hotels or in Portimão and taxis are cheap in Portugal, either being a means of escape from beach to mountain and from the usually tasteless 'International' hotel cooking to *ameijoas a Bulhão Pato*, a dish of clams cooked with garlic and coriander that should be found somewhere around the little restaurants at the back of Portimão's main square, Largo do Dique.

MONCHIQUE (Pop. 7000. Faro Airport 89 kms.) From Portimão a climb north to this cool hill town is a pleasant deviation. From February to May first the almond blossom, then the mimosa and then a profusion of wild flowers enhance the beauty of this Serra. En route the 17c. village, **Caldas de Monchique,** known for its hot springs and mineral water has been restored to include the 2-turret Albergaria Lageado (19 rooms May/October), two pensions and a bar or two.

Higher up, Monchique's surrounding hills and woods make pretty country with a great view south from Picota Hill. Going west towards Foia the charming Estalagem Abrigo da Montanha has six double rooms and four suites in its annex. Teresinha and Paraiso da Montana are two restaurants and the Monscicus Country Club has rooms and swimming pools. Foia's attraction is another stupendous view.

PORTIMÃO TO CAPE ST. VINCENT

Golf at Penina. Five kms. out of Portimão a left turning leads to the 5-star Penina Golf Hotel in the 360 acre Penina estate between the road and the Alvor beaches. The golf club now has two 18-hole courses designed by Henry Cotton. Many championships have been played on the South course, 6889 yards Par 73, so that after 25 years and a present imposition of 1000 rounds a week it is overworn and overgrown with weeds. Re-sowing fairways with more suitable seed and clearance of overgrowth elsewhere is now going on. The other *Composit* course, 6482 yards Par 71 has been completed by joining a new *Quinta* 9 to the existing *Monchique* 9. Handicap certificates must be produced in order to play on the Championship course.

Palmares. Frank Pennink's latest course, is to the east of Lagos close to Meia Praia, a long white beach marked on Michelin map 37. It has wonderful views across the broad bay of Lagos and in the northerly distance, to the Serra de Monchique. Five of its holes are among sand dunes bringing Palmares nearer to links golf than other Continental courses. 6615 yards. Par 71.

New Course Parque da Floresta, 9-hole 2782 yards, (2545 metres) now converting to 18 holes is by the coast at Praia de Salema, 12 miles west of Lagos.

GREEN FEES

In 1987 these were as much as £22 a day, but the Travel agencies are full of brochures offering all manner of winter packages to Portugal and elsewhere. From Britain the all-in cost of flight to Faro, full board and Green Fees should be around £50 a day in 1988. Membership of Eurogolf Ltd no longer benefits Algarve golfers. Balls are cheaper in Britain, it pays to take some.

Lagos (Faro Airport 82 kms.) Lagos enjoys an exceptionally sheltered position even for the Algarve because the coast, turning south for two miles to the Ponta da Piedade gives its spacious bay protection from the south and south west. A trading and naval port, Lagos shipyards built the caravels that Henry the Navigator sent forth on the voyages of discovery. His statue stands in the town's main square between the harbour and the town. From Nelson's times for over a century the British Channel Fleets were frequent visitors to this bay where international sailing regattas are now held.

The important things to see in Lagos are in the Praça da Republica.

Regional Museum 0930–1230; 1400–1700. Closed Monday and holidays. The entrance is up an alley way from the Praça. Contains interesting archaeological and ethnographical collections. **St. Anthony's Church** (Igreja de S. António). This little chapel adjoining the museum in the Rua de Silva Lopes, rebuilt after the earthquake in 1769, is completely lined with rich rococo woodwork. **Former Slave Market** (Mercado de Escravos). Now the 15c. Customs House, Europe's first slave markets were held in this arcaded building. **St. Mary's Church** (Igreja de S. Maria). Opposite the Customs House above, this church has a Manoeline window from which King Sebastian (1557–1578) addressed his men before sailing on the disastrous expedition to conquer Morocco, in which he and most of his army were killed at Alcázar-Quibir.

His successor Henry, the King–Cardinal (1578–80) favoured Philip II of Spain for the Portuguese throne, thus handing a weak, bereaved Portugal over to Spain for the next 60 years.

ACCOMMODATION, FOOD, WINE

The 4-star Hotel de Lagos with 287 rooms, in the town half a mile north of the Praça da Republica, caters for holiday makers with its own swimming pool, besides running its own bus shuttle service to the beaches.

Headed by Alprende there are plenty of small Portuguese restaurants to do justice to the fish brought in daily.

Lagão (Faro Airport 55 kms.) This small town on the N125 makes its own red table wine; Lagão Tinto, Alfonso III, Domelhor are some of the brand names. Wines also come from Tavira, Portimão and, though very little, there is a white Lagos.

Ponta da Piedade and the Coast. From this promontory, already mentioned, steps lead down to the sea and a scene described by one English writer as 'like a fantastic cathedral, with spires and arches weathered out of the soft orange rock and great caverns, towers and minarets in the cliffs'. **Praia Dona Ana,** where another 4-star hotel, the 259 room Golfinho has been built, is partly hidden by these cliffs. The name has no connection with the gulf or the game; Golfinho is a dolphin and appropriately the hotel offers nautical sports as well as tennis. **Praia de Luz.** Three kms. out of Lagos a turning off N125 leads to the village of Luz in a valley running down to its five mile beach. Around it the Luz Bay Club has planned and built a self-catering village of well equipped terraced villas, with two large swimming pools. On the hill above they have built a group of larger villas, many with their own private pools and all well furnished. Amenities include O Jardim, the Club's restaurant, with a charcoal grill. O Poco superbly sited on the beach, offering fresh fish *al fresco* from sardines to clams, and the Luz Bay Sea Sports Centre instructing in aqua-lung scuba diving, wind surfing and just plain sailing, with equipment hire as necessary. Reported favourably in *Country*, The Country Gentlemen's Association's magazine, I fancy Luz could become the last refuge of the breed, Old Etonian ties, Harrovian boaters, Panama hats and all. **Praia de Salema.** Reached by a turning off N125 beyond Budens this, the penultimate south-facing beach, adjoins Praia de Luz. The 4-star Estalagem Infanta do Mar with 30 rooms looks out to sea and the Maré run by Mr and Mrs Jones is a restaurant bar with rooms.

Sagres (Faro Airport 115 kms.) West of Lagos with less protection from the mountains, the south western promontory does become windswept and colder. Between Figueria and Raposeira, a right turn leads to the 13c. chapel of Nossa Senhora de Guadalupe, to which the coloured stone columns, some with human faces, impart a Byzantine air. It is said that coming here from his quinta at Raposeira to pray and meditate, Prince Henry became known as *O Infante de Sagres*.

N125 ends at Vila do Bispo, a white-washed village whose lovely church is lined with blue and white azulejos. A minor road winds on westwards to the Castelejo cliffs where the Atlantic rolls and roars below.

N268, the road that turns south across a desolate plateau except for a few rabbits and partridges, reaches the Sagres headland in ten kms, where there are more Atlantic rumblings, and Cape St. Vincent, Europe's south-westerly point, can be seen five kilometres across the bay. Short of the Sagres point Prince Henry established his 'School of Navigation' around 1435. The walls still stand and in the courtyard on the ground lies the large and famous stone compass dial. Inside the great gate there is a pretty white-washed church. Today the place is an attractive and popular youth hostel.

Vasco da Gama and Christopher Columbus were among those instructed here in the new celestial navigation by mathematicians from Majorca and the Middle East. The Astrolobe, and much later the Quadrant and Sextant, enabled men to measure altitudes of the Pole Star, and of the Sun when on the meridian at midday, to find their position when out of sight of land. Besides setting up chairs of mathematics and medicine at Lisbon, Henry – as Grand Master of the Order of Christ – founded a professorship of theology.

Some 120 years later, soon after the Armada, Drake occupied this last corner of Europe while pouncing upon the Plate fleet returning from South America. The Elizabethans, being no respecters of foreign property, possibly destroyed Henry's buildings unaware of his work. And in any case, observes Cedric Salter, had they been contemporaries, Drake would have regarded Henry as a half foreign Papist.

Sagres itself, a small fishing port primarily handling the excellent lobsters caught in the bay lies a little to the east at the foot of the cliffs, well sheltered by both the headland and its own jetty.

From the port back towards Faro a good five miles of south facing coast with cliffs and beaches extends to Salema and Luz. The modern 3-star Hotel Baleeira with 118 rooms and the Motel Gambozinos (17 rooms) are both close to it. High up, with views westwards over the cliffs to the open sea, the Pousada do Infante's 23 rooms have private baths and balconies. Nearby the Fortaleza do Beliche is an ancient fort made into a restaurant with four rooms.

Fishing boats for four people with crew, tackle and bait all provided, can be hired for the day.

Cape St. Vincent (Fim do mundo).

> Nobly, nobly Cape St. Vincent to the North-west died away;
> Sunset ran, one glorious blood-red, reeking into Cadiz Bay.

Before the Discoveries Robert Browning's *Home-Thoughts from the Sea* were by no means shared by the local land lubbers. From the Cape the sun sinking below the waves looked so immense that they believed it to be so close that sizzling was clearly audible.

The blood has been real enough. For the lives of thousands of European sailors Cape St. Vincent to Cadiz Bay has been a *Fim do Mundo* or World's end. Cadiz was repeatedly sacked by Drake, Raleigh and Essex before and after the Armada in 1588. In the Smyrna Convoy off Lagos in 1693 a hundred English merchantmen out of four hundred were lost when Tourville surprised Rooke.

Casualties are seldom mentioned in national history books. Apart from war, in *English Social History*, G. M. Trevelyan wrote:

'The fleet had to be maintained by the haphazard and iniquitous compulsion of the press-gang because voluntary recruitment was inadequate owing to the notorious conditions on board, where the food was foul and scanty, the pay inadequate and irregular, the attention to health nil, and the discipline of iron'.

We can only guess the magnitude of the disaster for the Spaniards in 1780 off Cape St. Vincent when Rodney captured six out of their eleven ships, the *San Domingo* having blown up with six hundred men on board and not one survivor.

In 1797, soon after making a disastrous alliance with France, the Spanish Government sent 27 ships out from Cadiz, undermanned and thoroughly neglected. Surprised by Sir John Jervis, later Earl St. Vincent, with 15 ships and prevented from escaping by Nelson's tactical brilliance, the Spaniards surrendered four fine ships as prizes before retreating to Cadiz without their Commander, de Córdoba, who had been killed in the action.

Trafalgar, over a hundred miles to the south-east so that the cannonade could not possibly have been heard at Cape St. Vincent as some books suggest, ended these great battles of the age of sail. Twenty ships (two thirds of the whole Franco-Spanish fleet) were taken as prizes; of their six flag officers three became prisoners and two were mortally wounded; a victory so decisive that naval power thenceforth sealed Napoleon's eventual fate. British casualties were 1663 dead and wounded; the enemy's 14,000, the majority killed or drowned.

Today, unless 'We, the peoples of the United Nations', really are 'determined to save succeeding generations from the scourge of war', *fim do mundo* seems likely to fall from the skies.

Meanwhile, at this focal point of world shipping, the lighthouse, 246 feet above sea level, projects its beam 60 miles out to sea as a safeguard 'for such as pass on the seas upon their lawful occasions'.

Bearing the name of the patron saint of wine makers (*Vin*-cent) it is always open to 'the peoples', a shining symbol of their own enlightened self-interest.

APPENDIX I

Bibliography

Guides

Spain: The Mainland Ian Robertson *Blue Guide* Ernest Benn 1980
Portugal Ian Robertson *Blue Guide* Ernest Benn 1982
Portugal Michelin Green Tourist Guide 1982, 1985
España Portugal Michelin Red Guide 1982, 1983, 1987
Portugal's Pousadas Stuart Ross APN Sociedade Impresion 1986

The Language

Discovering Portuguese Alan Freeland: BBC books 1987
The Portuguese Travel Mate Richard Drew 1982

General

They Went to Portugal Rose Macaulay: Jonathan Cape 1946
The Selective Traveller in Portugal Ann Bridge and Susan Lowndes: Evans Bros 1949
Portugal and Madeira Sacheverell Sitwell: Batsford 1954
Minho and North Portugal David Wright and Patrick Swift: Barrie & Rockliff 1968
Portugal Cedric Salter: Batsford 1970
Wellington: The Years of the Sword Elizabeth Longford: Panther Books 1971
Portugal Henry Myhill: Faber and Faber 1972

Food and Drink

Portuguese Food Carol Wright: J. M. Dent & Sons 1969
Portuguese Wine Raymond Postgate: J. M. Dent & Sons 1969
Oporto Older and Newer Gerald Cobb 1965/66
Guide to the Wines of Spain and Portugal Jan Read: Pitman 1977
The Story of Port Sarah Bradford: Christie's Wine Publications 1978
The Factory House at Oporto John Delaforce: Christie's Wine Publications 1979
Port George Robertson: Faber and Faber 1982
Rich, Rare and Red. The International Wine and Food Society's – Guide to Port Ben Howkins: Heinemann 1982
Guide to Visiting Vineyards Anthony Hogg: Michael Joseph 1982
The Wines of Portugal Jan Read: Faber 1982

The Arts

Portugal A pictorial essay with 144 colour illustrations, designed by a Portuguese/Florentine team of art historians Frederick Muller, London 1983.

APPENDIX II

Reigns and Dates

The following is a summary of Portugal's Kings and Queens mentioning important events with which they were associated. Reproduced with the kind permission of the executors of the late Henry Myhill and Faber and Faber.

FIRST OR BURGUNDIAN DYNASTY 1095–1383

Henry of Burgundy, Count of Portugal (1095–1112).

Afonso I Henriques (1112–85), took over rule from his mother 1128, declared himself King of Portugal 1139, was recognised by Leon 1143, captured Lisbon 1147.

Sancho I (1185–1211), occupied but soon lost western Algarve (1189–91).

Afonso II (1211–23).

Sancho II (1223–48), deposed for not ruling strongly enough.

Afonso III (1248–1279), finally conquered Algarve 1249.

Dinis (1279–1325), married St. Isabel, consolidated frontier which has never changed since, built castles, founded Coimbra University. His reign was a golden age of medieval Portugal.

Afonso IV (1325–57).

Pedro I (1357–67), lover of Inés de Castro.

Fernando (1367–83), weak and under influence of his wife, Leonor Teles, who succeeded him as regent (1383–85) for their young daughter, married to the King of Castile to whom Leonor planned to hand the country over.

DYNASTY OF AVIS 1383–1580

John I (1383–1433), an illegitimate son of Pedro I, thwarted these plans, leading a popular uprising, defeatng Castile at Aljubarrota in 1385, signing an alliance with England in 1386, and marrying Philippa of Lancaster in 1387. Their sons in 1415 captured Ceuta, first move in Portuguese overseas expansion and discoveries presided over by the third son, Prince Henry the Navigator until his death in 1460. Meanwhile there reigned

Edward (1433–38) his brother, and

Afonso V (1438–81) his nephew, who was more interested in campaigns in Morocco than in further discoveries, although these were now paying for themselves with the gold from Guinea. However,

Alphonso Apology. There are at least five different spellings in four languages of this popular name among Iberian royalty; among them 'Afonso' is Portuguese, 'Alfonso' Spanish. The author regrets his failure to make a clear distinction in his text.

John II (1481–95), a brilliant ruler, encouraged the explorers, with the result that his cousin

Manuel I, 'the Fortunate' (1495–1521), reaped the harvest which followed Vasco da Gama's opening of the sea route to India in 1498. This was the golden age of the second dynasty, symbolised by the elaborate late Gothic style called Manueline.

John III (1521–57) faced the severe problems of sudden empire by maintaining a prudent neutrality, but

Sebastian (1557–78), returning to the chimera of conquering Morocco, was killed there with most of his army.

Henry, the King-Cardinal (1578–80), his aged uncle, favoured as his successor Philip of Spain.

SPANISH DYNASTY 1580–1640

Philip I (II of Spain) (1580–98), had an excellent claim, and in any case the bereaved country was in no state to resist him. It remained a distinct kingdom, but was drawn into Spain's overseas wars. That with Holland was the most serious, leading to the loss of much of the overseas empire under

Philip II (III of Spain) (1598–1621) and

Philip III (IV of Spain) (1621–40).

DYNASTY OF BRAGANÇA 1640–1910

John IV (1640–56), head of the wealthiest family in the kingdom, was descended both from an illegitimate son of John I, and from a grand-daughter of Manuel I, and was the natural choice when Spanish attempts to raise taxes and reduce autonomy provoked a national rising. But the war of independence which continued until 1668 left Portugal bankrupt.

Afonso VI (1656–83) was mentally unstable, and

Pedro II (1683–1706) was *de facto* ruler from 1667. The disastrous economic situation only improved with the arrival of the first gold from Brazil in 1697, but it then improved very quickly, so that

John V (1706–50) presided over yet another, and literally golden age. His physical incapacity from 1472 led to a breakdown in government, which was repaired when

Joseph (1750–77) handed over executive power to the high-handed Marquis of Pombal. The gold of Brazil, still arriving in sufficient quantities

to rebuild Lisbon after the 1755 earthquake, was diminishing before the end of the reign: this explains why Pombal encouraged cotton to take its place, why he left the treasury empty, and why the reign of

Maria I (whose consort was Pedro III) (1777–1816) proceeded less ostentatiously. Its most dramatic moments occurred after she had fallen victim to religious mania in 1792: the French invasion, the departure of the royal family and government to Rio de Janeiro in 1807, and the subsequent victories of Anglo-Portuguese arms right across the Peninsula and in France itself.

John VI (1816–26), who had been Regent ever since 1792, only returned from Rio in 1821. The U.D.I. by Brazil the following year dealt the economy a blow which was exaggerated by the effects of the civil war between

Pedro IV (who reigned briefly *in absentia* in 1826) and his brother

Miguel (1827–34), an absolutist supported by the old nobility, who unhappily were removed from political life with the triumph of liberalism represented by Pedro IV's daughter

Maria II (1834–53), whose accession was marked by the suppression of the religious orders.

Pedro V (1853–61), a Saxe-Coburg through his father, had at least as many qualities as Victoria's Prince Albert. His early death is still grieved at, for his brother

Luis (1861–89) had neither the training nor the enthusiasm for kingship, making no attempt to guide a parliamentary system which failed to represent large sections of the nation, and which carried out a superficial modernisation only by means of ruinous foreign loans.

Carlos (1889–1908) had to face the 1890 British ultimatum demanding evacuation of central African territories, which might have linked Angola and Moçambique, and the subsequent rise of the Republican party. Unable to call on the alienated nobility, he showed more energy than his father, but in attempting to install a non-Parliamentary government provoked his own assassination and that of his son and heir.

Manuel II (1908–10) was unthroned by a revolt of part of the armed services, leading to the establishment of a republic.

FIRST REPUBLIC

	Presidents
	(or heads of provisional governments)
1910	Teófilo Braga
1911–15	Manuel de Arriaga
1915	Teófilo Braga
1915–17	Bernardino Machado
1917–18	Sidónio Pais
1918–19	*Adm.* João de Canto e Castro
1919–23	António José de Almeida
1923–25	Manuel Teixeira Gomes
1925–26	Bernardino Machado
1926	*Commander* Mendes Cabeçadas
1926	*Gen.* Gomes da Costa
1926–51	*Gen.* António Oscar de Fragoso Carmona (with António de Oliveira Salazar as 'Prime Minister' from 1932–68)
1951–58	*Gen.* Craveiro Lopes
1958–74	*Adm.* Américo Tomás (with Marcello Caetano as 'Prime Minister' from 1968–74)

SECOND REPUBLIC

1974	*Gen.* António Spínola
1974–76	*Gen.* Francisco Costa Gomes
1976–1986	*Gen.* António dos Santos Ramalho Eanes
1986	Dr Mário Soares

Geographical names are printed in Roman or bold type. The suffix (S) in brackets denotes a place in Spain. Names of people are printed in italics. Names of subjects are indicated in CAPITALS. Barragem (dams), cabos (capes), saints, serras (ranges of mountains or hills) and quintas (wine estates) are each sub-indexed. Figures in italics refer to illustrations.